PRAISE FOR
SERVANTS OF THE DAMNED

"Astonishing. . . . A powerful and important picture of how mega law firms distort justice."

—David Cay Johnston, *Washington Post*

"*Servants of the Damned* is a feat of thoughtful, detailed research, rendering with clarity and even compassion the moral drift of 'Big Law.' As an attorney, I found it illuminating—but this is important reading for anyone concerned about law and policy."

—Ronan Farrow, Pulitzer Prize–winning author of *Catch and Kill*

"This fascinating book is somehow both devastating and rollicking all at the same time. Enrich brings us into the room to watch how a modest law firm built on honorable service gradually becomes an ubershield for the worst of American greed and abuse—all in the quest for enormous billable profits and outsized power. From handling a fatal gas explosion to terrorizing a tobacco whistleblower to aiding Donald Trump, it's all in here."

—Carol Leonnig, Pulitzer Prize–winning coauthor of *A Very Stable Genius* and author of *Zero Fail*

"A deep dive into the law firm that became one of the key institutions in the president's orbit. . . . Jones Day lawyers figured prominently in Trump's rise to power and his exercise of it. Enrich treats the relationship as a sign of a broader decline in ethical standards at big American law firms."

—*Financial Times* (London)

"A withering study of how Big Law got into bed with the forty-fifth president. . . . Informative and disturbing."

—*The Guardian* (London)

"A fast-moving, damning book. . . . Essential reading."

—*Kirkus Reviews* (starred review)

"A vivid, crackling account of the law at its most bullying. Readers will be outraged."

—*Publishers Weekly*

"Enrich's stories provide a disturbing window into how the rules underpinning democracy have been weaponized by those meant to protect it."

—*New Statesman* (London)

"Enrich tells an important story of the gradual corruption of the rule of law, and of the broader corruption of our society."

—*The American Prospect*

ALSO BY DAVID ENRICH

Dark Towers: Deutsche Bank, Donald Trump, and an Epic Trail of Destruction

The Spider Network: How a Math Genius and a Gang of Scheming Bankers Pulled Off One of the Greatest Scams in History

SERVANTS OF THE DAMNED

THE
DARK SIDE
OF
AMERICAN LAW

DAVID ENRICH

MARINER BOOKS
New York Boston

A hardcover edition of this book was published in 2022 by Mariner Books, an imprint of HarperCollins Publishers.

FIRST MARINER BOOKS PAPERBACK EDITION PUBLISHED 2023.

Designed by Chloe Foster
Photograph on pages iv–v © Shutterstock Enterprise.

Library of Congress Cataloging-in-Publication Data
has been applied for.

ISBN 978-0-06-314218-3

23 24 25 26 27 LBC 5 4 3 2 1

To Peggy and Peter Enrich, who instilled in me a fascination with psychology and the law.

In memory of Alan Osur, a reliable source of facts, wisdom, and dad jokes.

I came to feel that the American lawyer should regard himself as a potential officer of his government and a defender of its laws and Constitution. I felt that if the time should ever come when this tradition had faded out and the members of the bar had become merely the servants of business, the future of our liberties would be gloomy indeed.

—Henry Stimson, secretary of war and state, in his 1947 memoir

From handguns to tobacco, Jones Day defends the powerfully damned and the damned powerful.

—*American Lawyer* magazine, January 2004

CONTENTS

PART III

AUTHOR'S NOTE

The information in this book comes largely from my interviews with more than 180 people. Most were current or former Jones Day lawyers, but they also included judges, opposing attorneys, witnesses, and others who have interacted with Jones Day or had notable experiences with the legal industry. Many, fearful of the professional consequences of discussing a powerful, secrecy-prizing law firm, spoke on the condition that I not identify them as sources. Others—including those whom Jones Day's leaders authorized to answer my written questions—were on the record.

When faced with conflicting accounts of specific incidents, I used the descriptions that struck me as the most plausible, based on factors including the credibility of different sources. In some cases, I have included dissenting accounts in the text or footnotes.

In addition to interviews, I drew on court documents, oral histories, family scrapbooks, university archives, academic research, many books, and contemporaneous media reports, as well as internal emails, memos, and other materials that I obtained via sources and Freedom of Information Act requests. These are detailed at the end of the book.

PROLOGUE

POWER PLAY

On a chilly evening in January 2017, shortly before the inauguration of Donald J. Trump, a large crowd gathered in Washington, D.C., for an extraordinary celebration. A procession of judges, senators, congressmen, and conservative power brokers trooped up to the top floor of a neoclassical art deco building near the United States Capitol. The eighty-two-year-old edifice—originally the headquarters of the Acacia Life Insurance Company—was designed by the same architects behind the Empire State Building. A pair of limestone griffins, each clutching eggs, guarded the twenty-two wide steps that led to the building's main entrance on Louisiana Avenue. Green marble columns loomed inside the cavernous lobby. Upstairs, the floors luxuriated under twelve-foot ceilings, and wood-paneled offices and conference rooms, some equipped with fireplaces, afforded breathtaking views of the Capitol dome.

The law firm Jones Day occupied the building. Founded in 1893 in Cleveland, it had grown into one of the planet's largest legal machines, with thousands of attorneys spread across dozens of offices in the U.S. and overseas. Cleveland had long since faded as a locus of power, which these days resided in Washington. There was no clearer sign of that shift than the men who were being honored this January night: These were the lawyers who were leaving Jones

Day to join the new Trump administration, where they would exert tremendous sway over the course of national events.

Jones Day's leader was a headstrong, bulldog-faced attorney named Steve Brogan. He was a religious man and the son of a New York City cop, and after faith and family, the law firm was his life. Brogan loved Jones Day, and he wielded unfettered power. He controlled who Jones Day hired, how much employees were paid, where the firm opened offices, and even who would succeed him as managing partner. (Technically, there were a pair of committees that could overrule such decisions, but they had never done so.) Brogan was king—or, as more than a few of his colleagues described him, the godfather.

Brogan very much liked the Acacia. "That is one great building," he had gushed shortly after signing the lease. (Jones Day beat out the Securities and Exchange Commission, which also had been eyeing the location.) Brogan ensconced himself in a suite so palatial that a colleague warned him that it would create the impression that Brogan viewed himself as emperor, not a member of a partnership. Brogan kept the office.

Soon after Brogan took over the firm in 2003, Jones Day had set out to greatly enlarge its ranks of Washington lawyers, in keeping with the firm's—and the industry's—governing principle over the past few decades, which boiled down to more lawyers, more offices, more clients, more money, more power.

Thanks to those wonderfully high ceilings, though, there wasn't space in the Acacia to cram in many more lawyers. In 2004, architects and engineers proposed leveling a neighboring parking garage to make way for a gleaming, twelve-story office annex. It would be connected to the Acacia by a triangular, glass-enclosed atrium and a series of translucent "skywalks" etched with the names of cities in which Jones Day operated.

The plans called for a zoning variance that would allow the new structure to exceed the area's 110-foot height limit by at least twenty feet. This was when the problems began. Law enforcement agencies, still skittish after 9/11, warned that the roof was so high that it could provide snipers with an ideal nest from which to pick off senators. The building's developers didn't deny that gunmen would have a clear line of sight onto the Capitol grounds; instead, they pointed out that there were plenty of other nearby sites that *also* would be suitable for assassination attempts. This was a less-than-persuasive argument—surely, creating additional platforms for snipers was undesirable, even if other options existed—but D.C. zoning bodies approved the plans.

Yet the Capitol Police kept pressing their case. They appealed to individual senators who, the cops emphasized, were the ones who might find themselves in the crosshairs of a rifleman perched on the roof of this sleek new mini-skyscraper. Not surprisingly, senators didn't like the sound of that. In June 2005 the chamber approved a measure that essentially blocked the building's construction.

Jones Day's lawyers thought this was an overreaction. "We were told at the time that there were only two sharpshooters in the entire U.S. military who were capable of making that shot," Ray Wiacek, a Jones Day partner who was responsible for handling the firm's leases, told me. (He added that Jones Day didn't plan to lease the top floors of the new building and therefore "had no dog in this fight." The building's developers, however, cited Jones Day's desire for more space as the reason for the requested zoning variance.) In any case, the developers were outflanked and had to back down. The proposed building's top floors were lopped off.

Construction finally got underway in 2008, and the finished campus became an appealing synthesis of old and new. Exposed yellow piping accented the stone and steel. All-glass elevators glided through the skylit atrium. Yet the delayed and downsized building—a product of a defeat at the hands of the political establishment—was a diminished monument to its primary occupant.

Over the next decade, Jones Day underwent a remarkable metamorphosis that ensured it would no longer lurk on the outside of that establishment, peering in. Soon, the firm wasn't only bigger, though it was that. It wasn't only richer, though it was that, too. It was more powerful, especially where it mattered most: in Washington.

Jones Day had enmeshed itself in the fabric of the capital's conservative firmament. The law firm had always leaned Republican. But lately it had become a champion of right-wing politics, organizing legal challenges to Obama's health care program, white-collar prosecutions, government regulations, and voting rights laws. Then came the 2016 presidential election. Jones Day took a gamble by representing Trump, helping the underdog build credibility in Republican circles and even using the law firm's majestic building as a campaign prop. The mastermind was Don McGahn, a shaggy-haired, guitar-playing Jones Day lawyer who, as the Trump team's lead outside counselor, took on a public role advising and traveling with the inflammatory politician.

That was why the well-heeled crowd was gathered on the top floor of Jones Day's offices on this January evening. The venue was an event space whose floor-to-ceiling windows overlooked the Capitol and opened onto a manicured roof terrace. In summer, it was a verdant landscape of plush lawns and colorful bushes and a garden that yielded lettuce, radishes, peppers, and carrots. In winter the terrace was beige and lifeless, but the views were still amazing—so much so that CBS News had received Jones Day's blessing to create a permanent broadcast studio up there, giving its anchors an impressive backdrop as they covered events like a State of the Union address or a presidential inauguration. The latter would occur in just a few days.

This night, hundreds of lawyers and lawmakers and dignitaries milled about the chilly veranda and the adjoining conference area. They had gathered to toast the large landing party that Jones Day was dispatching to get the Trump administration up and running. By Brogan's count, a dozen of his lawyers had lined up prominent jobs in the White House, Justice Department, and other federal agencies. There would be many more.

It was an unparalleled concentration of a single firm's lawyers inside a new administration, and it would position Jones Day to aid its corporate clients and advance the political agenda of men like Brogan. Leading the pack was McGahn, who would serve as Trump's White House counsel. Prior to helping elect Trump, his claim to fame had been the weakening of regulations restricting outside spending on political campaigns. Now McGahn was plotting something bolder: neutering the federal bureaucracy and remaking the judiciary. A fortunate handful of Jones Day attorneys would soon score lifetime appointments to the federal bench.

As the illuminated Capitol glowed in the night sky, the lawyers and politicians ate and drank and congratulated each other. Then it was time for speeches. McGahn, touched that Jones Day was throwing him a reception, thanked the firm for hiring him less than three years earlier and for its fearlessness in representing a polarizing campaign. His longtime colleague and onetime mentor, Ben Ginsberg, had flown in on a red-eye for the event, and he noted fondly how McGahn had first arrived in Washington "with long hair and a guitar." Brogan, a big smile plastered on his ruddy face, declared how proud he was of McGahn and his gang, who were elevating Jones Day's stature as a go-to political law firm.

The crowd that evening was festive and a little tipsy. It was mostly Republican, but a handful of prominent Democrats, includ ing Minnesota senator Amy Klobuchar and Michigan congresswoman Debbie Dingell, showed up, too. The event marked the arrival of this once-obscure law firm as a true power player.

FOR MORE THAN THREE years after that rooftop party, Jones Day flew mostly under the radar, even as it helped Trump sidestep Special Counsel Robert Mueller's investigation into the 2016 election and as it helped its corporate clients get their way in the capital.

Then, in the summer of 2020, people inside and outside Jones Day began sounding urgent alarms about its work for Trump and his allies. Even before Election Day, the firm had been laying the legal groundwork for Republicans to question the legitimacy of the results in the crucial swing state of Pennsylvania. Sure enough, Trump lost the election, and the subversion of democracy through a barrage of litigation became the president's best hope of clinging to power.

In a flash, Jones Day became a symbol of a well-orchestrated assault on the integrity of the American electoral system. Protesters chanted outside the firm's offices in New York and Washington. In San Francisco, where Jones Day had offices in a downtown skyscraper that was partly owned by Trump, activists painted a street mural depicting the firm stealing votes and demanded that it cease and desist. Inside Jones Day, angry partners and associates began complaining—a grave breach of decorum at a law firm where power was vested almost entirely in a single man.

The firm's work for the Trump campaign was what attracted scrutiny, but what if the general public knew what else was going on inside Jones Day—or, for that matter, any other elite international law firm? Here was a corner of the business world that, despite its size, money, and clout, had mostly escaped outside attention, allowing the legal industry to make the planet a more dangerous, less just place under the guise of providing trusted legal counsel.

Around the time that Jones Day's lawyers were trying to make it harder for mail-in ballots to count in Pennsylvania, a group of the firm's partners was helping the tobacco company R.J. Reynolds. The goal was to defang regulations governing the marketing of cigarettes. The lawyers insisted in court that government-mandated health warnings on cigarette packs violated tobacco companies' First Amendment rights. Elsewhere, Jones Day's lawyers were threatening municipalities that dared to discourage the sale or advertising of tobacco products.

Around the same time that these Jones Day lawyers were seeking to preserve a tobacco company's rights to express itself, another team was helping Walmart, whose pharmacies for years had been dishing out opioids with abandon. Before Covid-19, the epidemic caused by the spread of the highly addictive painkillers was the foremost public-health crisis facing America. Jones Day trotted out a variety of creative defenses—and tapped its alumni network inside the Trump administration—to shield Walmart from liability for the havoc it had helped wreak.

There was more. Jones Day was working for the Catholic Church as it tried to minimize the extent of its sexual-abuse scandals. And for Purdue Pharma, the maker of OxyContin, as it sought to protect its right to make and market its dangerous drug. And for Abbott Laboratories, as it dodged responsibility for babies being brain damaged after consuming the company's powdered formula. And for Fox News, as it waged war against employees who were the victims of sexual harassment or worse. And for Russian oligarchs as their conglomerates sought to expand internationally. And for Johnson & Johnson as it deployed a novel legal strategy to avoid payouts to cancer victims. And for a wide variety of companies that were trying to smash labor unions or prevent them from forming in the first place.

The point is not that Jones Day is uniquely terrible. It is not. Nor is the law firm the country's largest (though it is right up there) or most profitable (though it generates more than $2 billion a year in revenue). It is not an evil institution. Many of its more than 2,500 lawyers are consummate professionals, dedicated to zealously representing clients within the bounds of legal ethics. Jones Day prides itself on a culture of collaboration, in contrast to the backstabbing endemic to many of its rivals. And hundreds of Jones Day's lawyers—and the firm itself—have donated countless hours of lifesaving work for refugees and others desperately in need of legal assistance.

Even so, Jones Day's arc—from its founding in Cleveland to its current status as a global colossus—is a powerful encapsulation of the changes that have swept the legal industry in recent decades. Today, Jones Day and many of its peers have become enablers of the business world's worst misbehavior. Increasingly, that work bleeds into the political realm—as Jones Day's embrace of Donald Trump vividly shows.

For a long time, law firms weren't very big or profit crazed or power hungry. While some lawyers and scholars had long decried their profession's creeping commercialization, bar associations had responded to those concerns by erecting an interlocking network of firewalls to keep capitalism at bay. Lawyers didn't regard themselves as being in business; they were officers of the court, part of a centuries-old tradition that demanded allegiance to a code of ethics and honor. To be clear, this was no utopia. Plenty of lawyers crossed lines, and some legends of the bar, like the Supreme Court orator Daniel Webster, made their livings helping to carve out expansive rights for powerful companies. In addition, the legal profession was the nearly exclusive province of white men, who at times used their power for racist and sexist ends.

But most lawyers viewed their occupation as public spirited. They often turned down unsavory clients and assignments, because they and their firms didn't face an imperative to grow. That began to change in the late 1970s, thanks to a series of pivotal but long-forgotten events. First, the U.S. Supreme Court ruled that law firms were businesses, with the right to advertise their services. Today that seems obvious—and not unreasonable—but at the time it represented radical thinking for the legal profession.

Then, in 1979, came the debut of a monthly magazine called the *American Lawyer*. Law firms up until that point had treated their work—especially their inner operations and finances—like state secrets. The *American Lawyer*'s mission was to reveal those secrets and to cover the industry like other outlets did Hollywood or the NBA. Soon, lawyers could follow the ups and downs of their rivals and decide where to work based on how much they were likely to earn.

These dual developments unshackled the staid industry. An arms race ensued—for better lawyers, for more lucrative assignments, for prestige, for power. Growth begat growth. The more firms hired, the more their costs went up, which meant more revenue was needed. The simplest solution was to take on new clients or cases. It was not a coincidence that, just as Jones Day was starting out in what would become an international gold rush, it cast its lot with an increasingly risqué roster of clients, including Big Tobacco.

Thanks in part to the legal industry's private ownership, not to mention its practitioners' massaging of the media, law firms have long avoided much accountability for their actions. One way they have deflected attention is by espousing the largely self-serving notion that it is the patriotic duty of American lawyers to extend blind, everlasting loyalty to even their most monstrous corporate clients.

It is true, of course, that all accused criminals have the right to competent counsel. But the legal industry has warped this concept into something else entirely. Law firms and their leaders peddle the fiction that everyone—including, importantly, all companies—has the right to the best lawyers, in all situations and at all times. The corollary: Once a corporation becomes a client, the law firm is stuck, because ditching clients who find themselves in trouble is an abrogation of the lawyer's sacred vow.

These arguments are pocked with holes. While down-on-their-luck humans deserve access to high-quality legal services (which they often don't get, because so many of the best lawyers are lured to giant law firms, which overwhelmingly represent corporations), the same is not automatically true of companies or other institutions. The Sixth Amendment of the Constitution guarantees the rights of the accused in a *criminal* trial "to have the assistance of counsel for his defence." It says nothing about civil cases, much less about out-of-court legal services like helping companies skirt regulations or silence whistleblowers or dodge taxes. Almost by definition, the right to counsel is geared toward protecting the poor and weak, not the rich and strong, who can fend for themselves. Law firms don't even really believe in the principle that they often invoke; when it suits them, they trumpet their decisions to avoid impolitic work.

The problem is that it rarely suits them. It is profitable for lawyers and their firms to stand by giant companies—especially since abandoning them would send an unmistakable signal that other rich and powerful clients should look for more pliant counselors, of which there are plenty. Citing the constitutional right to counsel is a convenient way for giant firms to rationalize this representation and to preempt criticism—or even scrutiny—of whom elite lawyers serve and how they serve them.

By the dying days of the Trump presidency, with democracy hanging by a thread, the costs of this era of unaccountability were becoming clear. Almost exactly four years after the crowd had gathered on Jones Day's top floor to celebrate its lawyers' migration into the Trump administration, a much larger crowd assembled nearby. If anyone had been on Jones Day's rooftop on the afternoon of January 6, 2021, they would have enjoyed a splendid view of a violent mob storming the Capitol—the predictable culmination of a president whom Jones Day had helped elect, an administration the firm's lawyers had helped run, and an election whose integrity the firm had helped erode.

PART I

1

A HUSTLING BUSINESS

Four hulking steel tanks—three of them spheres, the fourth a towering fifty-foot cylinder—shone in the bright sun on a crisp Friday in October 1944. Nestled in Cleveland's densely packed Norwood–St. Clair neighborhood, barely a block from Lake Erie, the tanks were the fruits of an engineering breakthrough. Several years earlier, scientists at the East Ohio Gas Company had realized that if you stored natural gas at extreme low temperatures—minus 260 degrees, in this case—the gas converted into a liquid, which compressed its volume to about 1/600th of its usual size, which meant you could store a whole lot more of it in one place. That was important, because Cleveland was booming. Its factories were churning out machinery for World War II, its population was soaring, and its needs for energy were galloping higher.

To keep up with demand, East Ohio Gas had constructed the world's first commercial gas-liquefication facility in 1941. The first three tanks, double walled with steel, insulated with cork, each held about 50 million cubic feet of gas. Tank No. 4 was built two years later. Wartime rationing was in place, and to conserve scarce materials, it was insulated with rock wool rather than cork and was built in a cylindrical shape that allowed it to hold more gas per square inch of steel. It contained about twice the volume of gas as its three smaller siblings. Clevelanders regarded the facility with pride, "one of the scientific wonders of the country," as the *Plain Dealer* newspaper put it.

At 2:30 p.m. on Friday, October 20, the fourth tank sprang a leak. Liquid gas was escaping through a seam, mixing with air, reverting to its gaseous state. Neighbors noticed white mist circulating near the bottom of the tank. Then, as the volume of leaking gas increased, residents saw it pouring into a nearby sewer, flowing like water.

The explosion came at 2:41. One worker described it as "a big balloon of fire" inflating over the neighborhood. In an instant, the sky turned orange, flames leaping a half mile up. Red-hot shrapnel screamed through the air. As a square mile burned, the air temperature hit 3,000 degrees—hot enough to melt coins in victims' pockets. "It was as if a flame-thrower had been turned on you," a survivor said. Charred sparrows fell from the sky.

Twenty minutes after Tank No. 4 exploded, one of the spherical tanks detonated. Underground blasts rumbled through the city as gas that had drained into sewers and pipes combusted. Miles from the initial explosion, car tires blew out and streets were torn up, manhole covers shooting hundreds of feet into the air.

The fire smoldered for days. Through the smoke, shell-shocked residents confronted a scene of awesome wreckage. Much of the teeming Norwood–St. Clair neighborhood, home to a thriving community of Slovenian immigrants, was leveled. The occasional lonely tree trunk or wall stood amid endless heaps of ash and debris. Seventy-nine homes and two factories were destroyed, with others sustaining serious damage. One hundred and thirty people were killed, 225 hospitalized. The bodies of sixty-one people were so thoroughly incinerated that they couldn't be identified. Some were found kneeling in prayer. It was not lost on survivors that this was the sort of devastation that European cities were enduring during the war.

THE GRAND UNION COMMERCE Building was nearly three miles from the site of the explosion, but the tremors almost certainly were felt inside what at the time was one of the three largest office buildings in the world. One occupant of the building was a fast-growing law firm: Jones, Day, Cockley & Reavis.

Jones Day had represented East Ohio Gas for decades. The company had been part of John Rockefeller's Standard Oil empire, and Jones Day lawyers had a long-running relationship with the mighty industrialist. Within hours of the blast, a small team gathered inside Jones Day's offices. The lawyers' assignment was to assess the gas company's liability for the vast damage the explosion had caused. The lawyers spent twenty-four hours holed up in the firm's library. Clearly their client would shoulder some responsibility for this disaster, but there were plenty of other culprits the lawyers could also blame. There was the Pittsburgh steel company that had, it seemed, cut corners on the material for the cylindrical tank. There was the manufacturer of the rock wool, which, soaked with gas, ignited and transformed into fiery projectiles that sparked blazes all over the neighborhood. There were Cleveland's sewer and water authorities, whose networks of tunnels became channels for the gas to spread and catch fire.

In response to the inevitable flood of lawsuits against East Ohio Gas, the law firm could unleash delay-and-deflect maneuvers to wear down plaintiffs in the interest of getting them to accept the smallest possible settlements. Its lawyers could lowball the value of damaged property. They could blame homeowners for inadequate fireproofing. They could submerge plaintiffs in legal motions and other paperwork. If, that is, the law firm and its client wanted to take a scorched-earth approach.

A Jones Day lawyer named Pat Mulligan was close to East Ohio's management. On Sunday, two days after the explosion, Mulligan met with the company's general counsel, Bill Pringle, and explained the firm's thinking: East Ohio's best bet was to admit fault and make people whole. If the company hoped to remain in Cleveland, it had a powerful incentive—an obligation—to take care of a community that had suffered a tragedy. It might cost more in the short run, it might set a precedent of corporate culpability for out-of-the-blue catastrophes, it might mean waiving some plausible cover granted by the law, but it was the right thing to do. That was Jones Day's counsel.

The next day, East Ohio ran an ad in the *Plain Dealer*, inviting victims to come to the company's offices (which weren't near the explosion), detail their losses, and get paid. "It is not necessary to incur any expense or to employ anyone to aid you," the ad explained. Jones Day set up desks in the building's lobby to process the claims, and that morning hundreds of people lined up. Many had been injured; some had family members who were killed; more faced huge bills to repair their homes. East Ohio wrote checks on the spot. Within a few months, the company had paid nearly $7 million (about $100 million today) to thousands of people. Only twenty-four lawsuits were ever filed.

The gas company, today owned by Dominion Energy, remained in the neighborhood. The site of the explosion became a public park. Decades later, victims perceived East Ohio's process to have been fast and fair.

JONES DAY HAD BEEN established a half century earlier under a different name by a well-regarded former judge, Edwin Blandin, and a dapper young lawyer named William Rice. Blandin & Rice hitched itself to Cleveland's fast-growing railroad and coal companies, among others. The firm even represented a prominent actress, Olga Nethersole, who sued a local newspaper for libel for saying that her play was booed so loudly that she "had hysterics." (The Ohio Supreme Court ruled that a woman having hysterics "is so common an occurrence" that the accusation, though untrue, was not libelous.)

Just as the firm was hitting its stride, tragedy struck. On a Friday afternoon in August 1910, Rice played a round of golf at a country club near his colonnaded hilltop mansion. After dining there and watching a few hands of bridge, he set out for home. He never made it. Around 11:00 p.m. he was found lying on his back on the side of the road, bleeding from two bullet holes near his right eye and multiple stab wounds to his chest.

The law firm offered a $5,000 reward for information about Rice's murder. Pinkerton detectives were hired. A loaded revolver was found under the pillow in Rice's bed, and his colleagues speculated about the potential culprits, but no motive was ever established, and the case was never cracked. Generations of Jones Day lawyers would retell the story of the unsolved mystery, building a mythology about how their firm survived a calamity, defied expectations, and soared to greatness. (The murder also became a punchline. "It shows that there was lawlessness in Cleveland even in that early day," one of the firm's leaders, Jack Reavis, chuckled to a group of associates more than seventy years later.)

At the time, the concept of a law firm was just taking root in America. Up until then, most lawyers had operated solo. They viewed themselves as "independent craftsmen who served the needs of local communities in which they were leaders," Mitt Regan and Lisa Rohrer wrote in their book *BigLaw*. Lawyers who assembled into "firms" generally did so to share office expenses, not to function as a team. But as companies grew and their legal needs became more complex, small groups of lawyers in America's largest cities banded together. From the get-go, this trend appalled critics who viewed the profession of law as something akin to a religious practice, not to be corrupted by the pursuit of money or clients. "The practice of law has become commercialized," a commentator groused in 1913. "It has been transformed from a profession to a business, and a hustling business at that."

The profession's response to such critiques was to institute a system of self-regulation that discouraged, and often banned, businesslike behavior by practitioners. Soon bar associations prohibited lawyers from even soliciting clients. But there was no way to stop firms from growing.

• • •

Tom Jones, a recent graduate from Ohio State University and the son of a judge, joined Blandin & Rice the year after Rice's murder. In college, Jones had lettered in track and was the football team's quarterback and captain. He was an academic star, too, elected to Phi Beta Kappa. Jones desperately wanted to be a lawyer. Blandin & Rice enjoyed a growing reputation in Cleveland's business community; Jones showed up unannounced and asked for a job. He was told to go away. "This young man could not comprehend such an attitude, so he came to the office every day and just sat," his widow would recount. Finally, the firm's leader, Frank Ginn, gave him a job.

At the time, the firm, like its peers, was little more than a collection of isolated lawyers, "each practicing his own individual law business, just as local as a country doctor," as Jack Reavis, who joined the firm a decade after Jones, put it. Ginn was a stern, autocratic fellow who chopped wood for exercise and attended classical music concerts in a cape and top hat. With the title of managing partner, he could hire and fire unilaterally. (He refused to hire anyone who was engaged. "A young lawyer had to be married to the law before he took on a wife," Ginn's son explained.) He set employees' compensation. He was the arbiter of disputes. He could pick his successor. "He completely dominated the law firm and ran it with an iron hand," a colleague recalled.

Ginn established a principle that would guide the place for decades: "The firm must maintain its freedom and independence to turn down any representation." He once declined an assignment advising a company on a merger "because he was convinced it was the result of investment bankers pushing something that could never be accomplished." Marvin Bower, a Jones Day associate who went on to found the consulting firm McKinsey, liked to tell the anecdote. "If you are not willing to take pain to live by your principles, there is no point in having principles," Bower would say.

Ginn was fond of Tom Jones, and he handed ever more responsibility to his young associate. Before long, Jones represented many of Cleveland's most iconic companies and families: industrial businesses, utilities, railroads, lenders, real estate concerns, parts of the Rockefeller empire, and the Van Sweringen brothers, owners of everything from banks to department stores.

The lawyers viewed their firm as a brotherhood. Jones's son joined. Jack Reavis worked alongside his brother Tat. The lawyers went fishing and played poker and got drunk together. "We gave more parties than a neighborhood dance club," Reavis would recall. During Prohibition, the lawyers would buy "this god-awful alcohol from a cock-eyed bootlegger" and make gin together. (On one occasion, a colleague phoned Jones, pretending to be a U.S. Marshal who had been tipped off to the group's illegal liquor purchases. Jones dumped his entire stash into a river before realizing it was a prank.)

Before he died in 1938, Ginn selected Jones to succeed him at the helm of the thirty-four-lawyer firm. The power transfer led to an abrupt cultural change. Ginn had been tough, no-nonsense, "no gaiety or first-name greetings," a secretary remembered. Jones, by contrast, was so charming he "could have been in the movies." Ginn's criticisms stung; Jones's were so soft that you hardly realized he had criticized you. He insisted that everyone take their four weeks of vacation time. It was under Jones's leadership that the firm advised East Ohio Gas to put principles ahead of short-term profits and to quickly compensate victims of the explosions.

One of Jones's first big moves, the autumn after he took over, was to merge with an eight-lawyer Cleveland firm run by Luther Day, who was regarded at the time as "possibly the greatest trial lawyer in Ohio's history," in the words of a federal judge. With the addition of Day and his team, the firm's roster of clients expanded to include out-of-town goliaths like General Motors. In 1939, the merged firm was rechristened Jones, Day, Cockley & Reavis. Aside from that merger, Jones didn't try to expand. He focused on keeping clients and ensuring that the quality of services was top-notch.

• • •

In 1932, Chapman Rose—everyone called him Chappie—was the last clerk to serve under Supreme Court justice Oliver Wendell Holmes. The famed jurist was ninety and in his final term. Holmes's eyesight was failing, and he asked the pale-eyed, fair-haired Rose to read to him. Against all better judgment, Rose picked the novel *Lady Chatterley's Lover*. "Sonny, we will not be finishing this book," Holmes remarked. "Dullness is not diminished by pornography."

As Rose's clerkship ended, the young lawyer asked Holmes for advice. It was the middle of the Great Depression, but he had two job opportunities. One was in the Roosevelt administration. The other was in his native Ohio at the firm that would become Jones Day. Holmes didn't equivocate: Get real-world experience. "Sonny, go home," he advised.

Rose joined Jones Day; his starting salary of $200 a month was swiftly sliced to $140 as the Depression deepened. After a decade in Cleveland, he decamped to Washington to join the War Department. He helped it procure wartime supplies, eventually earning the rank of colonel. When World War II ended, Rose realized that Washington was poised to become the center of the free world. He thought Jones Day had an opportunity to prosper in the capital. He explained this to Tom Jones and his underlings back in Cleveland. There was a fair amount of skepticism; did a midwestern firm really need a beachhead on the East Coast? Jones, however, was sold. He authorized Rose to open a Washington office in 1946.

Jones Day was already building a national reputation, representing storied companies like American Greetings Corporation, J.M. Smucker, and Sherwin Williams. But the move into Washington vaulted Jones Day into a rarefied position. It was one of the only law firms in the United States with a presence in more than one city.

It would soon attract even more attention. In 1952, Harry Truman issued an executive order to seize the nation's steel mills. Republic Steel had been a client of Luther Day's, and the D.C. presence made Jones Day a natural choice to represent the company as it battled the White House. At the law firm's behest, the Supreme Court struck down Truman's order.

AROUND THE TIME THAT Tom Jones signed off on the foray into Washington, he had a heart attack. The doctors prescribed bed rest. When his son Brooks visited him in the hospital, he found Jones lying on his back, perfectly still, except for his fingers, which were moving vigorously.

"What in the world are you doing?" Brooks asked.

"This is the only exercise I'm permitted to do," he replied.

Two years later, when Jones was sixty, he was hospitalized again with more heart troubles. He was released after several weeks. Jones sat on the boards of directors of several companies that his law firm represented, and in April 1948 he and his wife drove to Baltimore for a board meeting of the Glenn L. Martin aircraft company. "They thought it would be a good opportunity to get away from the tensions of business in Cleveland," Brooks wrote in a notebook that he gave his daughter decades later. After the board meeting, the Joneses checked into a hotel. Around 8:00 p.m., Jones phoned Brooks to inquire about the status of his younger brother's divorce proceedings. "I couldn't give him a very happy report," Brooks recalled.

A half hour later, the phone rang again, and this time Brooks felt a sense of foreboding as he picked up. His mother was on the line. "Your father is dead," she said.

2

THE INDEPENDENCE PRINCIPLE

One evening in 1959, Jim Lynn, a Jones Day partner, was prowling the offices of the *Harvard Law Review.* He was looking for legal talent, and there were few places in the country—in the world, for that matter—packed with more raw, young brainpower than inside the old, white Gannett House. Decades of leather-bound legal texts lined the walls, and dozens of sleep-deprived students sat at desks, slumped in armchairs, and huddled with classmates.

The fact that Jones Day had sent a lawyer to Cambridge to scout for recruits was one sign of the firm's ascent. Notwithstanding its small Washington office, it was still very much a Cleveland firm that represented midwestern clients. It was among the scores of local legal powerhouses popping up in cities around America: Gibson Dunn in Los Angeles, Bryan Cave in St. Louis, Kirkland & Ellis in Chicago, Ropes & Gray in Boston, and King & Spalding in Atlanta, not to mention the bevy of firms that predominantly served Wall Street. (In addition to Jones Day, Cleveland was home to the firms that would become BakerHostetler and Squire Patton Boggs.) These firms would all become global behemoths, but at the time, their businesses revolved around their hometowns.

To be more precise, these law firms were barely "businesses," and the legal industry was hardly an industry. It was more like a collaborative club (one that was largely off-limits to anyone besides white men).

Ever since the 1920s there had been an unwritten agreement among the leaders of major firms to pay young lawyers the same starting salaries, known as the "going rate." Partners at these firms were disturbed by the notion that the career decisions of short-sighted law students might be influenced by small differences in salaries. So they decided to eliminate any such differences. Each summer, the firms' managing partners would gather for a luncheon to determine that year's going rate. (In the 1950s, it was about $4,000.)

For many decades, the act of recruiting employees was a restrained affair. Harvard Law's New York alumni chapter, for example, held a "smoker" each Christmas at which law firms could present their case for employment. Firms also sent notices to law schools' placement offices describing themselves to prospective job seekers. By the late 1950s, though, competition for the best students was beginning to warm. Some large firms—those with more than fifty lawyers—began inviting second-year students to clerk with them over the summer; they were called "summer boarders." The boldest were experimenting with what at the time was a cutting-edge recruitment tactic known as "wining and dining" of job candidates, which induced heartburn in the legal establishment. The practice "irritates many lawyers who must resort to this procedure, even though in only a limited way, for they feel it is not 'professional,'" a prominent sociologist wrote in 1960.

Poaching lawyers was simply not done. Once, a partner at another firm came to Jones Day looking for a job. The managing partner at the time, Jack Reavis, and others met with him. Toward the end of the meeting, Reavis checked to make sure the lawyer had withdrawn from the other firm's partnership. The lawyer replied that he had not, but planned to soon. "Well, then we're not going to talk to you," Reavis stated, and he ushered the man out.

• • •

YET JONES DAY'S AMBITIONS were growing, in a way that seemed suspiciously businesslike. The firm wanted to join America's elite. And to do that, it needed to hire from the Ivy League.

Inside Gannett House, Jim Lynn noticed a heavyset student bent over a manuscript. He had thick black hair and bushy eyebrows. Lynn approached him and introduced himself. They got to talking. By 2:00 a.m., Lynn had convinced the student to get eggs and bacon with him in Harvard Square. The kid was from the New York City borough of Queens. He told Lynn that another law firm, Philadelphia's Morgan Lewis, had offered him a job, which he planned to accept. But by the end of the predawn breakfast, Lynn had persuaded the student to visit Cleveland to interview for a job at Jones Day.

Two months later, true to his word, Antonin Scalia arrived in Cleveland. He attended a recruiting party at Lynn's house. The conversation turned to a recent *Harvard Law Review* article in which Scalia had defended "blue laws" that required stores to be closed on Sundays. Eight Jones Day lawyers encircled Scalia, pelting him with arguments against the blue laws. The debate got intense. *Boy, this is a terrible way to recruit a guy*, one lawyer, Dick Pogue, thought to himself after an hour of this. Pogue was a fast-rising attorney at the firm, destined one day to become managing partner, and he was impressed with this unflappable recruit. Scalia stood his ground, his eyebrows furrowed, relishing the intellectual combat. The debate wore on until 3:00 a.m.

Scalia summered at Jones Day, made a little money, got married, honeymooned on Cape Cod, went off to Europe by ocean liner, spent time in Germany, and returned to Jones Day as an associate in 1961. At the time the firm had about sixty lawyers in Cleveland plus a few in Washington.

Scalia fit right in. At office functions, he and Lynn were in a Jones Day quartet. Other times, Scalia played the piano and sang numbers from *Guys and Dolls.* ("I wouldn't say he's terribly good at [the piano], but he likes to hammer," recalled Lynn, who later would have top roles in the Nixon and Ford administrations and would run Aetna, the insurance giant.) Scalia got into a monthly poker game with colleagues; he tended to show up wearing a fishing hat. At lunch, he'd debate constitutional law with liberals. The guy was clearly going places.

Scalia had planned for Cleveland to be a brief way station on his road to academia, but he got sidetracked. He enjoyed the practice of law. He enjoyed Cleveland, at the time "pretty much an ethnic town." And he enjoyed Jones Day, which allowed him to rotate among different practice areas. He did litigation. He did wills. He did real estate. He did financings, contracts, labor law, taxes. "I got a really good look at the whole waterfront," he remembered years later.

After about two years, Scalia landed his first client, "my own little corporation," he said. "Any problem they had, they would call me up, and it was a really wonderful feeling." He spent nearly seven years at Jones Day. Until he became a federal judge, it was the job he held longest—and his only stint in private practice. "I enjoyed practicing so much that I just sort of forgot that I was going to go into teaching eventually and hung around probably longer than I should have."

Eventually, forced to pick a specialty, Scalia grew bored. It was time to leave. He got a job at the University of Virginia School of Law. On his way out, he addressed the firm's lawyers. "I'll be glad to get away from such a liberal place," he joked.

THE DAY AFTER TOM Jones died, Jack Reavis summoned the partners to the firm's library. He announced that Jones had anointed him as successor. Partners were not thrilled. "We knew him [Reavis] as a brilliant tax lawyer, with a mind like a steel trap, a short fuse on his temper, and a sharp tongue," one remembered. Unlike his personable predecessor, the bald and bespectacled Reavis had trouble keeping track of the names of partners' wives. (Reavis himself was a widower; the firm became his spouse.)

Under his leadership, Jones Day cemented its role as the firm of choice to the Midwest's biggest companies, many of which were heavy polluters and notorious for mistreating workers. Reavis and his inner circle were mostly Republicans, and the firm was seen as a hegemonic force in Cleveland politics. It became a bête noir of the local left. Roldo Bartimole, a legendary Cleveland muckraker, routinely had Reavis and his firm in his crosshairs. Citing the firm's extensive work for the giant iron and coal company Hanna Mining, Bartimole bestowed upon it the "Sierra Club 'Soot Award.'" He blasted Jones Day for wielding political power on behalf of clients. "Reavis is another fat cat living off the poor," Bartimole seethed.

But Reavis was also a pragmatist—and the culture in law firms at the time was that the profession's leaders should be embedded in the civic life of their cities. In 1963, Cleveland was being ripped apart by riots. Reavis wasn't a civil rights activist. But he recognized that for Cleveland to prosper, there couldn't be strife in the streets. He used his clout in the community to establish the Interracial Businessmen's Committee. It consisted of prominent white executives and less prominent Black business owners. Its goal was to foster dialogue, defuse tensions, and find ways to alleviate some of the economic pressures on the city's Black underclass. Polarization was not good for Jones Day's business prospects.

Against all odds, Reavis's initiative eased racial tensions, even if it didn't address the underlying problems. The NAACP honored Reavis with a human rights award.*

IN 1912, AN AXE-WIELDING maniac had terrorized the citizens of Villisca, Iowa. A suspect was apprehended and put on trial for murder. It was a sensational case, and the small courtroom was packed with spectators. One of them was a sixteen-year-old farm boy

* Bartimole was not impressed, calling it a "disgusting tribute."

named Lloyd Welch Pogue. He was wowed by the lawyers. *That's for me*, Pogue said to himself. He went to college, then law school, then Ropes & Gray in Boston. Among his clients were Bell Aircraft Corporation and Lockheed.

It was a thrilling time to be involved in aviation, the dawn of an age that would make the world a much smaller place. Pogue was hooked. In 1938, he got a job at the new Civil Aeronautics Authority. He soon was promoted to be general counsel, then chairman. In 1944, he helped negotiate a landmark pact that allowed civilian aircraft to fly through the airspace of other countries without having to stop in each jurisdiction.

Two years later, Pogue started his own D.C. law firm. Pogue & Neal specialized in aviation law and airline regulation. Over two decades, the little firm grew into a medium-sized firm with fourteen lawyers. Pogue by then was a giant in the field, to such an extent that *Aviation Week* established the L. Welch Pogue Award for Aviation Achievement—and named Pogue its first winner.

But Pogue's firm was completely reliant on the aviation industry. He wanted to team up with a more diversified operation. Pogue got to talking with Jones Day's brass in Cleveland. He immediately hit it off with Jack Reavis. Pogue could tell that these gentlemen were honest, had integrity, and had respect for the law as a profession, not simply as a business. (It didn't hurt that Pogue's son, Dick, was a partner there.) The 1967 merger of the two firms more than doubled the size of Jones Day's team in the capital. For the time being, the D.C. office would operate as a semiautonomous unit of Jones Day.

The timing was ideal. President Lyndon Johnson and Ralph Nader were ushering in an era of government regulation. Corporations needed a law firm that could help them navigate these tricky waters. The D.C. office, its walls lined with modern art, took flight, propelled by Pan Am, its biggest customer. Specialists in government contracts were brought in, toting enormous corporate clients. Then came Erwin Griswold, a Cleveland native who had recently stepped down as U.S. solicitor general; plenty of other top firms had tried to hire him, but Welch Pogue and Chappie Rose landed him by emphasizing the firm's Cleveland character.

Pogue insisted that his own values be reflected in the D.C. operation that he oversaw. He wasn't a big drinker, and when partners gathered for after-hours beverages in the office, they kept it a low-key affair so as not to attract the boss's unwanted attention. More important, Pogue refused to engage in lobbying or other common forms of Washington influence peddling, which he viewed as beneath the honorable calling of his profession. As the journalist Nicholas Lemann wrote in 1980, "It was his belief that that kind of work—political work—inevitably led to a lessening of a lawyer's respect in the community."

THAT IS NOT TO say that the firm lacked political connections. With scandals devouring his presidency, Richard Nixon regularly sought advice from Chappie Rose. They had first met when Nixon was vice president and Chappie worked in the Eisenhower administration; the two men became friends. Rose was a big donor to Nixon's presidential campaigns. Nixon and his deputies regularly called Rose for counsel on matters of politics, public relations, and of course, the law. (Rose's son, Jonathan, worked in the White House as a special assistant to the president.)

As Watergate intensified, a reporter in 1973 asked Chappie Rose whether he planned to keep advising Nixon. "Well, I don't know," he answered. "If the president wants help, I would be glad to offer it." The president wanted help. The White House pleaded with Chappie to represent Nixon when Congress demanded that he hand over his soon-to-be-infamous Oval Office recordings. Rose said sure—on one condition. Nixon needed to let him listen to the audiotapes first. Rose was a loyal Republican, and he liked the president, but neither he nor his law firm was interested in stumbling blindfolded into a situation where their ethics or judgment could be called into question.

Nixon refused to let Rose review the tapes. Rose wouldn't budge.

And so that was that—Rose and Jones Day would not represent the president. "He felt that it was just not a matter that he could undertake consistent with his responsibilities to Jones Day," Jonathan Rose would say.

Rose's stand would become a point of enduring pride, a seminal moment in the firm's history. Steve Brogan, a partner who worked closely with Rose, regarded it as "a supreme demonstration of the lawyer's prerogative to exercise independent judgment concerning a proffered engagement, even if the client is the president of the United States."

To this day, Jones Day's website boasts about the firm having walked away from the high-profile assignment. The vignette is recounted alongside the tale of Frank Ginn rejecting the lucrative merger assignment. Both are listed under the heading "The Independence Principle."

3

A TRULY NATIONAL FIRM

One morning in the early 1970s, a Jones Day partner named Allen Holmes was driving to work when he had an epiphany. For as long as Jones Day had existed, Cleveland had been a bustling center of American capitalism. The tradition went back to the 1870s, when the city was leading the way in the creation of things like electric lighting, chemicals, cars, and steel—"a hotbed of high-tech startups, much like Silicon Valley today," as a group of academics later described it. Well into the 1960s, northeast Ohio was among the country's leading locations for Fortune 500 companies.

This had been great for Jones Day. The firm was the best in town. It was on retainer at the vast majority of these companies.

But as Holmes drove through the city and approached the law firm's headquarters, something clicked. Cleveland was a financial and social mess. One by one, its greatest companies were being swallowed up in mergers, or relocating to faster-growing regions, or just not doing nearly as well as they once had. The economy of the city—in fact, of the entire region—was grinding down.

A brilliant but mercurial antitrust lawyer, Holmes was next in line for the throne at Jones Day. He was a determined and stubborn man, qualities born out of a lifetime of health battles. When he was seventeen, he had his first bout of muscular paralysis. It turned out to be Guillain-Barré syndrome, a rare disorder in which the immune system mistakenly attacks the body's nerves. Holmes would suffer recurring episodes, sometimes leaving him hooked up to a breathing machine for months. His wife said that Holmes spent so much time in bed during these forced convalescences that he needed only five hours of sleep a night when he was healthy. "He simply got tired of bed," she explained.

Now Holmes had a revelation. To thrive, maybe even to survive, Jones Day needed to move beyond Cleveland. It needed to expand. It needed to go national.

This was unheard-of. At the time, even the largest law firms were confined to a city or two; some, like Jones Day, had their headquarters plus an outpost in Washington or New York. Jack Reavis was still managing partner, but Holmes had his ear. "You know, there aren't any national law firms," Holmes ventured at a meeting with Reavis and other partners. "We should be a national law firm." Some in the room rolled their eyes. Holmes didn't care. The only reaction that mattered belonged to Reavis.

At first, Reavis wasn't terribly receptive, either. But he listened, and Holmes kept pushing, and an opportunity soon presented itself. One of Jones Day's largest clients was TRW, which was becoming a major player in the aerospace industry. It was moving to Los Angeles. So here was Holmes's pitch: *Let's follow it west*. Reavis didn't see the need; lawyers could serve TRW while still being based in Cleveland. Holmes persisted. Having an L.A. office would allow the firm to pursue new clients and could serve as a model for other outposts in the future. Finally, Reavis relented. In 1973, Jones Day opened an office in L.A. "No outside firm had ever tried to come into California before," Pogue said many years later. "It was a dramatic symbol of what was to come."

Dramatic, yes, but also a disaster. The California bar association insisted that top partners (those with their names on the door) at law firms operating in the state had to be licensed to practice in California. That was a problem for Jones Day, since Jones and Day were dead. The firm fought the rule, arguing that it unfairly stymied competition. Eventually, the bar association caved; it was a precedent-setting victory not only for Jones Day but also for other firms looking to expand beyond their home states.

The California experiment proved humbling—for fifteen years, Jones Day would struggle to attract clients or turn a profit—but when Holmes took over from Reavis in 1975 he remained steadfast that the firm's future lay outside Cleveland. He proselytized to colleagues and clients about establishing a "truly national firm"—a phrase that he repeated so frequently that it became a joke, with insiders shortening it to "TNF." Holmes, a man determined to overcome very long odds to get what he wanted, viewed the practice of law as a business, not just a profession. Everything was about to change.

IN 1978, HOLMES PERSUADED Jonathan Rose—the former Nixon aide and Chappie's son—to join Jones Day and, not long after, sent him to D.C. to help start an antitrust practice. The lawyers in the Washington office perceived the appointment as nepotism and a usurpation of their prized autonomy.

The way Holmes and his allies in Cleveland saw it, the folks in Washington were angling to build their office into a self-sufficient fiefdom that wasn't part of a firm with national aspirations. On a snowy Valentine's Day in 1979, Holmes arrived in Washington and expelled the leaders of the D.C. office's independence movement, as well as a bunch of their colleagues.

Partners spent the following weeks bickering over which lawyers, which secretaries, which furniture would stay and which would go to a new firm being launched by the outcasts. One day, Dick Pogue stopped by to check on the progress. He was surprised to see that a young man was handling the negotiations for Jones Day. He was only two years out of law school and had a thick head of dark brown hair, his bangs threatening to descend over his eyes. His name was Steve Brogan. Pogue was impressed.

Ultimately, about two-thirds of the Washington lawyers left the firm. Brogan was one of those who remained, and he could not have missed the lesson. The power at Jones Day would reside entirely with one man. For now, that person was Allen Holmes. Maybe one day Brogan would have his shot. In the meantime, he would be fast-tracked into leadership as a result of his loyalty.

AFTER LEAVING JONES DAY, Antonin Scalia had spent a few years teaching at the University of Virginia. Then he began pondering his next career move. Nixon was president. The White House's newly created Office of Telecommunications Policy was looking for a general counsel. The head of the office asked Jim Lynn, the Jones Day partner who had recruited Scalia and now was at the Commerce Department, if he knew anyone. Lynn endorsed Scalia, who got the job in 1970. It was Scalia's entree into Washington.

Four years later, following a recommendation from Jonathan Rose, Nixon nominated Scalia to run the Justice Department's Office of Legal Counsel. (By the time Scalia started the job in August 1974, Gerald Ford was president.) During the Carter administration, Scalia took a job at the University of Chicago, where he helped establish the Federalist Society in an effort to place more conservatives on the federal judiciary.

Then Ronald Reagan was elected. Among the people who joined his Justice Department were Steve Brogan and Jonathan Rose, who worked together in the Office of Legal Policy. Its responsibilities included drawing up lists of potential judicial nominees. Rose had an eye out for young, conservative academic stars. Here was Scalia, who had worked at Jones Day and in the Ford administration. Rose recommended him as a federal judge. In 1982, Reagan nominated Scalia to the powerful D.C. Circuit Court and then, four years later, to the Supreme Court.

It was a small preview of the power Jones Day would one day wield in shaping the federal judiciary.

4

ADVERTISERS-AT-LAW

John Bates was living in a one-room shack in a rundown neighborhood in Phoenix, Arizona, when he realized that he wanted to become a lawyer. His decision would change the American legal profession.

Bates was from a small town in the West Virginia panhandle, due west of Pittsburgh, steel country. His father was a minister; his mother helped at the church. They instilled in Bates a spirit of public service, and from a young age he was a liberal do-gooder. He also was a talented musician—tuba, French horn, piano—and he toyed with making it a career. But after graduating from Oberlin, it came time to make real-life decisions, and the prospect of roughing it in a big city, trying to land a scarce gig in a respectable orchestra, seemed . . . hard.

So Bates enrolled in grad school. But then he got to worrying: The Vietnam War was in full swing, and what if he got drafted? He started looking for ways to reduce the odds of that happening.

Johnson was president, and his administration had created a national service program called VISTA. It was essentially a domestic version of the Peace Corps. Young people could enroll to work—and live—in impoverished communities for a year or two. "Your pay will be low; the conditions of your labor will be difficult," Johnson had told the first class of VISTA enrollees. "But you will have the satisfaction of leading a great national effort, and you will have the ultimate reward which comes to those who serve their fellow man." That sounded pretty good to Bates, who figured that joining the program might also give him a way out of the draft. He applied to VISTA, got in, and was sent to Phoenix.

The job entailed helping locals do things like navigate government bureaucracies to apply for public aid. Bates didn't much mind the hardscrabble living conditions, but he found it tricky to effectively advocate for the people he was supposed to be assisting. He lacked the skills or credentials to make much difference. One day, Bates met another VISTA volunteer who was a lawyer. This man knew how to get things done. Bates craved that kind of efficacy. He decided to become a lawyer. It was his ticket to making the world a better place.

Bates was admitted to Arizona State University's small law school. On the first day of orientation, he met Van O'Steen, an army brat whose family had settled in Phoenix. During an orientation session, O'Steen had asked about opportunities for community service. Bates came up to him afterward and said that he, too, had a hankering to help. They became friends. They worked together in legal clinics that the law school ran, and in 1972 they both graduated with honors. They could've scored jobs at major law firms. Instead, they went to work for Maricopa County's legal aid society.

They were assigned to a tiny neighborhood clinic. They arrived the first day to find that they each had nearly one hundred open cases, and no supervision or training. They served mostly indigent people who needed lawyers for relatively simple legal services, but they had to turn away a procession of others: people who weren't poor enough to qualify for legal aid but couldn't afford a private lawyer, or those who needed routine legal services that the aid society didn't offer. It became clear to both lawyers that "there was this gigantic gap," as Bates put it nearly a half century later.

Bates and O'Steen decided to bridge that gap. In 1974, after eighteen months working for legal aid, they opened their own little shop that would specialize in low-cost legal services. They scraped together their savings and borrowed $2,000 from a friend, and that was enough to rent space in a small, two-story office building in downtown Phoenix, a block away from the courthouse and "with a neighborhood drunk taking up residence on the front sidewalk."

Their trick was to standardize much of the legal process: They printed questionnaires and forms and do-it-yourself kits. They relied on paralegals to collect information and help with the paperwork, a novel concept at the time. The two lawyers could spend their time on tasks that only lawyers were allowed to do, like making appearances in court. That would enable them to charge fees well below those of established law firms.

THE ORIGINAL PLAN WAS for word of the Legal Clinic of Bates & O'Steen to spread from one satisfied customer to the next. But the trickle of clients walking into their dingy offices quickly made clear that wouldn't be enough. So, what to do?

Back in 1908, the American Bar Association, trying to preserve the dignity of a profession that was veering ever closer to business-like mores, had promulgated the twenty-seventh rule of its Canons of Professional Ethics: "Indirect advertisement for business by furnishing or inspiring newspaper comments [about a law firm's work] . . . and all other like self-laudation defy the traditions and lower the tone of our high calling and are intolerable."

In case that left any room for ambiguity, state bar associations soon issued their own edicts. Arizona's was explicit: "A lawyer shall not publicize himself . . . through newspaper or magazine advertisements, radio or television announcements, display advertisements in the city or telephone directories or other means of commercial publicity, nor shall he authorize or permit others to do so in his behalf."

Over the years, lawyers had been busted for skating around the edges of these rules. Not only could you not run ads—you couldn't even promote yourself in the media. (A law firm had been disciplined for letting *Life* magazine reporters shadow its lawyers for an article.) You couldn't take out space in the Yellow Pages. (A lawyer had been nailed for paying to have his name and phone number in bold lettering in the phone book.) Even handing out business cards at a cocktail party could be construed as an improper act of self-promotion.

The ostensible purpose of these restrictions was to insulate the bar from the sorts of degrading commercial pressures that afflicted normal industries. Lawyers were not supposed to be businessmen. They were above the seamy profit-maximizing ethos of traditional capitalists.

But the practical implication was that it was all but impossible for lawyers to make an independent start, and that served the interests of large, powerful firms, which did not have to compete against upstarts that promised lower prices or better services. Nobody would even know they existed.

After giving up hope that their clinic would take flight on the back of referrals, Bates and O'Steen wondered if a newspaper might be inclined to write about this new legal clinic offering cut-rate prices. The problem was, the Arizona bar association might penalize them for reaching out to a reporter. "We were just down there in that little building, hoping," Bates told me.

It soon became clear that their venture was not going to be able to survive along its current trajectory. Their business model was low price, high volume. The reality they were facing was low price, low volume.

The two got to thinking. What was to actually stop them from buying an ad in the newspaper? The Arizona bar association would almost certainly come down hard on them, but what did they have to lose? Maybe the story of a powerful band of lawyers attacking a couple of recent grads who were just trying to help the needy would attract media attention, which would spread the word about their clinic, which would allow them to keep their doors open.

They came up with a small, rectangular ad. "*DO YOU NEED A LAWYER?*" it asked. "Legal services at very reasonable fees." The ad featured a simple image of the scales of justice. And it listed the prices of common services: divorces, $175; adoptions, $225; bankruptcies, $250. On a Friday in February 1976, Bates and O'Steen walked to the offices of the *Arizona Republic,* carrying a printout of their ad. For a small fee, they arranged to have it run in Sunday's paper.

That afternoon, the ad department called O'Steen. The *Republic* couldn't publish the ad after all. The newspaper had a policy against running copy that mentioned divorces. Now, figuring they might as well go all in, Bates and O'Steen made a phone call of their own: to the *Republic*'s investigative reporter, Al Sitter. They told him about their plan, how they were trying to upend the stodgy legal business with an eye toward helping the poor. Sitter made a few calls and, lo and behold, the *Republic* reversed course and agreed to run the ad.

That same day, Bates and O'Steen called their Arizona State constitutional law professor, William Canby, and asked if they could stop by to get his advice. At a restaurant near campus, they told Canby about their plan. The professor (he'd later become a federal judge) seemed to appreciate the provocative nature of what his former students were considering, but he urged them to slow down. *Don't run the ad yet.*

"We already have," Bates replied.

"Oh." Canby told them they were going to need a good lawyer—and he couldn't think of anyone better than himself.

The small ad for the small legal clinic ran on page A21 of the *Republic* on Sunday, February 22. On the front page was an article by Al Sitter. It described how two local lawyers were taking a daring stand against the mighty bar association. He quoted Bates and O'Steen saying the prohibition on advertising was a disservice to the public; he quoted the president of the bar association saying Bates and O'Steen were in big trouble.

That week was a blur. Bates and O'Steen were swamped with calls and visits from would-be clients who had seen the media coverage (if not the ad itself) about their low prices. That Friday, O'Steen hosted a party to celebrate their remarkable turnaround. Among the guests was Arizona's attorney general—and soon-to-be governor—whose wife had been a law school classmate of Bates and O'Steen. By then, the inevitable complaint, filed by the bar association's president, had arrived in the mail.

BATES AND O'STEEN WERE young and maybe a little reckless, but they also had picked an opportune time to challenge the hegemony of bar associations and their restrictions on self-promotion.

The prior year, the U.S. Supreme Court had issued a landmark ruling in a case called *Goldfarb v. Virginia State Bar*. The plaintiffs, Lewis and Ruth Goldfarb, had signed a contract to buy a home in a Northern Virginia suburb. Before they could get a mortgage, they needed a lawyer to conduct a title search on their property. Lewis Goldfarb called a list of lawyers, who all offered the same exact price—1 percent of the value of the property. Goldfarb, himself a lawyer at the Federal Trade Commission, got suspicious. He did a little research and learned that the state bar association required all lawyers in Virginia to adhere to a schedule of minimum fees. In the case of title searches, that minimum was 1 percent of the purchase price.

The rules, versions of which existed in many other states as well, represented another feeble attempt by local bar associations to strike a balance between maintaining the profession's non-capitalist posture while dealing with the reality that lawyers wanted to make money. Increasing competition among lawyers was driving down prices. Virginia's minimum prices were crafted to address the fact that "lawyers have slowly but surely been committing economic suicide as a profession," as a bar association committee put it when it proposed the fee schedule. The minimum fees were good for lawyers, but not for consumers. They were also, in the most literal sense, anticompetitive.

That was the argument made by the Goldfarbs' lawyer, a Ralph

Nader acolyte named Alan Morrison. The bar association insisted that it was exempt from antitrust laws because theirs was a "learned profession," not a traditional industry. In June 1975, in a unanimous decision written by Chief Justice Warren Burger, the Supreme Court sided with the Goldfarbs. Lawyers and law firms might be "learned," but they were also in business. They couldn't collude to set prices in unison.

Five months later, the court heard oral arguments in a case commonly referred to by the shorthand *Virginia Pharmacy*—also brought by Alan Morrison. It had nothing to do with the legal industry. Instead, Morrison argued that restrictions on ads about the prices of prescription drugs deprived consumers of valuable information, stifled competition, and violated the First Amendment. In May 1976, the Supreme Court agreed. It struck down government restrictions on commercial speech—aka advertisements—as unconstitutional.

The seven-to-one decision was widely hailed as a milestone for consumer rights. The lone dissenter was William Rehnquist. He predicted that the ruling would set off a chain reaction. The court's decision, he wrote, would open the door to the "active promotion of prescription drugs" and other products directly to consumers—and to the invalidation of restrictions on ads by other professions. Sure enough, cigarette companies, casinos, the liquor industry were all soon citing the court's decision to knock down bans on ads for their addictive wares. "Rehnquist's dissent in *Virginia Pharmacy* would turn out to be one of the most farsighted opinions in the history of the Supreme Court," Adam Winkler wrote in his 2018 book, *We the Corporations*.

With those cases fresh in their minds, Bates, O'Steen, and Canby had good reason to be confident that they would prevail in their legal battle in Arizona.

THE ARIZONA BAR WAS represented by a prominent constitutional lawyer, John Frank. A decade earlier, he had counseled Ernesto Miranda in a case that went to the Supreme Court and established the right to remain silent. Frank and Canby discussed the Bates and O'Steen case. They both felt that the question of lawyer advertising was ripe for Supreme Court refereeing; similar skirmishes were breaking out around the country. They agreed to do everything they could to fast-track the case.

The bar association imposed token one-week suspensions on Bates and O'Steen, but it allowed them to be served at different times, so their clinic wouldn't have to close. Canby quickly appealed the punishment to the state supreme court, arguing that the *Goldfarb* and *Virginia Pharmacy* cases showed that advertising restrictions violated antitrust laws and the First Amendment. The state court rejected their arguments. Canby next appealed to the U.S. Supreme Court. It granted certiorari—it would hear the case. Oral arguments were scheduled for January 18, 1977.

Bates and O'Steen came to Washington, which was abuzz with preparations for Jimmy Carter's inauguration in two days' time. They stayed with one of Bates's friends. The morning of January 18 was bitterly cold; at 9:00 a.m. the temperature was 13 degrees. The two Arizonans stepped outside, and it was like their faces were burning. O'Steen was pretty sure his nostrils were frozen; he felt ice every time he inhaled. The men made their way to the Supreme Court. Here they were in this temple of the law, and its nine august jurists would be hearing a case with national implications, and it was all because of them. The thrill thawed them.

"Mr. Chief Justice, may it please the court," Canby began. "This case is about two lawyers who advertised in their local newspaper and were disciplined for it. But, as I intend to show, it's also a case about the delivery of legal services in the United States." He explained how advertising was the only way for poorer people to realize what legal services were available to them. Justices Stevens and Burger interrupted to ask about what to do about misleading ads; could they be regulated? Canby said yes. Where does one draw the line? Could hospitals ban employees from handing out leaflets? Sure, Canby said. What about TV? Could lawyers broadcast their ads? Canby said yes.

Then it was Frank's turn. Canby was a plain speaker; Frank sprinkled his speech with quotes from Plato. "What you are asked to believe is that if you give your permission, the nation will be dotted with noble souls who will, by advertising, communicate . . . their desire to perform worthwhile and needed service at very low cost," Frank orated. "This frankly visionary speculation overlooks the human experience, which tells us that you would be unleashing quite a different flood. The plain truth of the matter is that advertising law business leads to incompetence at best. . . . It leads to lying, cheating, and swindling at its worst."

Frank went on to claim that the prices Bates and O'Steen were offering weren't all that low. Justice Stevens asked what he thought the prevailing fee was for an uncontested divorce. (Bates and O'Steen advertised a $175 price, plus a $20 court fee.) Frank said that they normally ran from about $150 to $300. "I've handled them myself for anything in that whole zone," he asserted. "It is not some spectacular bargain."

Bates had to restrain himself from shouting. This guy was one of Arizona's most prominent lawyers; he wasn't taking on divorce cases and, even if he were, he'd be charging ten times the nominal amounts that Bates and O'Steen were asking. "Did you hear that?" Bates whispered to O'Steen. A guard nearby pointed at Bates, mouthed "next time," and motioned with his thumb to signal he'd be kicked out.

Frank ended his speech with a plea for the justices not to allow the legal profession to pollute itself with self-promotion: "May it never be said that this profession was cheapened here, in this, its highest sanctuary."

FIVE MONTHS LATER, O'STEEN was getting ready for work when his phone rang. A reporter with the Associated Press was on the line. The decision in their case was just coming in over the teletype. O'Steen could hear the machine clattering in the background. The reporter started reading the ruling aloud. "You won," he said.

The decision was five to four. Harry Blackmun, writing for the majority, crafted what was supposed to be a narrow opinion. The only type of advertising that the court was explicitly upholding were ads that listed "routine" services and prices. The Arizona rule "serves to inhibit the free flow of commercial information and to keep the public in ignorance," Blackmun wrote.

But the minority saw what lay ahead. In his dissent, Lewis Powell noted that there was no reason that the ruling should not apply to other media—whether television or park benches. And "routine" was such a subjective, malleable word as to be almost meaningless. "I am apprehensive, despite the court's expressed intent to proceed cautiously, that today's holding will be viewed by tens of thousands of lawyers as an invitation—by the public-spirited and the selfish lawyers alike—to engage in competitive advertising on an escalating basis. Some lawyers may gain temporary advantages; others will suffer from the economic power of stronger lawyers, or by the subtle deceit of less scrupulous lawyers."

O'Steen called Bates and Canby. They met in the clinic's office. "We were overjoyed," Bates recalled. "We felt like we were on top of the world." That afternoon, the Arizona bar association called a news conference to discuss the ruling. Bates and O'Steen showed up, uninvited, wearing suits and ties. The event was in a large meeting room in a downtown high-rise. As it ended, the journalists realized that Bates and O'Steen were in the audience, and a scrum formed around them. An *Arizona Republic* photographer snapped a shot of them, O'Steen clean-shaven with a shaggy head of hair, Bates with a bushy beard and a receding hairline. The photo ran in *Newsweek*—along with an image of "their landmark ad"—in a piece headlined "Advertisers-at-Law."

The court's decision would soon unleash havoc. One early

harbinger involved the breakup of Bates and O'Steen. Bates saw his mission as helping the poor. Same with O'Steen, except he didn't see anything wrong with making money in the process. He sensed an opportunity to cash in on his newfound fame and the end of the prohibition on self-promotion. O'Steen told Bates that he wanted them to go their separate ways. Bates, surprised and hurt, could tell O'Steen had made up his mind and didn't bother arguing.

Soon, the new O'Steen Legal Clinic was hitting the airwaves—the first TV ads for lawyers in Arizona. A camera followed O'Steen as he walked around his smart new offices, talking about divorce, about personal injuries, about how he had fought all the way to the Supreme Court to make legal services available to the masses. Each time a spot aired, the office's switchboard would light up with calls. His little clinic grew into a decent-sized firm, with ten lawyers and five thousand square feet of office space. He'd land in a special issue of *Esquire,* alongside Eddie Murphy and Bruce Springsteen, as a member of "America's New Leadership Class." The magazine ran a photo of a smiling O'Steen showing off his firm's ad in the Phoenix Yellow Pages.

Bates was left with a sour taste in his mouth. There was something off-putting about O'Steen's self-promotion—and how effective it was. Not long after, he returned to public service, working in the Arizona attorney general's office. In 1992, he and his wife and their one-year-old son moved to Ohio. Bates now has a small law practice focused on personal bankruptcy cases. The two old friends haven't spoken in many years.

SOON THERE WOULD BE newspaper ads and radio spots and billboards for lawyers blanketing the country. Other changes were subtler. It wasn't just that ads were now permissible; as bar associations loosened their chokeholds, all manner of self-promotion became kosher.

By 1985, there were forty law firms that employed marketing directors (up from zero), and the number would soar to two hundred by the end of the decade. There was even a National Association of Law Firm Marketing Administrators. To raise their public profile, lawyers were encouraged to speak to journalists without fearing penalties from their local bar associations.

Dick Pogue had been closely tracking the *Goldfarb* and *Bates* cases. He briefed Allen Holmes on their significance. Holmes "was very farsighted, and he could see there would be significance if it came down the wrong way, which it did," Pogue recalled. He tasked Pogue with explaining to the firm's partners that it was now "perfectly proper" to solicit business, to market themselves. The partners gathered at the Union Club, around the corner from Jones Day's offices. More than forty years later, Pogue could still remember the shock on the lawyers' faces as he informed them that they were freed from centuries of professional norms. "They looked at me like I was from Mars," Pogue told me. "They just couldn't accept it. It was so drastically contrary to everything we had learned to accept."

After briefing the skeptical partners, Holmes and Pogue went to see Henry Eaton, whose PR firm, Dix & Eaton, was the best in Cleveland. "We'd like to see if it would be appropriate to get our name out," Pogue ventured to the spin doctor. The goal was to spread the word about Jones Day's accomplishments. Soon, Dix & Eaton was issuing a steady stream of press releases trumpeting Jones Day's victories. "It worked!" Pogue marveled. New clients noticed and hired the firm.

Others took things even further. One of the country's oldest firms, Cadwalader, set out to shed its stodgy image. Branding experts recommended a complete overhaul. Ditch the ancient maritime practice. Stop requiring people to wear three-piece suits. The firm went all-casual—and then decided to announce it to the world. Cadwalader brought in folks from Polo Ralph Lauren and *Esquire* magazine to teach the lawyers how to pull off casual attire with style and flair. A flurry of articles about lawyers in pastels popped up, thanks to the firm's newly ambitious marketing department.

Then someone came up with the idea of a fashion show. The venue was the Polo Ralph Lauren store on New York's Madison Avenue. Cameras flashed as Cadwalader's lawyers strutted their khakis on the catwalk.

5

CREATING A MONSTER

Around the time that Bates and O'Steen placed their ad in the *Arizona Republic,* Steve Brill made a fateful trip to a vending machine in New Haven, Connecticut. A native of Queens in New York City, Brill was a student at Yale Law School. Things came easily to him; he didn't attend classes much. What Brill was really into was writing. Back in college, he'd caught the journalism bug when the *New York Times* published his op-ed about a homeless man named Chicago, who regularly came by his parents' liquor store for a pint of port. ("Try to put yourself in his world for a moment," Brill wrote. "Live with Chicago and his wine, and his stench, and his beaten body, and his filth, and his loneliness, and his utter nothingness—or at least think about it so that it occupies your thoughts for one minute the way it must occupy his for a lifetime.")

By the time Brill was in law school, he'd finagled a gig writing for *New York* magazine. One day, he went to get a soda from a machine next to the school's recruitment office. He noticed a bulletin board crowded with letters from law firms, generically addressed to Yale law students. "Dear Potential Applicant," they would begin. Printed on thick paper stock, the letters all had the same pitch: Join us and join the best and get paid well to do fascinating work. Brill thought to himself, *Surely there are differences between all these law firms.* He decided to explore it in an article. He made some phone calls and quickly heard about two guys who were revolutionizing the industry: Joe Flom of Skadden Arps and Marty Lipton of Wachtell Lipton. They were working on hostile takeovers, a booming but slightly shady business that Wall Street's traditional law firms had shunned.

Brill's article ran in *New York* in June 1976. It narrated a takeover fight involving the gunmaker Colt Industries. But the story was really about these two idiosyncratic Jewish lawyers who were making gobs of money—millions and millions of dollars—for their firms playing the mergers-and-acquisitions "game." The ten-page article treated them like pro athletes—the good, the bad, the ugly. It glamorized their wealth and strategic brinkmanship.

This was unusual fare—one of the first times the legal profession had been written about as if the law was a cutthroat business or a sport, with attorneys from corporate firms playing starring, larger-than-life roles. (Of course, there was a long tradition, predating Brill, of do-gooder lawyers being valorized in the media and literature for their courtroom heroics: Thurgood Marshall fighting for civil rights, Clarence Darrow defending the teaching of evolution, even Atticus Finch in *To Kill a Mockingbird*.) Letters poured into *New York*. The piece had gone viral, 1970s-style, and Brill, having graduated from Yale, parlayed that success into a full-time job at the magazine. Months later, Rupert Murdoch bought *New York*, and Brill quit. He soon landed at *Esquire*, writing a regular column about the legal industry.

Imbued with his parents' entrepreneurialism, Brill figured he could take this a big step further: He would start his own magazine—all about lawyers and their firms, and he would cover them not as an aloof, isolated profession, but as a collection of ambitious individuals and institutions hustling for money, prestige, and power. He would call it the *American Lawyer*. All he needed was someone with deep pockets willing to take a risk.

A happy coincidence: A British company, Associated Newspapers, had just bought *Esquire*. Brill, twenty-seven years old, arranged to meet two Associated executives, Vere Harmsworth and Mick Shields, at the swanky Pierre hotel in Manhattan. On the appointed Friday in January 1978, Brill parked on Madison Avenue and put money in the meter for an hour. He had already provided Harmsworth and Shields a nineteen-page pitch. "The law is moving rapidly from a nineteenth century cottage industry to a modern profession and business," the document read. "In every community, large and small, lawyers are becoming openly more competitive for money and for clients . . . [and] are increasingly curious about the finances and affairs of their colleagues." The *American Lawyer*, Brill promised, "will be the nation's first trade paper for lawyers—about lawyers." The potential market, he noted, was considerable. There were some 400,000 lawyers practicing in the United States.

In their suite at the Pierre, Harmsworth and Shields sat in plush armchairs and asked a few questions. Brill kept glancing at his watch to see if he needed to feed the meter. But things zipped along. "Let's have a go at it," Harmsworth said. Brill left with a multimillion-dollar commitment. When he returned to his car, the meter had fifteen minutes left.

Now there was the small matter of figuring out how to create a magazine from scratch. Brill's wife, Cynthia, worked at a Wall Street law firm, and she knew a smart, gossipy young lawyer at the elite firm of Cravath, Swaine & Moore. His name was Jim Stewart. Brill and Cynthia took Stewart out to dinner in the West Village. Brill showed off a prototype of the magazine. Stewart lit up, effervescent. He was tiring of the Big Law life; his Cravath colleagues seemed to be experiencing joy, and while Stewart liked his job, he didn't love it. Growing up in Quincy, Illinois, he had written for the *Herald-Whig* newspaper, and his father had worked at the local TV station, so journalism was in his blood. Being a reporter had been fun! At Cravath, Stewart had kept a notepad in his desk drawer where he jotted down ideas for "stories that should be written" about law firms. Brill had his first employee.

More talent soon arrived: Jill Abramson, Ellen Pollock, Connie

Bruck, David Margolick, Steve Adler, Jim Cramer, Bob Windrem. It was a small army of cub reporters who would go on to be among their generation's leading journalists.

BRILL HAD PAID CLOSE attention to the Supreme Court's decision in *Bates*. By then he'd become all too familiar with lawyers' favorite refrain when fielding phone calls from reporters: As much as they might love to help, they were not allowed to speak to the press. It was against the rules. They couldn't risk being censured. Now, thanks to *Bates,* that self-serving excuse went out the window. Brill knew this would make his life easier.

The problem was that others knew it, too. Virtually overnight, a small cottage industry of legal publications had sprouted up. At the American Bar Association's annual meeting in 1978, attendees were besieged with staff shoving free copies of new publications into their hands. There was the *Legal Times,* which covered the industry with a D.C. slant. There was the fusty *National Law Journal*. And there was a "preview issue" of the *American Lawyer*—which Brill himself was handing out at the New York Hilton, where the convention was taking place. With all this competition, Brill knew his publication would need to be fresh and irreverent. The preview issue featured an article about an ugly fight between the law firm Kirkland & Ellis and an ousted partner—and a scoop that New York lawyers were paid, on average, $161,000 a year (about $690,000 today). An editor's note promised that "if you're curious about your colleagues—across the hall, across town, and across the nation, you'll want to read *The American Lawyer*."

That set the tone for what was to come, a saucy mix of scoops and gossip. The lead article in the inaugural issue the following February was about Joe Flom and his partners at Skadden: They were making more money than any other lawyers in the world. The cover featured an illustration of Flom's face on a dollar bill. ("In Flom We Trust," the money said.) For an industry that tried to downplay the financial aspect of the craft, this was the equivalent of a slap in the face. It was impossible to ignore.

The tabloid mentality continued in the subsequent issues. "Escaped Mental Patient Drives Judge Crazy," read one early headline. Some of the stories were accompanied by outlandish illustrations, including a judge with fangs. (Jones Day's first appearance was in May 1979, when Jim Stewart recounted the breakup of the D.C. office.)

The legal establishment treated Brill and his reporters like parasites. The American Bar Association refused to sell him its mailing list because the group considered the *American Lawyer* to be "a scurrilous publication." At one point, Brill was summoned to a meeting at a Wall Street law firm. He was escorted into a conference room with a table that looked to Brill like it was about the size of a tennis court. He sat at one end, the firm's chairman at the other. "I think your magazine is completely disgusting, and I think you're scum," the chairman spat. Another time, the managing partner of Shearman & Sterling phoned Brill: "We're the biggest firm in New York, and we're going to run you out of town." The greatest indignity might have been when, shortly after the *American Lawyer* launched, Cynthia Brill was forced out of her job at Winthrop, Stimson, Putnam & Roberts (a predecessor of today's Pillsbury Winthrop) because her husband's magazine was bringing "disrepute" upon the legal profession.

Brill and his troupe of young reporters, toiling away in a corner of *Esquire*'s Midtown Manhattan offices, reveled in their outcast status. The scruffy reporters looked and acted the part. Jill Abramson would bring her baby daughter to work one day a week; she'd nap on a blanket on the floor. On Friday afternoons, a group of reporters would smoke pot on the opposite side of the floor from Brill's glass-walled office. The pay was terrible. Jim Stewart had gone to Harvard Law, and an alumni publication collected data on how much its graduates were earning and then published the highest and lowest figures in anonymous form. Stewart was embarrassed to see he was dead last among his former classmates.

For all his take-no-prisoners gusto, for all his ambition to shake up this stodgy, cosseted industry, Brill seemed to hanker deep down for acceptance in it. He wanted the power and the status—or at least that's how his reporters saw it. Perhaps as a result, Brill favored pinstriped suits and two-toned shirts. He wore his hair slicked back like Gordon Gekko, and an unlit cigar often jutted from the corner of his mouth.

The reporters vacillated between worshipping and fearing Brill. He was a bully. When he marked up reporters' drafts, he'd scrawl insults in a red, felt-tipped pen: "What are you, a moron?" "Is English your second language?" "You should be fired for this crock of shit." Even his sister remarked that "he can be a real S.O.B." On one occasion, a young woman threatened to stab Brill with a pair of scissors after he made an especially nasty series of comments. Inside the *American Lawyer*'s offices, there was a small, windowless room with a vinyl couch where reporters would go to cry; a wet-cheeked Jim Cramer, now famous for his bug-eyed theatrics on CNBC, was spotted in there more than once. (Brill acknowledges that he used to behave badly. "I'm not proud of that," he told me. "I think about that stuff a lot now.")

But Brill was also fearless (and a tad cavalier). If a powerful lawyer called him to accuse a reporter of bias, Brill would put the man on hold and shout for the offending journalist to step into his office. In came the reporter. Brill would put the lawyer on speakerphone and say to the reporter, *Such-and-such lawyer is furious with your biased coverage. You're doing a fabulous job if you're pissing them off.* And that would be the end of the phone call. What's more, there was no question that Brill was a gifted journalist; listening to him work the phones himself, reporters picked up strategies and style through osmosis. "I learned everything I know about journalism from Brill," said Jill Abramson, who would later run the *New York Times*. "Seriously."

• • •

STEWART, WHO WOULD GO on to be a bestselling author and *New York Times* columnist, came up with the idea for one of the *American Lawyer*'s first big innovations. Tall and thin, Stewart was into running, and he'd recently come across a piece in *Runner's World* magazine that ranked the best sneakers. That inspired Stewart to propose ratings of which firms had the best programs for summer associates (the students between their second and third years of law school). His brainchild, which debuted on the cover of the October 1979 issue, became a popular fixture. Law firms angled to improve their images by offering new perks, more money, and boozy parties to law students—and, in the case of one firm, having a top partner secretly fill out surveys on behalf of summer associates. (Jones Day in 1980 drew high marks for its $2,300-a-month summer salaries and outings to the Cedar Point Amusement Park on the banks of Lake Erie.)

Taking a page from law firms' playbook, Brill began hosting summer outings for his staff. The venue was a home he rented in the New York suburbs. Brill was a water polo fanatic, and he pushed his employees to participate in matches in his pool. One sunny afternoon, he was facing off against a team that included Stewart and Cramer. Cramer was poised to score the tying goal. Brill swam toward him and sank his teeth into Cramer's cocked throwing arm. Cramer dropped the ball. He had to be led out of the pool, leaving a swirling trail of blood in the chlorinated water. (Decades later, Brill alternately insisted to me that he didn't bite Cramer and that he didn't draw blood.) By the end of the game, Stewart, too, had bloody scratches crisscrossing his torso. "That was Steve all over," Cramer would write. "He stopped my attempt, won the game, and gave new meaning to unsportsmanlike conduct, all with one bite."

Most Friday evenings, Brill would drive up to his country house. He'd pour himself a Scotch and sit outside, alone, and stare at the stars. He often came up with what felt like great ideas, which he would excitedly share with his staff on Monday mornings, only to realize, as he described them out loud, that they weren't quite as brilliant as they'd seemed under the starlight and the influence of whiskey. His staff talked him out of many a half-baked epiphany.

So when Brill showed up in the magazine's offices—by now it had its own digs, on an upper floor of an art deco building on Park Avenue—on a Monday in early 1985 with the fruits of another Scotch-infused brainstorming session, his employees were ready to roll their eyes. His idea was this: a ranking of the top law firms based on their revenue and profitability. He proposed calling it the "AmLaw 100"—in other words, they'd rank the top hundred firms in the country. This sort of financial data wasn't publicly available, yet it was the most objective way to judge the size and success of the nation's leading firms. Lawyers and law students would surely salivate at this type of information.

The staff started discussing this idea. They were reluctant. It would require an enormous investment of time and energy. In various articles over the years, the *American Lawyer* had figured out the relevant metrics for maybe twenty firms. Reporters would have to identify sources at the other eighty firms and get them to divulge their innermost financial secrets. "Everyone said I was nuts to do the AmLaw 100," Brill told me. Ellen Pollock* was among those who managed to talk him down to the AmLaw 50. From there, the staff started cooking up different ways to crunch numbers. One was a metric called profits per partner (a firm's total profits divided by its number of partners), which seemed like a decent proxy for which firms' partners were the most lavishly rewarded. "We were sort of making it up as we went along," Brill said.

Tracking down the information was complicated. Reporters would go through phone directories and cold-call partners. (To nail down the data for one especially impenetrable firm, Pollock made sixty-two calls.) "Some of the lawyers were just appalled,"

* She is now the business editor—and my boss—at the *New York Times*.

Bob Windrem, who would go on to a long career as an investigative reporter at NBC News, told me. "They would make you feel you were doing something highly improper by calling and asking for these numbers," Jill Abramson added. "They just thought we were nosy and low-class. It was really horrible work."

Then someone made a discovery. Leading lawyers in those days tended to sit on the boards of the companies they advised. Publicly traded companies were required to report in securities filings how much they paid their board members—and any transactions they'd done with anyone or anything directly connected to those board members. Buried in corporate filings, there'd often be a footnote revealing that a company paid, say, a million dollars in legal fees to a board member's law firm. Reporters could use the clue to pry more information from their sources.

The rankings debuted in a special edition in July 1985, with a special "AmLaw 50" logo on the cover. There were several categories: the highest-grossing firms, those with the most revenue and profits per partner (a metric that would soon become known in the industry as PPP), and an "Am Law Profitability Index," which basically combined all the metrics into a single number.

Jones Day was all over the map. It was tied with Cravath for eighth in terms of gross revenue, with $82 million. (Skadden topped the chart with $129 million.) It ranked fortieth in terms of profits per partner, at $210,000. (No. 1 was Wachtell Lipton, at $795,000.)

In a long article accompanying the rankings, Brill noted that many lawyers would view the focus on finances as "emblematic of how crass a business the profession has become. In fact, some suggested that the very existence of a survey like this is destined to make things worse." Brill defended the AmLaw 50 by citing the keen interest that lawyers expressed about their competitors' finances during the magazine's reporting process. "To put it mildly, everyone was anxious to know how his firm was going to rank. Were we creating not only a good story but also a monster—a set of dollar rankings that would further obliterate the old values of the profession? Will partners become obsessed with how they rank this year—or next, when we will probably expand our effort to 100 or 200 firms? Yes, this survey may accelerate the growing competitiveness among firms and the awareness that it's a tough new world out there. Better market information often has that effect in a free, vigorous economy. And, yes, for some that may mean an increased willingness, even an enthusiasm, for throwing professionalism aside."

Some of Brill's reporters shared that queasiness. They felt that distilling law firms down to profit-making entities debased the profession. No right-minded journalist doubted the value of aggressively covering law firms, and there was no question that publishing detailed data about their finances was fair game. But was it good for the world?

BEHOLD THE CHANGES THAT swept the legal industry, whose practitioners not all that long ago would have strenuously objected to being described as part of an industry.

Lawyers could see how much their peers at rival firms were making and then threaten to leave if their firm didn't match the pay. They could even compare what they were earning to the Big Swinging Dicks of the 1980s: Wall Street's investment bankers and traders. Students at top law schools could now pick firms based not only on their reputations and starting salaries but also on how their profits per partner stacked up.

What happened next should not come as a surprise. Firms started paying more to retain and recruit talent. Cravath fired the starter pistol in 1986—the year after the *American Lawyer* unveiled its rankings—by hiking salaries for first-year associates to $65,000 from $53,000. Rivals scrambled to match this new going rate. The move was greeted by horror and indignation within the industry. It was "one of the most antisocial acts of the bar in recent history," a Stanford Law professor fumed. "It drives impressionable young associates toward consumption patterns and expectations of opulence that will be hard to shake off if they want to change careers."

A vicious cycle began to spin. To afford higher salaries, law firms needed more revenue. They could get that by opening new offices and hiring new lawyers, but that meant their costs went up. Lawyers came under pressure to increase their billable hours and to accept clients that, not long ago, might have caused heartburn. That was what it took to compete and to boost your all-important profits-per-partner figure.

The size of the legal industry exploded. The number of firms with more than fifty lawyers doubled between 1985 and 1998. In the mid-1980s, no law firm had more than one thousand lawyers. A decade later, seventeen did. The industry—with dozens of firms raking in at least a billion dollars a year in revenue—soon rivaled the auto sector in economic value.

Firms abandoned the quaint notion of not poaching each other's lawyers. And lawyers, who used to worry that jumping from one firm to another would reflect poorly on them, now did so with gusto, enticed by the money. The number of recruiting firms focused on the legal industry tripled between 1984 and 1989. The greater mobility between firms imperiled smaller shops' financial security. The loss of a rainmaker—and a corresponding drop in revenues of even 5 percent for a year—"can create immense risks to the stability of a firm," a longtime partner at Arnold & Porter wrote in 1989. That fear led to compromises. If a star lawyer was an asshole, would you risk penalizing him? Come down too hard, and he might just bolt, taking his clients with him. More often than not, such dilemmas were resolved by ignoring allegations of abuse or misconduct.

Round and round this went. The more people joined a partnership, the more the firm's profits got divvied up, and the more pressure there was to expand that pie. That meant the firm needed to hire more associates, and to push them to bill tons of hours, so that the firm could keep increasing its revenue. The problem was that this hiring put more lawyers on a partnership track. It was a path toward exponential growth. "Growth changes the character of the firm," two professors, Marc Galanter and Thomas Palay, wrote in their seminal 1991 book *Tournament of Lawyers*. "Informality recedes; collegiality gives way; notions of public service and independence are marginalized; the imperative of growth collides with notions of dignified passivity in obtaining business."

Billable hours became arguably the single most important determinant of a young lawyer's success. In the 1950s, the American Bar Association found that lawyers at big firms couldn't reasonably work more than 1,300 billable hours a year—about twenty-five hours a week, not counting any vacations. (Keep in mind that not every working hour is generally billable.) In the early 1980s, billing 1,600 hours a year was considered great. By the late 1990s, most large firms pushed associates to bill at least 2,000 hours a year. A decade later, 2,500 billable hours would be common.

Cheating ensued. One law firm billed 12 hours a day for months on behalf of a lawyer who was comatose following a car accident. Another lawyer billed 62 hours in a single day. At a Chicago firm, a lawyer billed about 5,500 hours in a year—roughly 15 hours a day, every day—and claimed to have pulled 52 consecutive all-nighters while working on bankruptcy cases.

Attorneys under pressure to perform financially were more likely to cross ethical lines. In a national survey of lawyers in the 1990s, one-third said lawyers today were more likely to lie than in the past; three-quarters said lawyers had become more "money-conscious." Satisfying corporate clients was key, and their general counsels—these were the guys who doled out jobs to law firms—liked hearing things that would please their C-suite bosses. In this context, "it is likely that ethical gray zones will get resolved in the client's favor," Galanter and another professor, William Henderson (who had briefly worked at Jones Day), wrote in 2008. What was the point of saying no to a client if the client would just dump you and go find another firm willing to say yes?

"The leaders of the law in America, historically, have been men who could say no, who preserved their autonomy, who served their clients with their hearts, their skills, their advice, their advocacy, and their friendship—but not with their souls or with their citizenship," Sol Linowitz, a famed lawyer and diplomat, wrote in *The Betrayed Profession* in 1994. "Not many years ago . . . law firms were jealous of their reputation and would not risk having their name associated with shady operators." That credo became roadkill. "The only question that counts now is whether a client will bring money into the firm," Howard Fineman, a senior partner at the law firm Loeb & Loeb, told a journalist in 1998.

As he was researching his book in the early 1990s, Sol Linowitz asked Brill about the vicious cycle. "It's all my fault," Brill admitted.

6

KEEPING UP WITH THE JONES DAYS

Dick Pogue was in his office when the call came from London. Allen Holmes was on the line. The iron-willed Holmes hadn't let his precarious health get in the way of his pursuit of the good life. It was February 1984, and he was in England for a meeting of the International Wine & Food Society, a gastronomic club of which he had recently been named president. Then his Guillain-Barré syndrome struck. Holmes, calling from a hospital and paralyzed from the neck down, informed Pogue that he was hereby appointed as Jones Day's managing partner.

Like Holmes, Pogue was a tireless worker. He hardly slept; even as a baby, he would stay up until 11:00 p.m. and wake six hours later, pounding on his crib to get out (and causing his parents a fair amount of worry about their sleep-deprived infant). This didn't change in adulthood, though Pogue found time for poker and the saxophone. He "puts in more hours than I do, and I was doing what amounted to about 3,000 hours a year," Holmes would say.

Now, as the managing partner of the firm he had joined twenty-seven years earlier, Pogue had two main priorities. One was to gain the respect of the firm's partners. The other was growth. The combination of the Supreme Court's rulings in *Goldfarb* and *Bates* and the emergence of the legal media had convinced Pogue that a new era was dawning for his revered profession. Expansion wasn't just a goal; it was a prerequisite. "Everyone else was going to do it,"

Pogue recalled decades later. Jones Day had to move fast or be left behind.

The firm had a jump on most of its rivals. After moving into L.A., Jones Day had opened an office in Columbus, Ohio, and then, in 1981, in Dallas. That made Jones Day the first out-of-state law firm in Texas. The *New York Times* had seized on the deal as proof of an emerging trend of law firms becoming national, ending "the traditional identification of law firms with single cities."

With 335 lawyers in five offices, it was not crazy to argue that Jones Day had achieved Holmes's ambition of becoming a truly national firm. When Jack Reavis addressed a group of Jones Day associates in 1983, he remarked wistfully how much the firm had changed. Only one of its five largest clients was based in northeast Ohio, and the rest had "practically nothing to do with Cleveland."

Now in the driver's seat, Pogue stomped on the gas. The U.S. economy was booming, with the Reagan administration's deregulation acting as a shot of adrenaline. This go-go period would come to be regarded as a time of recklessness and greed, but in the moment it seemed like a golden opportunity for Jones Day to get bigger. Three months after he took over, Pogue decided to open an office in Austin, which was among the fastest-growing cities in the U.S. The move would set the tone for the rest of his tenure.

Pogue asked Rick Kneipper, a lawyer who'd helped open the Dallas office, to start thinking strategically about how Jones Day could keep growing. The two men discussed shedding the traditional lawyer mentality and thinking more like investment bankers. Kneipper and a small team began analyzing the business landscape and looking for areas—industries and regions—that were poised for growth and where other law firms hadn't already established positions of dominance.

The firm's next leap would be much bigger. Globalization was in full swing. "If we wanted to be at the forefront of the profession, we needed to be international," Pogue explained.

The first step, he concluded, was to establish an outpost in New

York, which was the port of entry for many European and Asian companies seeking to do business in America. "People didn't take you seriously without a New York office," Pogue told me. His team drew up a list of potential acquisition targets and then started putting out feelers. After a few aborted attempts, Pogue's crew came across Surrey & Morse, a venerable New York firm with offices in Washington, London, Paris, and Riyadh. The firm's leaders were nearing retirement age, and their frugality appealed to Pogue, who, for all his ambition, favored austerity.

The deal was completed on January 1, 1986. At the time it was the biggest law-firm merger ever. With the addition of Surrey & Morse's 79 lawyers, Jones Day now had a total of 572 worldwide. Pogue got on the phone with the *New York Times* to tout the acquisition. "The international offices were the primary attraction," he explained. The firm had become the country's second-largest, behind only Baker McKenzie.

JONES DAY GOT MORE than just an international law firm when it bought Surrey & Morse. It also got a lobbying shop. For years, Surrey & Morse had represented foreign governments as they sought to influence Washington. Now the lobbying business—which Welch Pogue had shunned when he was running Jones Day's Washington office because he considered it demeaning—belonged to Jones Day.

Jones Day had already established a pedigree as a politically wired firm with a clear rightward tilt. It went beyond Chappie Rose's counseling of Nixon. In 1980, Jones Day had filed a lawsuit against President Carter on behalf of Marathon Oil, protesting the imposition of an import fee on crude oil. Jones Day won. Months later, the firm represented Reagan's presidential campaign when the Carter campaign sued to prevent him from collecting $29 million in federal election funds. Once again, Jones Day beat Carter. The back-to-back victories became a point of pride. "Jones Day has the unique distinction of having defended one president and sued another in the same year," wrote Albert Borowitz, a Jones Day lawyer, in his 1993 history of the firm.

Even so, Jones Day had avoided trying to sway federal officials on behalf of clients. That made the firm an outlier. Other large firms in the capital—like Patton Boggs and Akin Gump, among many others—had made this sort of work a foundation of their Washington practices. Now Jones Day plunged into this rough-and-tumble world. Surrey & Morse's lobbying clients included the South African Sugar Association, which wanted to defang international sanctions against the country's apartheid government, and the Chinese government on issues including Tibet and China's one-child policy. Such work might have left the old guard at Jones Day feeling queasy, but it was lucrative. And with the firm growing rapidly, it was incumbent upon all offices to generate as much revenue as possible, as quickly as possible.

That was how, a couple of years later, Jones Day found itself capitalizing on a crisis in the Libyan desert. In November 1988, the U.S. government issued a warning to European countries that Muammar Gaddafi's regime had built a poison-gas factory with the help of Western companies. Before long, the names of those companies were made public. One of them was West Germany's Preussag, which had built a water-purification plant that ended up serving the weapons factory southwest of Tripoli. Preussag officials denied wrongdoing, but the company was already in hot water for allegedly having helped build a chemical weapons factory in Iraq.

American lawmakers were angry. In January 1989, Senators Bob Dole and Jesse Helms introduced bills to punish companies that aided outlaw countries in developing chemical and biological weapons. Helms entered into the Congressional Record a list of companies, including Preussag, that were accused of assisting in proliferation. Senator John McCain blasted the members of this "Roll of Dishonor." "Such companies must be judged guilty until proven innocent," he thundered. "One strike and you're out!"

Lawyers at Jones Day smelled an opportunity. Six days after the bills were introduced, a partner in the newly acquired Paris office wrote a letter to Preussag. The letter warned that Preussag faced possible sanctions that would prevent it from importing products into the U.S. "Jones Day is uniquely qualified to be of assistance to Preussag to represent its interests on the Hill and the executive branch," the partner wrote.

Attached was a twelve-page "Proposal for Representation of Preussag." It was a blunt articulation of how Jones Day hoped to use its growing roster of well-connected insiders to influence events in Washington—and specifically to help a company avoid punishment for helping Libya develop dangerous weapons.

The proposal recommended that Preussag "embark upon a series of meetings" with key officials throughout the George H. W. Bush administration and on Capitol Hill. "Jones Day would be prepared to set up and attend these meetings," the proposal explained.

The letter outlined why Jones Day was right for the task. It wasn't the firm's international reach or its expertise on sanctions or its skillful lawyers. It was that Jones Day had people with access to the country's leaders. There was former GOP senator Charles Mathias, who had joined Jones Day in 1987 after eighteen years on the Senate Foreign Relations Committee. There was Herbert Hansell, who had spent years at the State Department and "is currently actively involved with the State Department on behalf of many of the firm's international clients." There was Jonathan Rose, who "has close relations with many individuals currently serving in the White House." There was Randall Davis, who had served in the Reagan and Bush White Houses "and has maintained a close working relationship with many individuals now on the White House staff." Finally, there were Victor Raiser and Jane Harman, who were in touch with Democratic congressional leaders "as a result of their fundraising activities" and would be involved "should this project involve contact with the Democratic leadership."

It was a compelling pitch, in part because of its unusual candor in outlining exactly how the firm intended to exploit its connections. Preussag signed on as a client. Davis reached out to folks on the Senate Foreign Relations Committee and assured them that Preussag wouldn't service the water-purification equipment it had provided to the Libyans. Senate aides said they'd take that into consideration if the legislation began to move.

The legislation never moved; the bills died without a hearing. But the successful pitch showed Jones Day the power of capitalizing on its lawyers' political comrades and their prior work for the government. The lesson would resonate for decades to come.

AFTER THE SURREY & Morse acquisition, Dick Pogue went on a spree. Later in 1986, Jones Day opened a Hong Kong office. Then it acquired a Chicago firm and opened an office in Geneva. A Pittsburgh outpost came in early 1989. Four months later Jones Day bought a firm in Atlanta. That was Jones Day's tenth U.S. office, and it left the firm with more than one thousand lawyers. It went on to open offices in Tokyo and Brussels that year, followed by Taipei and Frankfurt.

In the space of about a decade, Jones Day had gone from being an unremarkable regional firm to being one of the largest and most important in the world. It became the envy of the industry. "The clients flow from one city to the other and back again," marveled a partner with Akin Gump. "It's awesome to behold." In Brussels, the firm hired so many people that local lawyers coined the phrase "keeping up with the Jones Days" to reflect the race for talent that the firm had kicked off.

Jones Day prospered. By 1988, it was the country's second-largest firm in terms of revenue, behind only Skadden. Under Pogue's watch, Jones Day expanded from 335 lawyers in 5 U.S. cities to more than 1,200 lawyers in 20 offices around the world.

POGUE RULED HIS DOMAIN with an autocratic air. He was a micromanager. If a memo was being sent out about the vacation policy for secretaries, Pogue would insist on reviewing and editing it beforehand, to the frustration of even his admirers. He was often gruff. The journalist Mark Stevens noted in 1987 that Pogue's "assets do not include a sparkling personality." In interviews, Pogue was prone to repeating, over and over, that he was in charge, that he was the monarch: "In the end, I make all decisions." "I have the authority to run the firm." "There are no appeals."

It would be easy to lump Pogue in with that era's imperial CEO: strong-willed, supremely ambitious, arguably narcissistic men like General Electric's Jack Welch who lavished themselves with nine-figure paydays. But Pogue differed from that breed in a key respect. He wasn't in it for himself. All he cared about was Jones Day. Yes, his power was absolute. But he viewed that as crucial to the firm's ability to make quick decisions, unburdened by the never-ending committees and consensus-building that bogged everything down at other firms. Pogue didn't see a problem with this approach, so long as the managing partner exercised his power on the firm's behalf, not his own. And that was what Pogue did. He eschewed the trappings of wealth and power, showing up to business meetings in ill-fitting suits and ties that didn't match his cheap printed shirts. He drove a Chevy. He flew coach.

On one occasion, a junior lawyer boarded a plane for a business trip and settled into his first-class seat at the front of the cabin. Then, to his surprise, he spotted Pogue getting on board. The lanky managing partner shuffled past the associate to his seat at the rear of the aircraft. The associate nearly had a panic attack; had Pogue spotted him sitting in his expensive seat? What would he think? The plane took off and reached cruising altitude, and the young lawyer calmed himself by considering the unlikelihood that Pogue would even recognize a lowly associate. That is when he felt a tap on his shoulder. It was a flight attendant. "There's a fellow in the back who says you wouldn't mind changing seats with him," she said. On that rare occasion, Pogue enjoyed a first-class flight.

7

THE GREATEST CLIENT

In early 1985, Pogue and a couple of his colleagues boarded a flight from Cleveland to Greensboro, North Carolina. Their destination was the headquarters of the tobacco company R.J. Reynolds. Years earlier, Pogue had lost his luggage on a business trip, and now he refused to check his bags, so the lawyers trudged through the Greensboro airport, hauling suitcases, on their way to catch a quick connecting flight to Winston-Salem.

The Jones Day squad had been invited to Winston-Salem by Harold Henderson, who for many years had been the general counsel of Firestone Tire in Ohio. Firestone had faced ruinous litigation because its car tires had a nasty habit of exploding, and Jones Day's team—led by one of the country's best litigators, Pat McCartan—had successfully defused lawsuits and federal investigations. (McCartan's defense was that yes, the tires were flawed, but hey, the process of binding rubber and steel wasn't perfect.)

Henderson had recently decamped to RJR. From a legal standpoint, at least, the tobacco industry was coming off a successful few decades. Suits brought by smokers generally got tossed out of courts, a reflection of the industry's savvy at obscuring the evidence that smoking was addictive and deadly. And cigarette companies were determined to never settle cases—only fight, fight, fight. There would be no easy wins for plaintiffs' lawyers. Remarkably, the tobacco industry had never been forced to pay any damages.

By the mid-1980s, even as nearly one of every three American adults smoked, the landscape was shifting. Thousands of scientific reports had meticulously documented the health hazards of smoking; the annual death toll was estimated at 350,000 Americans. "No smoking" signs were becoming common. And courts increasingly held manufacturers liable when they produced dangerous products—like asbestos or faulty breast implants—even if others shared some of the blame for the health consequences.

Now the bill was threatening to come due for the tobacco industry. In the fall of 1985, a pair of closely watched lawsuits against RJR—one in Tennessee, the other in California—were set to go to trial. Henderson surveyed RJR's defense teams. They consisted mostly of small local firms. He got the feeling that his new employer, lulled by years of placid waters, was sailing into a gale.

After Pogue and his colleagues met with RJR brass in Winston-Salem, Henderson consulted with his board of directors and got permission to appoint Jones Day as RJR's lead litigation counsel. First, though, he needed an assurance. He warned Pogue that he, Henderson, would be going "far out on a limb" by hiring a Cleveland law firm for this "bet-your-company" assignment. Pogue promised Henderson that Jones Day was prepared to stand "shoulder-to-shoulder" with its new client.

This would turn out to be a momentous decision for Jones Day, but the lawyers scarcely thought twice about representing a tobacco company. Smoking was not nearly the cultural kryptonite it would become. More than that, the attorneys saw the gig as a validation of all the hard work they had put into years of thankless litigation on behalf of Firestone and other companies. Of course, it didn't hurt that this new client would likely become an extravagant moneymaker for Jones Day. "I do not recall that anyone at the firm had 'qualms' about representing Reynolds," Pogue wrote to me in an email. "It has always been my personal philosophy that everyone is entitled to counsel, no matter how unpopular their cause happens to appear in some circles at any particular time, and so it never occurred to me that anyone would question the firm's representation of a successful, law-abiding organization." Assuming that was true, it reflected a jarring lack of imagination and foresight on the part of a brilliant lawyer.

The reality was that the Jones Day litigators didn't see these tobacco lawsuits as a matter of justice. Sure, the cigarette companies were selling deadly products. But plaintiffs' lawyers were just trying to make a buck, and prosecutors were just trying to make names for themselves. (Jones Day lawyers would joke that the letters "AG," which typically stood for "attorney general," actually were short for "aspiring governor.") This was a cynical but not entirely unfounded view, and it allowed the lawyers to avoid moral judgment and instead adopt a mercenary approach to the practice of the law. There were no good guys or bad guys in this type of litigation, the attorneys assured themselves. It was more like a game, and everyone was doing whatever they could to win.

JONES DAY OFFICIALLY CAME on board as RJR's defense firm on April 1, 1985, and the following months would be frenzied. In downtown Winston-Salem, a large team set up shop on the tenth floor of the Integon building. The lawyers began the arduous and top-secret process of sifting through millions of RJR's documents to understand the lay of the land. Small squads of attorneys fanned out to interview current and former scientists, executives, and in-house lawyers.

One result was a long report detailing the history of RJR's work to oppose government regulations—a history that included destroying documents, hiring scientists to create smokescreens, and moving controversial research projects overseas to improve the odds that they'd be kept secret. The Jones Day document made clear that RJR knew that, at least for some people, its product was addictive. The law firm also produced a manual laying out its litigation strategy, which consisted in large part of blaming smokers for their own misfortune. "The key defense strategy in smoking and health litigation is (and must be) to try the plaintiff," the manual explained. Another tenet was muddying the science. "The defense must not concede that cigarette smoking has been proved to be addictive," Jones Day instructed. "Indeed, there are substantial benefits to be derived over waging a definitional battle" over the meaning of words like "addiction." A group of lawyers was directed to find experts who would be willing to testify that cigarettes weren't addictive or harmful.

John Strauch, a renowned Jones Day trial lawyer and Camel Lights smoker, commanded this army of attorneys. By the fall of 1985, he had emerged as a public spokesman for the tobacco industry. The fact that cigarettes cause health problems "has not been scientifically established," he falsely told the PBS show *Frontline*.* "There is a real controversy raging about what science has and has not been able to establish yet." He denied that smoking was anything more than an enjoyable habit. Otherwise, he asserted, "you end up claiming that chocolate is addictive."

Another Jones Day attorney, Bob Weber, was on a team prepping for the trial that was soon to start in Santa Barbara, a beach town in Southern California. Weber, who was in his mid-thirties, would go on to become one of the firm's most successful lawyers and a top contender to one day run the place. This trial would be a crucial proving ground.

Weber had grown up in small-town Ohio, where he was a high school football star. Yale recruited him for its team, but during the first scrimmage of his freshman season, he ripped up his shoulder, and that was the end of that. It slowly dawned on Weber that he'd need to come up with a career plan. Maybe he could return to Geauga County and become a football coach. He toyed with going to grad school. Instead, he became a substitute teacher for a year, which was more than enough time for him to realize he wasn't cut out to be a teacher. So, like countless other young people looking to

---

* Strauch insisted to me that he wasn't lying.

buy time before committing to a career path, Weber decided to go to law school. He got into Duke.

Weber didn't know anything about the legal industry, and he wasn't alone. It was 1973, before *Bates* and the *American Lawyer*. He didn't realize there was such a thing as large law firms, until recruiting season got underway during his second year. Weber was studying in a cubicle in the basement of Duke's library when a lawyer from Jones Day came by to introduce himself, having gotten his name from one of Weber's professors. The lawyer invited Weber to lunch—and then to Cleveland for a weekend of interviews. After graduating in 1976, Weber joined Jones Day as an associate.

At first, he was stuck on boring assignments. When a Jones Day client was preparing to issue bonds to raise money, he had to sit around the facility where the prospectuses were printed, going through draft after draft. There was booze and a round-the-clock buffet and a TV with porno movies in the back. Weber must have wondered whether this was the best use of his time and talent.

When he wasn't hanging around printing plants, he played on the Jones Day softball team, along with a bunch of guys from the litigation department. Weber liked them and soon finagled a job from John Strauch, who ran the group. Weber started small, helping defend General Motors in a lawsuit, then moved on to the Firestone cases. Strauch would mark up Weber's deposition transcripts, dispensing little tips, as they flew from one city to the next to interview witnesses and experts.

Under Strauch's tutelage, Weber became a great trial lawyer. He mastered the psychology of juries. During jury selection, he learned to ask open-ended questions about what these men and women read, what their interests were. He wanted jurors who had a positive outlook and believed they could make a difference in the world. Folks like that were more likely to embrace individual responsibility than to blame corporations for misfortune. During trials, he emphasized his rural roots while avoiding a patronizing aw-shucks demeanor. "He was raised not to be presumptuous," his wife once said. He was highly attuned to how jurors perceived lawyers. He pushed his colleagues to think less about impressing the judge and focus more on the jury. *Don't sit around whispering to each other or passing notes—jurors hate that.* "They watch how you treat the people you work with. They watch how you react when our witness is on the stand," Weber would explain. The goal was "communicating with that jury that we know what's going on, that nothing is surprising us, and that we're in control."

Years later, Weber composed a handbook, divulging to his colleagues the trial tactics that had made him largely invincible in a courtroom. "That's how I wanted the jury to see me; as an advocate to be sure, but not an unfair or nasty one. Not an advocate using sharp tactics or trying to win at any cost; instead an advocate who, just like the jury, was interested in putting out the full story and reaching the 'right' result," he wrote. "To carry out that persona, the lawyer must be fair with witnesses, fair with evidence, and fair with the jury." This was a bit of a shtick—a persona, as Weber put it—but if followed carefully, it translated into ethical conduct: *Don't quote things out of context. Don't mislead. Don't adopt self-serving interpretations of ambiguous documents.* "Let your sense of fundamental decency and ethics motivate you throughout trial," he concluded.

Not all of his colleagues would follow Weber's advice. And in any case, it only applied to how the firm behaved in the presence of jurors.

TWENTY-FIVE YEARS EARLIER, MELVIN Belli had lost the first-ever tobacco lawsuit to go to trial. He'd sued tobacco companies twenty times since then. He'd never won. Now, in John Galbraith, Belli thought he'd found his silver bullet, a plaintiff who would finally knock Big Tobacco to its knees.

Belli was one of America's most famous lawyers. His roster of clients ranged from Jack Ruby to Muhammad Ali, with plenty of politicians, movie stars, musicians, and millionaires mixed in. But he was best known for his exploits as a plaintiff's lawyer. He pioneered the use of graphic evidence—gigantic photos of accident scenes or gruesome injuries, sometimes even a skeleton—to drive home his points to a jury. In the 1950s, *Life* magazine dubbed him the "King of Torts," and the moniker stuck. Once, after winning a big case, he hoisted a Jolly Roger flag atop his firm's offices and fired a cannon to signal the start of the celebration. With a mane of silver hair, he generally appeared in court wearing fine tailored suits, lined with red silk, and black snakeskin boots. "When you're the king of torts, you've got to live like the king of torts," Belli explained.

Belli had filed a $100 million lawsuit against RJR in 1981 on behalf of John Galbraith, who'd started smoking in 1930 when he was eighteen. Every day for the next fifty years, he'd consumed at least two packs of Camel, Winston, or Salem cigarettes, all made by RJR. Even on his deathbed, kept alive by an oxygen tube snaking up his nostrils, Galbraith would sneak smokes. That's how addicted he was. He died in the summer of 1982 at sixty-nine. (His widow and adult children took over as plaintiffs in the suit.)

In 1984, the U.S. surgeon general had branded smoking as the "chief single avoidable cause of death in our society," and the director of the National Institute on Drug Abuse had deemed cigarettes more addictive than alcohol or even heroin. With the science clear, Belli was confident this case would be a turning point in the war against tobacco. He planned to make addiction the centerpiece of his case. If the Galbraith family won, it was sure to trigger a tidal wave of new suits by smokers and their families. Already, there were about seventy-five similar lawsuits against RJR pending nationwide.

Weber, Strauch, and the Jones Day squad had a simple objective: Crush this lawsuit. Pulverize it. Make Belli rue the day he had pursued RJR. Doing so would signal to other would-be plaintiffs and their lawyers that RJR was not going to roll over. It was going to continue to fight with all its strength.

From the start, the battle was lopsided. Lawyers for RJR submitted thousands of pages of motions and briefs, burying Belli's team in paperwork. Jones Day demanded that the Galbraiths hand over

Christmas cards, phone logs, lists of attendees at family members' weddings and birthdays. The RJR contingent subpoenaed and then deposed just about anyone who had ever been in contact with Galbraith: distant relatives, former employees, an ex-wife from more than forty years ago. After tracking her down in a trailer park in the Arizona desert, a team of six lawyers spent hours interviewing her about Galbraith's hobbies and eating habits. Did he use bug spray? Did he eat peanut butter? Did he read books? Meanwhile, whenever Belli's side wanted to depose an RJR witness, Jones Day strenuously objected. That meant the plaintiffs had to go to court to force the witness to sit for an interview, which ate up more time and resources. A couple of years later, a Jones Day lawyer would sum up the strategy: "The aggressive posture we have taken regarding depositions . . . continues to make these cases extremely burdensome and expensive for plaintiffs' lawyers. To paraphrase General Patton, the way we won these cases was not by spending all of Reynolds's money, but by making that other son of a bitch spend all of his."

Shortly before the Galbraith trial began, Jones Day and its client faced an important choice. Belli had filed the lawsuit in state court against not only RJR but also the store that for years had sold Galbraith cigarettes. The fact that one defendant was from California meant the case had to stay in state court. But then Belli dropped the retailer as a defendant. RJR now could seek to remove the case to federal court. Normally, this would have been a no-brainer. Federal courts tend to be more hospitable to big companies, and just as important, it would have restarted the entire process, pushing a trial years into the future and putting pressure on the plaintiffs to give up.

But Weber and Strauch were increasingly confident they'd prevail. Galbraith, the lawyers had learned, had lived an unhealthy lifestyle; it would not be hard to pin the blame for his illness on things other than cigarettes. And a win in this bellwether case would be worth much more than just kicking the can down the road. The lawyers decided to go to trial now.

It began on November 8, 1985, in Santa Barbara Superior Court, a white building with a red-tiled roof and a clock tower, designed to evoke a Spanish castle. The judge surveyed the crowded courtroom. "How many of you *are* there?" he asked. "I don't think I want to be here today." RJR had twenty-two representatives in the room: seven lawyers, five publicists, an errand boy, three men who assisted with jury selection, a woman who took notes for those men, a couple of legal secretaries, and three others whose precise roles reporters at the courthouse couldn't immediately discern. Jones Day knew this wasn't a good look, and it convinced the judge to prohibit Belli from mentioning to the jury how many lawyers were there representing RJR.

The courtroom also had a regular audience of analysts from Wall Street firms. The outcome of the case could have market-moving implications for the shares of RJR and other tobacco companies.

The defense strategy was simple: Blame the victim. Galbraith wasn't addicted to cigarettes, Strauch insisted. He just didn't try hard enough to quit. Tobacco didn't kill him, Strauch asserted; Galbraith had a host of other ailments, ate junk food, drank too much. His parents and siblings had died young; by that standard, Strauch suggested, Galbraith had lived a surprisingly long life. Another RJR lawyer argued that if cigarettes were indeed bad for Galbraith, the blame lay not with the tobacco company but with his wife, "who helped him obtain cigarettes after he became seriously ill." And on and on. All of this was supplemented with Jones Day's well-rehearsed experts, whose sworn testimony cast doubt on the fact that cigarettes were deadly and addictive.

Halfway through the five-week trial, news came from Knoxville, Tennessee, where Jones Day was defending RJR in another lawsuit brought by a smoker. A federal judge had tossed it out of court. For Jones Day and its client, this was an encouraging omen.

In Santa Barbara, the jurors deliberated for nine hours before returning with their verdict on the morning of December 23. It was a balmy day, the temperature in the sixties, and a gentle breeze blew in from the Pacific as the lawyers made their way to the courthouse. The vote was nine to three (just enough to avoid a hung jury): RJR was not responsible for Galbraith's death. As the decision was read and the jurors were surveyed, Galbraith's widow and children stared ahead, fighting to suppress their emotions. A Wall Street analyst sprinted out of the courtroom to call his colleagues with the great news for Big Tobacco. "People said we were in a new era, a new ballgame, and somehow things have changed," Strauch crowed to reporters afterward. "But we said personal responsibility was still the issue."

The lawyers headed to the Santa Barbara airport. Their grateful client had sent a corporate jet to fly the team home to Cleveland.

AROUND THAT TIME, A Jones Day lawyer showed up at the University of Texas Health Center in Tyler, Texas. The attorney was there to see a doctor named Gary Huber. More than a decade earlier, in 1971, a representative of the Tobacco Institute, the industry's leading trade association, had approached Huber, who at the time was a respiratory scientist at Harvard Medical School. The lobbyist had proposed bankrolling a new research center focused on tobacco. Huber said yes; the industry would eventually spend nearly $3 million on the Harvard center. At the time, cigarette companies were desperately searching for evidence that maybe, just maybe, their products didn't kill their customers. Partnering with Harvard had obvious attractions, namely "the P.R. value of the Harvard name," as an industry executive put it.

The results, however, were not what the industry was looking for. Huber tested how the lungs and hearts of lab animals reacted to cigarette smoke. The animals got sick. Huber tested the effect of low-nicotine cigarettes on humans. People compensated by smoking more cigarettes and inhaling the smoke deeper into their lungs. Huber published his findings, and tobacco executives publicly pooh-poohed them. "So what?" shrugged the medical director of the Tobacco Institute, saying Huber's conclusions would only be of interest to "people who worship at the temple of health."

In 1980, Huber went from Harvard to the University of Kentucky, where he hoped to continue his research. But the anticipated funding from the tobacco industry never materialized. It was hard to miss the message: His independent-minded research was not appreciated. Five years later, Huber relocated again, this time to the University of Texas. That's when he got the visit from Jones Day. The firm arranged for Huber to be paid to critique research on the connections between smoking and diseases like emphysema.

By now, Huber understood the game, and he was ready to play. He published papers downplaying the risks of secondhand smoke. Research that documented its health risks was "shoddy and poorly conceived," he claimed. Secondhand smoke, Huber wrote, "is so highly diluted that it is not even appropriate to call it smoke." In another report, he pondered, "Is smoking beneficial to your health? I believe that for some individuals, it may be." When damaging studies about the health risks of smoking came out, RJR and other tobacco companies pointed reporters toward Huber's research.

Before long, Huber had become "one of the most cited researchers in America," as one newspaper put it. "Modern Puritans want to control us through government," a syndicated columnist warned about tobacco regulations, pointing to Huber's work, which also was picked up in a Congressional Research Service report. RJR and Philip Morris cited Huber's research in ads and in a lawsuit against the U.S. government. Jones Day covered Huber's tab, which stretched into the millions of dollars.

WELL INTO THE 1990S, RJR and its lawyers were lying about tobacco's dangers. "Cigarette smoking is no more 'addictive' than coffee, tea, or Twinkies," the company said in a written statement to a congressional committee in 1994. Jones Day helped craft the testimony that day by RJR's chief executive, James Johnston. Lawmakers pummeled Johnston. "I was shocked and appalled that the Congressmen would treat a man of your stature, and a representative of such a fine company, in such a disgraceful manner," a Jones Day employee wrote to Johnston afterward.

The relationship between the two institutions was tight, sealed over many a boozy weekend. Chuck Blixt, RJR's general counsel, was often up in Cleveland, attending cocktail parties and NBA games with the firm's partners. "Jones Day's representation of RJR over the past ten years has been invaluable to the company," Blixt wrote in a thank-you letter after one jaunt in 1995. "On a more personal level, the friendships that have developed from this relationship have meant a great deal to each of us at RJR." The Jones Day team, and sometimes their wives, would go down to North Carolina or Florida for a weekend of golf, tennis, and meetings with politicians at a lush resort.

Both sides had reasons to be happy. Weber beat back one legal assault after another, including a $2 billion racketeering case brought on behalf of more than one hundred union health plans. At RJR's instruction, Jones Day whipped up white papers—"Does Advertising Really Control Cigarette Consumption: The Surprising Answer"—and then RJR cited those papers as evidence in response to allegations that cartoon spokesman Joe Camel led people to start smoking. This went beyond normal lawyering or the zealous representation of a longtime client. Jones Day was creating science fiction.

For the law firm, the rewards were obscene. In 1985, when Jones Day took on RJR as a client, the tobacco company was spending a total of about $1 million a month on legal fees, only a fraction of which was going to the firm. Thirteen years later, RJR was paying Jones Day alone $7.8 million in a typical month—or nearly $94 million a year. This single client was responsible for 19 percent of the firm's total revenue. Let that sink in: Nearly one out of every five dollars that Jones Day earned came from RJR. Month after month, year after year, you could count on this gusher continuing. "It's a huge stabilizing force," a retired partner, George Manning, told me. "It's the reason why the firm was able to continue to grow."

Yet despite the best efforts of RJR and Jones Day, the science on the dangers of smoking had gone from being very strong to being bulletproof. Their decades of deceit now known, tobacco companies had become public villains. Texas and dozens of other states were suing the industry to recover the many billions of dollars in costs associated with caring for ailing smokers. In 1997, Gary Huber was subpoenaed for a deposition by Texas's lawyers. Huber called a Jones Day lawyer, Bob McDermott, and told him that he planned to comply. McDermott was "extremely angry," Huber later said. He warned Huber that he wasn't permitted to talk about his tobacco work with outside parties. "What have you done?" McDermott demanded. If Huber cooperated, "the weight of Jones Day could come down on you." McDermott ended the conversation on an ominous note: "My prayers are with you."*

Huber asked the state's lawyers to buy him a life insurance policy. "I did feel concerned . . . for my family," Huber later said under oath. His wife "has cried herself to sleep many nights, lost weight, just worried about a lot of things." A judge offered him the protection of U.S. Marshals.

Huber went through with the videotaped deposition, and he backed away from his research that played down the risks of secondhand smoke. He essentially admitted to having been a stooge for the tobacco industry. (He also recounted what McDermott had said.) The industry would eventually settle Texas's lawsuit for a record $14.5 billion.

---

* McDermott denied this. He told me that Huber (who died in 2013) fabricated the allegations against him in an unsuccessful attempt to disqualify McDermott from representing RJR at trial.

Yet for years afterward, Huber's research continued to reverberate. "WHERE THERE'S SMOKE, THERE'S DISTORTION," an *Arizona Republic* headline blared on a 2002 opinion piece. "The oft-stated claim that secondhand smoke is dangerous to others is utterly unsupported by scientific findings," the columnist wrote, falsely. Huber's debunked research was a crucial piece of his argument.

8

AIDING AND ABETTING

Around the time that Jones Day signed on with RJR, the firm began a marketing campaign. It didn't involve TV ads or radio spots or highway billboards. This was a much more discreet, narrowly targeted pitch, and it represented a principal way that the Supreme Court's *Bates* decision had revolutionized the legal industry. No longer were law firms content to stick with their clients and to field incoming calls from companies looking for new representation (as had happened with RJR). Passivity was passé. Now it was possible to be proactive, to go out and promote yourself and solicit business.

The consequences of this were more than just opportunities to make money. Law firms had long been able to justify doing business with dodgy companies that were long-standing clients or had come seeking representation. Now they were in a different position. Firms were able—arguably required—to make value judgments when they solicited companies or industries or people. If a firm had moral or ethical qualms about representing, say, gun companies, well, it shouldn't start marketing itself to gun companies.

This Jones Day marketing campaign was aimed at the savings-and-loans industry. S&Ls—also known as thrifts—were a type of bank that took customer deposits and lent them out, often to finance real estate purchases. With the housing market red-hot, and the Reagan administration having loosened restrictions on thrifts' size and practices, the industry was booming. Yet regulators were getting nervous about the dubious business practices—ranging from reckless lending to illicit insider transactions—that were rampant in the industry.

When Rick Kneipper conducted his strategic planning at Dick Pogue's behest, he had homed in on these savings banks as a promising place for Jones Day to trawl for clients. With its rare national footprint and decades-old presence in Washington, the firm could pitch itself as ideally suited to help S&Ls traverse the treacherous regulatory terrain. Jones Day began luring federal regulators to the firm with generous salaries and signing bonuses. The more the firm hired, the easier it was to recruit their government colleagues—and to impress prospective clients with the firm's roster of former feds. In a matter of years, about two hundred thrifts would hire Jones Day. It was a remarkable success, except for one thing: The firm's envelope-pushing work for some of these clients would land Jones Day in deep trouble with the U.S. government.

One new recruit was William Schilling. Immediately before arriving at Jones Day in January 1986, he had been the chief examiner at the Federal Home Loan Bank Board, which was responsible for regulating thrifts. One of his last official acts was to write a memo to his government superiors alerting them to problems at a large thrift called Lincoln Savings & Loan. The memo warned that Lincoln was making risky investments in apparent breach of federal banking regulations, "the same type of violations that have led to some of the worst failure in [the regulator's] history."

Pogue had persuaded Schilling to operate out of Jones Day's Los Angeles office, which had been losing money ever since it opened. His hope was that Schilling could help the L.A. outpost make inroads with thrifts in the western United States. Schilling was a hardworking, straightforward guy, eager to show his new colleagues that he could be an asset in the private sector. An opportunity soon appeared. Lincoln and its parent company, American Continental, were owned by a politically connected businessman named Charles Keating. Word had reached Jones Day that Keating was looking for lawyers. Kneipper wrote an eleven-page letter to Keating touting Jones Day's experience advising thrifts and its bench of former regulators like Schilling.

Keating invited Schilling and Kneipper to Phoenix for lunch. Their pitch was that Jones Day could scrub Lincoln's books to prepare for upcoming government audits. Kneipper was impressed with the articulate and personable Keating. Yes, he was a bit "on the aggressive side," but that's what it took to compete in the cutthroat S&L business. "I didn't see any red flags going up," Kneipper told me. (Schilling, of course, in his time as a regulator, had spotted plenty of those flags at Lincoln.)

Jones Day got the job—a big win for the flailing L.A. office. An internal memo noted that Keating "does not care" about how much he spent in legal fees. "It appears to us that [American Continental] is made for us and we for them," the memo gloated. To reinforce to associates just how important this assignment was, a Jones Day partner at one point showed off the $250,000 check that Keating had written the firm as a retainer. (A second $250,000 check, this one unsolicited, would arrive a few weeks later.)

In the spring of 1986, Schilling and about thirty colleagues deployed to Lincoln's offices in Arizona and Southern California. It was a round-the-clock operation. Jones Day had somehow learned that regulators would be showing up any day for an intensive on-site examination, presumably at least in part because of Schilling's warning to his government colleagues months earlier. Jones Day's mission was to conduct a dry run of the regulatory investigation. It was a slightly paranoid operation. Convinced that the feds might have planted listening devices inside Lincoln's black-glass building, the lawyers spoke in whispers. Outside the offices, they referred to Lincoln only as "the client."

Within three weeks, the lawyers had identified serious holes in the bank's financial paperwork; there were missing documents, and dozens of large loans had been made without anyone at Lincoln gauging their risks. Jones Day found that a Lincoln employee, apparently trying to rectify those deficiencies, had backdated documentation and forged board members' signatures on meeting minutes. Upon seeing this, the lawyers told their client to cut it out.

The trouble was that Lincoln's problems stemmed in part from self-dealing by executives. In one transaction, a Lincoln subsidiary had sold a hotel to an entity controlled by Keating and members of Lincoln's legal department—in other words, the same group that Jones Day was urging to stop messing around. "They reported the crimes and corporate wrongdoing to the very people who were committing them," a federal regulator would later say.

In any case, despite its instructions to stop tampering with documents, Jones Day soon learned that documents were still being tampered with; a bank employee told the lawyers that she'd been asked to backdate more paperwork. At this point, Jones Day could have resigned or escalated the issue to regulators or to the board of directors of American Continental, Lincoln's parent. The firm did neither. Instead, it helped craft documents for Lincoln's board that essentially ratified the backdated documents. The retroactive cleanup would allow the thrift to tell federal regulators, accurately but deceptively, that its board had signed off on everything.

When the regulators showed up to conduct their examination, they found some of the same problems the Jones Day lawyers had identified—but not all of them. It would take the government another two years to recognize the full scope of the misconduct.

WHILE JONES DAY LAWYERS were sifting through Lincoln's loan files, Keating made a strange request. He was a prolific contributor to political campaigns, and he had used that largesse to curry favor in Washington. Five senators in particular had been his beneficiaries and then pushed federal regulators to go easy on Lincoln. (This would eventually explode into the "Keating Five" scandal.) But Keating wanted to be able to influence state politics as well as federal, and he apparently wished to do it in a way that would remain under the public radar.

Jones Day at the time had three political action committees that contributed money to candidates. One, the Good Government Fund, focused on federal campaigns, while the other two supported state candidates. They reflected Jones Day's flirtation with building a serious lobbying and political practice in Washington. By 1988, the Good Government Fund was the largest PAC run by a law firm, doling out more than $300,000 to candidates nationwide—a significant sum in an era of relatively low-budget campaigns.

In June 1986, a Keating representative asked Jones Day to have one of its state PACs donate $10,000 to a candidate for governor of Arizona. In exchange, "we could bill liberally in future with recognition of this," Kneipper explained in a handwritten internal memo. In other words, the Jones Day PAC would make the $10,000 payment, but the law firm could recoup that and more from its client. Once again, Jones Day was going far beyond the call of lawyerly duty, this time to help a client covertly influence an election. "Shame on them," an expert on legal ethics told the *Los Angeles Times* when the scheme came to light. "It's not the kind of thing people of honor do."*

Jones Day wasn't done. After another law firm was hired to handle Lincoln's compliance issues, Jones Day got a new assignment. The real estate market had cooled, and regulators were getting tougher, and that combination was shoving hundreds of thrifts into a death spiral. Lincoln and its parent company were hemorrhaging money. If American Continental could find a way to raise funds, it might be able to ride out the storm. But the industry's woes were becoming so well-known that it was hard to find anyone willing to invest.

---

* Kneipper told me that he didn't recall billing Keating extra in exchange for the $10,000 contribution.

That is where Jones Day came in. Someone came up with the idea that American Continental could issue bonds and sell them to Lincoln's customers, who tended to be elderly and not very financially savvy. This was a fraught area; regulators frowned upon companies hawking any securities to unsophisticated customers, but especially when the company had a direct financial stake in those instruments. It was a recipe for rip-offs. Nonetheless, in early 1987, Lincoln's bank branches began peddling American Continental's bonds. In short: The parent company was borrowing money from its subsidiary's customers. Jones Day prepared the necessary legal paperwork to issue the bonds. The bonds, which came in $1,000 denominations, offered much higher interest rates than ordinary Lincoln savings accounts. To a discerning investor, there were neon warning signs. The bonds had not been underwritten by a reputable investment bank. Nobody was attesting to their riskiness or value. But few of the customers who showed up at the branches' teller windows were all that discerning.

As it happened, there was a Lincoln branch on the ground floor of Jones Day's L.A. office building. Signs in its window noted that Lincoln's deposits were federally insured and also advertised the sale of American Continental bonds. A passerby might well have gotten the impression that the bonds themselves were government-guaranteed, which they were not. When a secretary at Jones Day noticed the ads and asked a lawyer whether she should buy the bonds, the lawyer pointed out the risks and steered her away, according to a 1994 investigation by the journalist Rita Jensen.

More than twenty thousand Lincoln customers didn't have the benefit of that advice. They moved their life savings from federally insured bank accounts into the supposedly safe bonds.

THE REAL ESTATE MARKET soon went into free fall. Borrowers defaulted on loans. Thrifts collapsed. The S&L industry began melting down. Recriminations over who was responsible ricocheted back and forth. The government would conclude that Jones Day deserved a substantial share of the blame, and not only because of its work for Keating.

In fact, the problems had begun more than a year before Lincoln was even a Jones Day client. The firm's newly opened office in Austin, Texas, had signed up a couple of local thrifts—which were attracted to Jones Day in part because of its roster of former regulators—and they quickly became cash cows. So prized were these two clients that Dick Pogue flew down to Texas to woo one's chairman over an expensive lunch at the city's University Club.

These two banks were involved in what regulators later would describe as fraudulent, self-serving transactions designed to paper over each other's losses and to create fake profits in order to pay millions to their owners. And Jones Day, according to the regulators, went along with it. Between 1984 and 1986, the law firm collected as much as $10 million in fees, a former bank employee told the *American Lawyer* in 1991.

Regulators eventually opened an investigation. Jones Day dispatched a partner (another former bank regulator) to Capitol Hill to meet with the House majority leader, who urged regulators to ease up. That delayed the action, but it didn't prevent it. In September 1988, the government seized both teetering banks.

It was about seven months later that the government shut down Lincoln, in what at the time was one of the largest bank failures ever. American Continental filed for bankruptcy; customers who had bought its bonds were out of luck. (So was Keating, who was convicted of racketeering and fraud and sentenced to ten years in prison.) Then came the lawsuits. In 1990, the Federal Deposit Insurance Corporation sued Jones Day for negligence, malpractice, and having "aided and abetted" executives in illegal transactions at the two Texas thrifts. Another federal agency, the Resolution Trust Corporation, soon filed its own lawsuit. It accused Jones Day of concealing the improper practices at Lincoln and American Continental. If Jones Day had loudly blown the whistle, regulators said, they would have forcefully entered the picture, and billions of dollars in losses, ultimately borne by taxpayers, might have been averted.

It was rare for a major law firm—supposedly a bastion of ethics and legal rule-following—to end up in the government's crosshairs. Now, in the space of barely five months, one of the country's largest, most esteemed firms had been sued twice.

Pogue was furious; he felt the feds were trying to cover up for their own ineptitude. There was probably at least a kernel of truth to that—not that it excused Jones Day's conduct.

Ironically, the firm had only recently hired another former federal regulator, Rosemary Stewart, to join its Washington office. As a top regulator, Stewart had been involved in the investigations of Lincoln—fellow regulators and lawmakers criticized her for not having acted swiftly to shut it down—and the two Texas thrifts. Now she worked for Steve Brogan in Jones Day's D.C. office. Her hiring was controversial; a Republican congressman decried it as "an example of the legal ethics problem we have in Washington today." Brogan noted that Stewart wouldn't work on cases related to her old job. "This type of thing happens all the time in Washington," he said.

POGUE WASN'T SLOWING DOWN—HE would keep working twelve-hour days for the next two decades—but he knew his tenure as managing partner was nearing its end. In 1991, he asked Pat McCartan to craft a plan for Jones Day in the twenty-first century. McCartan was perhaps the country's most gifted trial lawyer. More than anyone else, he had helped build Jones Day into a litigation powerhouse. The sheer size of its litigation department—hundreds of lawyers, hundreds of millions of dollars in annual revenue—and its impressive track record were more than enough to intimidate those who considered suing a Jones Day client. That kind of success built on itself. Big companies that polluted or lied to investors or evaded taxes or sold faulty products or sold products (like cigarettes) that worked exactly as intended and still killed people flocked to the firm.

The fact that Pogue had entrusted this plotting to McCartan strongly suggested that McCartan would one day succeed him as managing partner. And sure enough, Pogue typed up a secret memo naming him as his successor. The memo was stashed in a safe deposit box, "in case I was hit by a truck," Pogue told me.

Under the firm's retirement policy, managing partners had to step down at the end of the year in which they turned sixty-five. That was 1993 for Pogue. But McCartan was not a young man, and Pogue decided that the right thing to do was to step down a year early so that his successor would get a solid eight or nine years. He invited McCartan to lunch at the Union Club and delivered the good news. McCartan was all smiles, and he thanked Pogue for the graciousness of leaving early.

IN 1992, JONES DAY agreed to pay $16 million to settle the FDIC's lawsuit about the firm's work for the Texas thrifts. The payment barely made a dent in the nearly $1 billion cost of bailing out the two lenders. Jones Day that year also agreed to pay $24 million to settle allegations, by the unfortunate customers who bought American Continental's bonds, that the law firm had duped them into purchasing the doomed securities. Jones Day was not apologetic. "There was an increasing risk that jury sympathy for the [victims] . . . would overwhelm the facts concerning the correctness of our actions," Pogue stated.

But the ongoing Resolution Trust lawsuit about Jones Day's work for Keating posed a serious long-term threat. McCartan had taken the reins on January 1, 1993, and this would be one of his first tests as managing partner. There had been on-again, off-again settlement talks, but the government appeared perfectly willing to let the case go to trial. McCartan had plenty of experience with brinkmanship, but this was a scary prospect for Jones Day partners.

The government was seeking up to $500 million in damages. The partners themselves—as owners of the firm—would be on the hook for most of that money.*

The trial was set to begin in Tucson. A jury was selected. Opening arguments were scheduled for a Monday in April 1993. When the day came, the judge, his voice raspy with allergies, called in sick. The start was delayed a week. McCartan now had seven days to find a way to avoid having the firm's fate hang on an unpredictable jury.

After a week of frenzied negotiations, a settlement was reached minutes before the trial was set to begin. Jones Day agreed to pay $51 million, while denying any wrongdoing. At the time, it was the most ever paid by a law firm to resolve a malpractice suit—and the largest penalty levied during the S&L crisis. As part of the settlement, Jones Day had to sign a "cease and desist" order and was forced into the embarrassing position of agreeing to conduct additional reviews before bringing on new banking clients. The deal made the front page of the *New York Times*. "This is really an instance of lawyers, who knew better, making an affirmative decision to chase the riches," an attorney for the government said.

The deal left a bitter taste in McCartan's mouth. Settling was not his style. But this was what leadership meant: putting aside your pride, and doing the right thing, the safe thing, the humbling thing, for the sake of your thousands of employees. And the reality was that this was a pretty easy pill to swallow. Most of the settlement would be covered by insurance; the remainder would be paid in six annual installments of $3.25 million. It was an average of $8,125 for each of the firm's four hundred or so partners—or, as one Jones Day lawyer smirked, less than what the firm spent in a year on photocopying. (Jones Day's revenue in 1993 was $395 million.) Even so, McCartan was pissed. "If it was me alone, I would have tried it," he

---

* Jones Day, unlike many other law firms, is not a limited liability partnership. Instead, partners personally share both the financial upside and downside.

grumped to a *Plain Dealer* reporter a few hours after signing the deal. He stabbed a pencil into a legal pad as he spoke.

The Lincoln episode became a teachable moment for the legal profession—a powerful reminder that lawyers should *not* do whatever it takes to please a client.* "The oft-heard justification . . . is that the client is entitled to undivided loyalty and zealous representation," Keith Fisher, a law professor, wrote in 2004. "That argument, of course, fallaciously conflates the duties of a trial lawyer, operating in a system of procedural checks and balances that offset zealous advocacy, with those of a business lawyer providing services to clients that desperately need sound, dispassionate, and, above all, independent advice and counsel."

The role, in other words, was not so much to be an agent of a client as to be a wise counselor, to be willing to say no as well as yes.

---

* Jones Day wasn't the only law firm punished for its work for Lincoln. A smaller firm, Kaye Scholer, had to pay $41 million to settle a government complaint about its conduct.

9

JUDAS DAY

Pat McCartan was from Youngstown, Ohio, the son of an Irish immigrant who was a local policeman. "His playground was a field down by the railroad tracks," McCartan's wife, Lois, would rhapsodize. "Pat grew up in the school of the street." That was until he discovered the magic of the courtroom. He would sit in the gallery watching trials the way other youngsters were glued to the TV. These real-life legal dramas thrilled him. After high school, McCartan headed to Notre Dame, determined to become a lawyer.

As an undergrad, he worked at the college radio station, inveighing against Richard Nixon and Joe McCarthy, much to the annoyance of campus conservatives. A few years later, after graduating first in his class from Notre Dame's law school, he landed a coveted Supreme Court clerkship, working for Justice Charles Evans Whittaker. Eating lunch with other clerks in the court's cafeteria, he was prone to liberal outbursts, especially on cases involving civil rights and school desegregation.

McCartan joined Jones Day in 1960, the same year as Scalia. (The two became lifelong friends.) He initially was headed for the dry world of tax law, figuring he wasn't cut out for the glamour of being a trial lawyer. But Jack Reavis saw something in the young man. He told McCartan that there was a glut of workers' compensation suits—derisively known as "slip and fall" cases—and asked the partner in charge of that litigation to throw some work McCartan's way. The partner was happy to lighten his load, and soon McCartan was taking his first case to trial. He won, trotting out a chalkboard to document the contradictory statements by the plaintiff, who claimed to have hurt his back at a Chevy plant.

That was the beginning of McCartan's vaunted career as a trial lawyer. A series of impressive victories followed. He successfully defended Firestone Tire in what had looked like an unwinnable patent case. He managed to convince a jury that GM's notorious Corvair—unsafe at any speed—was a decade ahead of its time in terms of safety. McCartan fended off Mobil's attempted hostile takeover of Marathon Oil, a longtime Jones Day client. The triumphs earned him a front-page *Wall Street Journal* profile with the headline "Top Trial Lawyer Gets Firms Out of Trouble With Quiet Efficiency." (The *Journal* memorably described McCartan as such a pristine dresser that he appeared "as primped and pressed as a Brooks Brothers mannequin.")

The decision to defend giant corporations for a living required you to either embrace their worldviews or to consistently subordinate your core beliefs. McCartan, it seemed, had prioritized his career over his politics. Perhaps trying to suppress his idealistic side, he avoided cases involving people, preferring institutions. Once, he had been stuck at a county jail on Christmas Eve, having been assigned by a court to represent an indigent defendant. "In a way, that was more difficult than corporate law," McCartan said in 1982. "I was dealing with an individual who was in that situation because he didn't understand the things I was trying to tell him." He paused. "I guess I just get too involved in my cases."

McCartan inspired his acolytes—few more so than Steve Brogan. Part of it was that McCartan was a renowned litigator. His preparation and work ethic were legendary. But it was more than that. He knew the lawyers' wives. He knew what their kids were up to. Young attorneys at Jones Day "are intensely loyal to him," Brogan told an interviewer in 1993. "He taught them to be lawyers."

One result was that by the time McCartan became managing partner, he had the self-confidence to move quickly—and in a slightly new direction. Soon after settling the savings-and-loans lawsuits, he decided to do some pruning. The law firm had grown very large, very fast. When he took over, Jones Day had about 1,200 lawyers scattered all over the world, more than three times its size a decade earlier. The breakneck growth was exhausting. "I would like to think that the expansion of the firm has reached a plateau, or, at least, that the firm would not expand further for a while," Erwin Griswold, the former solicitor general and longtime Jones Day partner, wrote in his 1992 memoir. "There is a point where the administrative problems will exceed the capacity of even the ablest managing partner. The development has already gone far beyond anything I would have thought possible when I joined the firm."

McCartan seemed to agree. He told an interviewer in January 1993, just as he took the helm, that law firms in general had grown too quickly. "I think it's now apparent that supply exceeds demand," he said. "Law firms are going to have to concentrate more on what their clients think they need." That year, Jones Day's roster of lawyers declined by 117. (It still had 1,066 and remained the country's second-largest firm.)

Soon McCartan shut down the firm's Austin office, one source of the trouble with the FDIC. Next, he closed the firm's PACs, which, as Jones Day had just learned with Keating, invited scandal.

McCartan's career had been spent in litigation, and that's where his heart remained as managing partner. The litigation department was the engine behind Jones Day, thanks in part to the steady thrum of tobacco work, but also a slew of other large, lawsuit-prone clients. It was a halcyon period for Jones Day's trial lawyers. Not only was one of their own leading the firm, but its litigation department boasted two of the country's best courtroom practitioners: John Strauch and Bob Weber.

Strauch was a master, in particular, at destroying opposition witnesses. One fabled episode took place in 1994. He was representing a bankrupt computer company called Alpex in a lawsuit against Nintendo. Alpex had patented one of the first technologies for home gaming systems where you could stick different cartridges into a console to play different games. The invention was a radical advancement from consoles that were hardwired to play only one game. A few years after Alpex's patent, Nintendo introduced its own cartridge-based gaming product. The underlying technology was similar. The crucial difference was that Nintendo's console came with blockbuster games like *Super Mario Bros.,* which would revolutionize the industry.

Alpex sued Nintendo, accusing it of violating its patents. The case went to trial in the summer of 1994. Nintendo's defense hinged on the argument that its Nintendo Entertainment System used more advanced, faster technology that allowed fully animated characters—visualize the curves on Mario's and Luigi's bellies—instead of the "linear player images" in use on consoles that relied on Alpex technology.

Nintendo's expert witness was an impeccably dressed MIT computer scientist named Stephen Ward. He explained to the jury the superiority of these animated graphics, which he said simply weren't possible using Alpex's clunky technology. Then Strauch stood up to conduct the cross-examination. It was a hot day, and the air-conditioning system at the federal courthouse in downtown Manhattan wasn't working. The judge invited the lawyers to shed their jackets, and Strauch happily did so, rolling up his sleeves. The opposing lawyers kept their jackets on, looking uncomfortable.

Strauch had prepared carefully for this cross-examination. He asked Ward to pinpoint the difference between the animated and linear images. Ward dodged, saying it was hard to define but that he could easily recognize them. Great, Strauch said. He wheeled out a large pad of white paper on an easel. He took a marker and drew a stick figure, which he said was supposed to be a hockey player. Which was that, Strauch asked, a linear or animated figure?

Ward said it was obviously a linear figure. Strauch colored the stick figure red. Now which was it? Still linear, Ward answered confidently. Strauch added a bulge around the figure's waist. Now? Still linear. This went on for a while, and everyone could see where it was going. Strauch added a nose. Then a tail. (It was a "combination human-animal cartoon," he explained, his hands smeared with ink.) Ward allowed that the image was inching closer to the description of an animated cartoon, not a linear graphic, but that it was in an ambiguous zone.

Finally, Strauch scribbled on a beard, and Ward acknowledged that the figure had now crossed the invisible threshold from stick figure into three-dimensional cartoon.

"Okay, so now I know how you are drawing the line," Strauch deadpanned. "If we have a nose, two little arms, a tail, more hip, and the configuration I have drawn, except for the beard, you don't know whether it is a linear image player or not. But if we add the beard, it is not."

The arbitrary nature of the distinction was clear for everyone in the courtroom. The jurors loved it. Some of them ducked behind the rail of the jury box so the judge wouldn't see them laughing.

After a few days of deliberation, the jury delivered a stunning verdict: It found for Alpex and awarded more than $200 million in damages, an embarrassing blow to the almighty Nintendo. It was one of the largest awards ever in a patent-infringement case. That cross-examination became a legend inside Jones Day. Strauch would regale lawyers about the strategy behind it, how he had prepped it in advance, how he knew that Ward would eventually snap. "There comes a time when the witness will know his next answer will be absurd," Strauch explained. "That is when they'll give you what you want."

Bob Weber, too, had a knack for dismembering witnesses, pouncing when they left out small details. If they're hiding this one little thing, what else might they not be sharing? In one case, defending RJR in a lawsuit brought by Minnesota's attorney general, Weber grilled a professor who was a witness for the state. Weber asked her to read aloud a press release. She skipped a word here, a sentence there. Weber had her. "You didn't read that quite right, did you, professor?" he asked.

"I read what I wanted to."

"You skipped over a sentence, didn't you?"

"It wasn't part of my point," the professor answered, falling into Weber's trap. Jurors rolled their eyes.

Like all experienced trial lawyers, Weber had suffered his share of setbacks. One came in 1984, on his first case after being named partner. Jones Day was representing Art Modell, the principal owner of Cleveland's cherished Browns football team. Modell was in a financial dispute with one of the team's minority owners, and the fight went to trial. Weber tried the case with McCartan. They lost. The next day, McCartan stomped into Weber's office with a copy of that day's *Plain Dealer*. The verdict was on the front page. McCartan threw the newspaper onto Weber's desk and snapped at the junior partner: "One thing I hope for you is you don't wake up on your fiftieth birthday and find out you're the biggest loser in town."

THE INDIANS BASEBALL TEAM for decades had played at Cleveland's Municipal Stadium alongside the Browns. But in the early 1990s, the city had blessed—and agreed to partly finance—a new sports complex that included Jacobs Field for the Indians. The stadium, named for Dick Jacobs, the team's owner, opened on a sunny Monday in April 1994. Bill Clinton, wearing an Indians jacket over his suit, strode to the mound, shook some hands, and fired a ceremonial strike to Sandy Alomar Jr. behind home plate. The president then watched the game from Jacobs's suite.

When Jacobs Field was being built, a number of Cleveland-based companies had ponied up $1 million apiece to help defray the costs. At Pogue's behest, Jones Day was one of them. The decision ticked off partners, who demanded to know why Pogue was spending the firm's money—*their* money—on what felt like a charitable endeavor. But it wasn't long before the contribution paid dividends. The Indians held a lottery among big contributors to see who would get which luxury box. Pogue drew the first pick and selected the box right next to the owner's. "I became an instant hero with the partners," he reminisced.

On Opening Day, Pogue, McCartan, and Weber were in the Jones Day box. Clinton had been leaning over a railing and chatting with McCartan. "Then he jumped across the bar separating the two loges and started talking to me," Pogue recounted. They chatted for five minutes. Pogue, a staunch Republican, couldn't help but be impressed with the charismatic young Democrat.

Weber, too, was in a jovial mood. Clinton's national security adviser, Anthony Lake, briefly left the loge and upon his return asked if anybody had come looking for him. A crisis was underway involving North Korea, and Weber joked that yes, there had been a phone call for Lake, and the voice on the other end had been shouting in what sounded like Korean, and the only decipherable phrase was "Anthony Lake." Lake chuckled. At another point, Clinton mentioned that he was flying to North Carolina that evening for the NCAA basketball finals. Weber slung his arm around the president. "Another tough day at the office," the lawyer joshed.

The Jones Day partners had company that memorable afternoon: Art Modell was in the box with them. Modell wasn't known as a bitter man, but he must have been hurting as he sat there, accompanied by an American president, watching as his city celebrated this state-of-the-art stadium, named for another team owner. For the past few years, Modell had been pressuring Cleveland to spend more than $150 million to upgrade the dilapidated Municipal Stadium. ("A crummy old silo with plumbing like a Calcutta sewer," a local columnist called it.) City officials had balked at the nine-figure price tag, leading Modell to threaten to sell the team. Even so, he vowed that as long as his family owned the Browns, the team would remain in Cleveland.

About a year later, Modell had a confidential discussion with McCartan. He was in the final stages of secretly negotiating a deal to relocate the Browns to Baltimore, where officials were dangling all sorts of financial incentives. Modell knew his move would be greeted with a flood of litigation—not to mention local fury—in part because it was a clear violation of his public promise. He needed his lawyers prepped for battle.

McCartan called Weber into his office. "Get ready," the managing partner said. Weber would be in charge of representing Modell.

Weber took over a Jones Day conference room and started getting people organized. The city was likely to sue for breach of contract; the Browns had a long-term lease on the stadium, which Modell planned to abandon. There would be delicate negotiations with the NFL. And there would almost certainly be other problems, though it was hard to predict exactly what form they might take.

The news began to leak in early November 1995. A television station in Baltimore reported that Modell had made a "handshake deal" to move the team there. All hell broke loose in Cleveland. Reporters tracked down Modell at the Browns' suburban training facility, and he initially declined to comment on the reports, simply saying that he had no intention of selling the team. (That was true, but not the point.) The deal was announced at a celebratory news conference in Baltimore days later.

To a sports-crazed city, this amounted to treason. "I always liked Art Modell," Pogue told me, "but like everyone else in Cleveland, I was devastated." Modell became a public enemy. Death threats poured in. So did anti-Semitic slurs. (Modell was Jewish.) Modell started wearing a bulletproof vest and traveling with bomb-sniffing dogs.

As expected. the city sued, accusing the Browns of violating the terms of the team's leases. In another lawsuit, season ticket holders accused Modell of fraud; his vow to keep the team in Cleveland had induced fans to shell out for season tickets in part because that would ensure that they had priority access to Browns games far into the future. Now there was no future.

Barely a week after the Baltimore move was unveiled, Jones Day entered the public crosshairs. "I'm for anything that will make Art Modell's life miserable. Same goes for the hired guns who are aiding him in his treachery," a *Plain Dealer* columnist wrote. "I trust Cleveland will long remember the commitment to the community Jones Day is demonstrating by representing Modell." Lawyers and editorial writers called for Weber to resign as president of the Cleveland Metropolitan Bar Association. Weber reported getting "serious personal threats" from Browns die-hards who left menacing messages on his home answering machine. The NFL hired off-duty Cleveland cops to stand sentry outside Weber's home, as well as police protection for other Jones Day lawyers and staff. Clients pulled their business. The firm's fax lines were sabotaged.

In court, Jones Day rolled out different defenses in different venues. Responding to claims that Modell had defrauded people by promising not to move the team out of Cleveland, Weber and his colleagues argued that holding Modell accountable for that statement would "have a chilling effect on comments by team officials to the media, which will be to the detriment of sports fans and the public at large." In the Painesville Municipal Court, Browns fans and local lawyers squared off against some of Jones Day's most experienced litigators, who flattened them with procedural maneuvers. "It was kind of comical," one of the fans sighed afterward. "We definitely were overmatched."

At one hearing, a battalion of Jones Day lawyers occupied three full rows of the courtroom. "It looked like they sent half the office," a columnist remarked. "Gazing upon wave after wave of Jones Day lawyers sitting there so earnestly as the billable hours rolled by, one word kept running through my mind," he wrote. "Ka-ching!"

Fair enough. But money was only part of the story, at least for

Jones Day. The firm by now was accustomed to representing radioactive companies; you couldn't help but develop a thick skin after years of defending RJR. There was no question of abandoning a long-standing client the way Modell was abandoning Cleveland. Weber, forty-four at the time, adored the Browns; he held four season tickets near the fifty-yard line and had been known to show up to games in orange face paint. Now, though, he had a job to do. "The life of a lawyer is that you defend the clients that come to you," Weber said at the time.

So when an editor at the *Plain Dealer* phoned McCartan with what sounded like a threat, he was playing right into Jones Day's hands. The headline on the front page of the next day's newspaper, the editor warned, would read: "JUDAS DAY." By aiding a public enemy, the law firm was betraying its hometown, or so the argument went. McCartan curtly responded that if the editor was trying to intimidate him, it wasn't going to work. "Professionals do not walk away from a client just because the media or those controlling or having access to the media don't like what they have done," McCartan explained.

McCartan and Weber's defiance in the face of violent protest would become one of the proudest moments in Jones Day's history—a tale recounted in orientation sessions and other settings to generation after generation of Jones Day lawyers. The "Judas Day" epithet would serve as a reminder of the importance of standing up to politicians and the media and everyone else when principles dictated. There was nobility in sticking up for a years-long client, even as his needs evolved from the resolution of anodyne business disputes to the defense of what felt like a public betrayal.

Over the years, though, the episode would evolve into something more than a unifying point of pride. It would become an all-purpose justification for Jones Day taking on toxic clients and going to great lengths to keep them happy.

PART II

10

THE FULL FREDO

One day in October 2002, McCartan summoned Weber to his office. The two men worked on opposite sides of the same floor of Jones Day's Cleveland headquarters. Weber walked down the long hallway to McCartan's corner suite. It boasted panoramic views of Cleveland, stretching from the airport to the downtown skyline. Directly outside was the Rock & Roll Hall of Fame, designed by I. M. Pei.

It wasn't hard to guess why McCartan wanted to see Weber. All year, the firm's partners had been speculating about who McCartan would pick to succeed him as managing partner. McCartan had reached Jones Day's mandatory retirement age a couple of years earlier, but the firm had amended its partnership agreement to let him stay. It was the first time that such an exception had been made. "That tells you the incredible amount of admiration and affection the partners have for him and the confidence they have in his leadership," Steve Brogan said at the time. McCartan used those extra years to restart the firm's growth, which he had paused at the beginning of his tenure. Jones Day opened offices in Shanghai, Madrid, Singapore, Silicon Valley, Milan, and Houston. (It also bought a Tokyo law firm.)

Now, though, his tenure was nearing its end. Per tradition, McCartan had stashed a memo naming his replacement in a safe deposit box. "It's been in there for quite a while," he told the *Plain Dealer* in January 2002.

While a handful of lawyers had been jockeying for the job, only two were serious contenders: Brogan and Weber. For its entire history, Jones Day had been led by men with plausible claims to being the best lawyers in the firm. Frank Ginn was. Tom Jones and Jack Reavis may well have been. Allen Holmes was. Dick Pogue was an antitrust star. McCartan was perhaps the finest trial lawyer in America. Weber was right up there. Brogan, however, was not. He was perfectly competent, and very hardworking, and some of his colleagues regarded him as a great strategist. But would anyone mistake him for the best at Jones Day? Probably not. His experience was more bureaucratic. Pogue had promoted him to run the D.C. office in 1989, when Brogan was only thirty-seven, and he'd been doing the job ever since.

By all accounts, Brogan had done a good job in this leadership position. The Washington office had been struggling when he took it over. Brogan ushered out underperformers and lured new lawyers. Soon the office was booming. That was one of the reasons that Brogan had moved the firm out of its musty, rabbit warren–like space near the White House into the Acacia, the landmark neoclassical building on Capitol Hill.

Some of Brogan's colleagues were turned off by his arrogance. On cross-country trips, he would book multiple first-class and coach seats, and a crew of associates would rotate between the two cabins to brief Brogan on various cases he was juggling. (The extra space in first class, one of his associates told me, made it easier to have confidential discussions.) When the plane landed, the associates would get right back on another flight to return from wherever they'd just come.

Once, in a meeting of the firm's advisory committee, the discussion turned to Jones Day's associates. "Within two years, I can tell who's going to make partner," Brogan boasted.

"How the fuck do you know that?" scoffed Rick Werder, a

longtime partner. Associates develop at different speeds, Werder pointed out. Brogan told Werder, basically, to shut up. He seemed to believe in his own omniscience.

Several partners used the word "cronyism" to describe Brogan's way of operating. He surrounded himself with a tight-knit circle of loyal advisers. As McCartan neared his decision on who would succeed him, a rumor circulated among senior lawyers that Brogan's band was ironing out contingency plans in case their man didn't get the job. They supposedly were contemplating creating their own law firm—a traitorous move inspired, perhaps, by the splintering of the D.C. office decades earlier, which had first put Brogan on the path to power.

Yet McCartan was inexorably, almost magnetically drawn to Brogan. He asked Brogan to help craft a strategic plan for Jones Day. The men's families vacationed together on Florida's Gulf Coast. When an ambitious partner sent a memo to McCartan raising his hand for the top job, McCartan faxed the document right to Brogan.*

What explained the exceptionally close ties, which many colleagues described as akin to a father-son bond? It may have been that McCartan saw shades of himself—as a person, if not a lawyer—in his protégé.

BROGAN WAS AN ONLY child. When he was a boy, his mother suffered from health problems and was unable to raise him. That task fell largely to his father, a lieutenant in the New York City Police Department. Brogan and McCartan were both brought up by cops.

As a lawyer, Brogan never tired of telling colleagues about his dad being a policeman; that detail found its way into an extraordinary number and range of conversations. Brogan emphasized

---

* A Jones Day partner, Chris Kelly, told me it was "completely unsurprising that Pat McCartan would circulate such an unabashed exercise in self-promotion to other leaders in the firm."

the loyalty, the honor of policing—qualities he wanted to transpose into his law practice. "He grew up with a dad who was the kind of rough, tough guy that you had to be to be a New York City cop in those days," said Rick Kneipper, whom Brogan used to regale with tales from his childhood during late-night drinking sessions. One nugget that Brogan liked to share involved his father's retirement party. A sergeant had leaned over and whispered to Brogan: "Your dad just reeks of manhood."

Like McCartan, Brogan was a devout Catholic. At Bergen Catholic High School in New Jersey, "Brog" was a middling student who bickered with teachers. He played baseball—his senior year, he was the Crusaders' starting catcher—and had a reputation as a bruiser. "He didn't back down from anybody," a high school friend said. "I thought he'd possibly end up in the Marines." In his senior yearbook photo in 1970, Brogan stared straight ahead, unsmiling, his lips tight, wearing a bow tie and a white blazer.

Brogan toyed with following his father into the police force. Instead, after graduating from Boston College with a degree in English, he went to law school at Notre Dame—just like McCartan. He spent the summer after his second year at Jones Day and then, newly married, joined the firm full-time the following year. At first, he wasn't sure the Big Law life was for him. Maybe he should work in public service; he still fantasized about being a cop. But he quickly grew close to McCartan. "I needed to see somebody who could be as fine a lawyer as Patrick is, who I'd still want to introduce to my dad," Brogan would say. McCartan "was an accomplished guy, but he had his head on straight." Aside from a two-year stint alongside Jonathan Rose in Reagan's Justice Department, Brogan would spend his entire career at Jones Day.

As an up-and-coming lawyer, he represented RJR, defense contractors, Persian Gulf royals, members of the bin Laden family, targets of independent counsel investigations, and many others. Brogan exuded the same unpolished brawler vibe that he'd been known for in high school. He sometimes made boorish remarks. He cursed a lot. After a few rounds of drinks, he'd slide into a clipped New York accent. (At other times, he was happy to discuss his favorite authors, who included Faulkner and F. Scott Fitzgerald.)

Legend had it that, when Brogan was running the D.C. office, a partner had walked into his suite to complain about his compensation. This was never a good idea at Jones Day; lawyers' pay was unilaterally set by the managing partner, and you were not to discuss your compensation—much less gripe about it—under any circumstances. But something possessed this partner to go to Brogan. Brogan's reaction was simple: "You're done." The stunned partner trudged back to his office. By the time he arrived, staff were already there boxing up his belongings.

While McCartan was refined and discreet, Brogan maintained a snarly side, even as he matured. He encouraged his underlings to act on their killer instincts, whether that meant firing poor performers or acting mercilessly in court. "Brogan loves blood on the floor," one of his confidants told me. If a good lawyer resigned to go to a rival firm, Brogan would sometimes fire off furious letters and memos trashing the departing colleague. It became such a familiar occurrence that some Jones Day partners gave it a name: "the full Fredo." It was a reference to the scene in *Godfather II* when Michael Corleone watches from the shore as his older brother, Fredo, is murdered on his orders.

WEBER COULDN'T HAVE REALLY expected to be named managing partner. But that hadn't stopped him from talking to his allies about what he might do on the off chance he did get the job. (John Strauch told me that he was among those who favored Weber for the role.) Weber had long believed that Jones Day concentrated too much power in the hands of a single man. It worked all right with a benevolent dictator like Pogue, who put the firm's interests above everything else. But as Jones Day grew, a system that empowered one person to make every important decision felt less viable. For starters, it meant the entire firm was hostage to one man's whims;

if his judgment was off, thousands of jobs and billions of dollars could be on the line.

What's more, the unitary power structure was making Jones Day a less attractive home for some top lawyers. Other big firms had strong leaders, of course, but their cultures encouraged consensus-building. Long-serving partners could expect to have a voice in major strategic or financial decisions; after all, it was their firm as much as it was the top guy's. Not at Jones Day. While plenty of the firm's veterans appreciated the speedy decision-making that was possible under its unusual structure, others found it emasculating to spend decades at a place where, no matter how much revenue they generated or hours they put in or courtroom victories they pulled off, they would always be on the outside.

The place, in short, could use a little more democracy, Weber thought.

But when he reached McCartan's corner office that day in October 2002, McCartan got right to the point. He had chosen Brogan.

Weber wasn't one to throw a tantrum. But for the sake of the firm to which he'd devoted his entire career, he wanted to voice his concerns about the choice of Brogan.

"There are two things you've got to talk to him about," Weber urged McCartan. First, there was Brogan's reputation for cronyism; he needed to learn to resist the temptation of withdrawing even more into his small circle of advisers, of surrounding himself with yes-men. "You've got to get him to change his way of operating," Weber pushed. Second was the issue of Jones Day abandoning its midwestern heritage. Brogan had always been based in D.C., and anyone who had glimpsed his office on Capitol Hill could surmise that he would be remaining there. What would that mean for Jones Day's identity as a Cleveland-centric law firm? "It's always been our secret sauce," Weber reminded his fellow Ohioan.

Dick Pogue similarly cautioned McCartan about this. He pressed McCartan to press Brogan to relocate to Cleveland. McCartan broached the subject, but Brogan wouldn't budge. Even before he was formally elevated, Brogan knew he had the power.

ABOUT A MONTH LATER, Jones Day's partners traveled to the luxurious Esmeralda Resort near Palm Springs for one of the firm's periodic retreats. Convening hundreds of lawyers from all over the world in the middle of the Southern California desert was not particularly convenient, but McCartan loved the venue because of its thirty-six-hole, championship-caliber golf course. The hotel, whose pool had waterfalls and a sandy beach, was designed for large corporate events. Attendees could roam from air-conditioned meeting rooms directly onto landscaped lawns and gardens with sparkling views of the Santa Rosa Mountains.

At the start of the retreat, a group of about two dozen of the senior-most partners sat down in a conference room. McCartan informed them that he had chosen Brogan. Weber was there, doing his best to maintain a poker face, though some attendees thought he looked crushed.*

Later that day, on stage in a ballroom, McCartan formally handed the gavel to the fifty-year-old Brogan. To honor his mentor, Brogan read a congratulatory letter from President George W. Bush, who hailed McCartan's leadership of Jones Day as "an important asset to the American legal community." Then, via a satellite hookup, Justice Scalia appeared on a big screen, his deep voice booming through the room. With the partners watching, he and McCartan reminisced about their time together at Jones Day.

Partners weren't surprised that McCartan had tapped Brogan. He had been strutting around for years like he knew he'd inherit the throne. Some—in particular those who worked for Brogan in the D.C. office—welcomed his ascent. But many others were displeased. The partners worshipped Weber, and now some were

*It's possible these partners were projecting their own unhappy emotions.

angry at McCartan for having strung him along. They figured that Weber would soon resign and that others who had clashed with Brogan probably would be gone, too.

The news was announced to the world a few days later. Sensitive to the appearance that the firm was giving up on the Midwest, McCartan hosted a cocktail reception in its Cleveland offices to celebrate Brogan's coronation. Some four hundred judges, executives, lawyers, and local politicians showed up to pay their respects. So did Weber, signaling that he remained committed to the firm. McCartan told attendees that he liked how Brogan viewed being a lawyer as a profession, not a business.

Brogan put on a show of folksiness. Attendees noticed he was wearing scuffed leather loafers. "Cop shoes," Brogan remarked. After chatting with him, the founder of a local duct-tape company was all smiles: "He's an Irish Catholic with six kids, and his old man was a cop. What could be bad about that?"

In private, though, Brogan dropped the façade. On a plane ride to Washington around this time, he boasted to a longtime ally that he hoped to remake Jones Day in the image of one of Wall Street's most powerful investment banks.

"We're going to be the fucking Goldman Sachs of the law firm world," he declared.

11

TRY TO SAVE THE CULTURE

Brogan officially became managing partner on January 1, 2003. Change came quickly. First was the firm's name. It was in its seventh iteration since the firm's founding in 1893, as named partners came and went. Its most recent incarnation was Jones, Day, Reavis & Pogue. Brogan regarded that as unwieldy, and as his first official act he shortened it to simply Jones Day. "The move to 'Jones Day' is a symbol of change and an extension of our determination to capitalize on our brand-name recognition around the globe," Brogan announced.

A more important shift followed. Under McCartan, the firm's lawyers had been organized in a handful of groups: corporate, litigation, tax, and so on. Those departments were run by powerful partners, whose clout derived from the large number of lawyers they managed and the awesome amount of revenue those attorneys generated. Brogan smashed the groups into smaller pieces. The stated explanation was that it would create a nimbler organization. But it was hard not to notice that the restructuring diluted the power of the partners who had led the large groups—the closest thing Brogan had to internal rivals. Adding to that impression, he didn't consult with some of the partners whose powers were being stripped. "That was not the firm I grew up in," Weber would lament in an email to a colleague, noting how he and others had been blindsided.

While Brogan projected confidence, there were subtle signs of insecurity. One of his closest colleagues at the firm was Tim Cullen; multiple Jones Day partners described him to me as Brogan's professional conscience. So it was telling that, not long before Brogan became managing partner, Cullen emoted to a reporter about how, when Jones Day attorneys competed with Wall Street firms for assignments, they heard their New York competitors make disparaging remarks like, "We're the investment banking people—they're the Cleveland people."

That chip on the shoulder was shared among the firm's senior lawyers. Brogan often acted like he had something to prove. And one thing he quickly set out to establish was that he—and his firm—intended to be dominant all over the world.

ON FEBRUARY 8, 2003, A Jones Day jet touched down in London. It was a cloudy and cool morning, though the air felt mild compared to the near-freezing temperatures in Washington the evening before. A car drove Brogan into the City of London, Britain's ancient financial and legal hub, and pulled up next to the Old Bailey courthouse. This was the home of the century-old Gouldens law firm. It now belonged to Jones Day.

Barely a month into his tenure as managing partner, Brogan was in London to sign the paperwork on the deal, which had been unveiled the day before. Jones Day already had about fifty lawyers in London, but Brogan wanted to be bigger. Gouldens had roughly 150 attorneys of its own. Just like that, Jones Day's presence quadrupled. The addition of this venerable British firm nudged Jones Day into sixth place in the rankings of the world's largest law firms, with more than two thousand lawyers.

Gouldens had a strong team of corporate lawyers who advised European companies on mergers, acquisitions, and other transactions. (It also had a legendary wine cellar filled with many of the world's finest vintages.) After sealing the deal, Brogan and four other men posed for photos on a carpeted stone staircase in

Gouldens's offices. Brogan, standing in the center, struck an imperious stance: his hands clasped in front of his crotch, his left foot a step up from his right, no trace of a smile.

He was just getting started. Later that year, Jones Day agreed to buy a 120-year-old New York firm, Pennie & Edmonds, and opened offices in San Francisco and Beijing. In 2004 came San Diego. Jones Day was expanding so quickly that it was opening outposts before it even secured office space. Since 1999, the firm had doubled in size.

The firm's thirtieth office, in September 2004, was in Moscow. Brogan noted that Russia's rapid economic growth "makes it an important market for our clients and, therefore, for us." Before long, Jones Day was one of the firms to which Kremlin insiders were turning for professional services. The head of the Moscow office became an adviser to oligarch-owned conglomerates like Alfa Group and Rosneft. One of the firm's senior associates left in 2012 to run the legal department at a company controlled by Alisher Usmanov, a billionaire in Russian president Vladimir Putin's inner circle.

DISCRETION WAS IMPORTANT TO Brogan. No business leader—no person, for that matter—wants their dirty laundry aired in public. But Brogan insisted on a level of secrecy inside the firm that caught many longtime partners by surprise.

When he emailed memos to the staff, the text wasn't in the message; you had to click a link, which brought you to the firm's intranet, which was programmed to block people from printing or copying and pasting the text. The firm's official spokesman was regularly instructed by Brogan's office not to return reporters' phone calls, much less divulge anything about the firm. ("A firm spokesman declined comment on Brogan's age" was an actual sentence in a news story about Jones Day.)

Jones Day had long ordered its lawyers not to discuss their pay with anyone. The confidential compensation system—known in the industry as the "black box"—was unusual. Most major law firms used transparent, or at least translucent, pay models in which partners and associates alike generally knew how much their peers earned. They also usually knew how their compensation was determined. Not at Jones Day.

Brogan and his allies argued that keeping people's pay under wraps encouraged collegiality and reduced jealousy. But it also bred fears that Brogan was playing favorites. This wasn't the thinking of one or two disgruntled lawyers. It was a widely held belief among longtime partners whom I spoke to that Brogan rewarded his friends and penalized his real and perceived rivals. A member of the firm's exclusive partnership committee told me that Brogan's colleagues in the D.C. office tended to make vastly more than partners elsewhere at the firm and that the ratio of what the highest to lowest paid partners were making had grown so lopsided—more than six to one—that the firm risked no longer being considered a partnership in any real sense. Another partner, a former federal prosecutor, said that when he joined Jones Day in the McCartan era, the firm felt like a meritocracy. Under Brogan, "meritocracy turned into high school, a cool kids' club," he said. "We all want to be surrounded by people who like us. If you aren't careful, you simply end up promoting your friends."

For years, partners had considered the idea of using a private jet as anathema. It ran counter to the image the firm was trying to project of a no-frills culture that cared about representing clients and nothing else. At one point, as the firm's international empire grew under Pogue, there was a brief debate about whether the firm should buy its own plane. One partner pointed out that it might pay for itself within a few years. "He was laughed at," Rick Kneipper told me. "We're not the kind of people who want to fly private."

That resistance had begun to fade under McCartan, who sparingly used a corporate jet, including to fly himself and clients to Augusta National for golf outings. As managing partner, Brogan adopted private planes as his primary mode of air travel.

Quite a few lawyers compared Brogan to a mob boss, not because he was a crook but because he demanded deference. Associates once made a parody video depicting the harrowing moment when they had to go and kiss Brogan's ring as if he were a godfather. His worldview hewed toward the authoritarian: *Do what you're told, whether you like it or not*. Now that was becoming Jones Day's philosophy. (Some of Brogan's supporters disputed that, saying he built consensus and delegated responsibility.)

Every two years, all of the firm's partners convened at a sunny, golf-friendly venue like the Orlando Ritz-Carlton or the Breakers resort in Palm Beach, Florida. In addition to group meetings and a golf tournament, everyone was required to gather for a long afternoon in a cavernous ballroom. Onstage, Brogan would deliver interminable PowerPoint presentations. Before the speech, a group of partners would place bets on how many slides would be in Brogan's show this year. Eight hundred was not out of the question. Lawyers mainlined coffee; nobody wanted to be spotted losing focus, checking his phone, or, worst of all, nodding off.

Brogan covered everything: the firm's finances, his outlook for the year to come, a hearty helping of cultural indoctrination. He illustrated his points with stills from popular movies like *The Godfather*. Some slides listed books Brogan had been reading or quotes he found inspiring. And there were slogans: *Because we're the best* or *Nobody does it the way we do*.

One slide almost always appeared: a picture of a guy on a skyscraper washing windows, alongside the phrase "We do windows." The idea was that Jones Day had a culture of service to clients. The firm would do whatever it took to get the job done. It didn't matter how big or small, glamorous or dull, the task might be. You had to do it.

TOP LAWYERS SOON BEGAN stomping for the exits, frustrated with what they saw as Brogan's autocratic style. Rick Cieri, who ran the firm's bankruptcy practice: gone. Rick Werder, a leading litigator: gone. Jamie Wareham, another litigation star and a Brogan acolyte: gone.

Wareham's departure, in 2003, was especially acrimonious. He had spent seventeen years at Jones Day, quite a bit of it complaining about what he perceived as his insufficient pay. ("Jamie was obsessed with money," one of his longtime colleagues, Mike Gurdak, told me. "I knew him well back then, and he is the proverbial character who, if he saw a dime on the floor, would dive on it.") At one point, Brogan had walked into Wareham's office in the D.C. building and informed him that he was getting a raise: from $500,000 to $550,000. This was a nice chunk of change, but it struck Wareham as inadequate given how much money he was pulling in for the firm.

Brogan soon returned with a $100,000 check, written from a Jones Day bank account, payable to the exclusive Congressional Country Club in Bethesda, Maryland. Brogan told Wareham to use the check to pay his dues there. Wareham was dumbfounded. You couldn't just go around handing out six-figure checks to golf clubs as a form of compensation. He handed the check back to Brogan.

Not long after, Wareham decided to leave for another firm. "I knew you were gonna leave when you wouldn't take that check," Brogan growled.

"I knew I was going to leave when you offered me that check," Wareham shot back.

It took Bob Weber a few years, but he would be gone, too. He told acquaintances that he'd been unhappy with Brogan's imperious ways—and his apparent disinterest in Weber's clients. Shortly after Brogan became managing partner, Weber had asked him to come meet top executives at long-standing Jones Day clients like Cardinal Health and IBM. The idea was for Brogan to make these crucial customers feel special. Brogan came to the meetings—he flew in via private jet—but uttered maybe four sentences. Weber later vented his frustration to colleagues.

In 2004, Weber successfully defended IBM against workers who claimed they had developed cancer because of exposure to chemicals at a company factory. (In an argument that surely would have caused RJR to blanch, Weber noted that one of the plaintiffs was a pack-a-day smoker; maybe that's what caused her cancer.) Afterward, IBM's CEO, Sam Palmisano, invited Weber to dinner at the luxurious Homestead Inn in Greenwich, Connecticut. Sitting in the quiet back patio, Palmisano asked Weber if he'd be interested in joining the company in the newly created role of senior vice president for legal and regulatory affairs. (IBM's general counsel would report to him.) Palmisano told him it would be a new adventure—and he could make a killing if, as Palmisano hoped, IBM's undervalued stock price took off.

It was hard for Weber to come to terms with leaving Jones Day, but he eventually realized the job offer was a gift from God. For decades, he'd been grinding it out, constantly on the road, feeling like he was never able to really catch his breath. It was getting old.

In the fall of 2005, Weber said yes. Before anyone else could find out, he sent Brogan a confidential letter. "The reason for this memo is that, after almost thirty uninterrupted years at the firm (my only 'real' job), I have decided to accept an offer to join IBM," Weber wrote. "I am very happy for you," Brogan replied the next day. "This development is a great credit to your standing as a lawyer in the whole of the profession."

No doubt, it was a plum gig—IBM was one of America's most iconic companies—but it was a body blow to Jones Day. Weber was soon deluged with emotional messages from his shocked colleagues. One admirer after another lamented the departure of someone with such high standards and professional and personal ethics. And they mourned—in some cases, using their work email accounts—what felt like the end of the golden days at Jones Day. It was as if, two years into the Brogan regime, lawyers were waking up to the fact that things had changed irrevocably.

"I fear now for the future of the Firm," one partner—who would eventually run a key region for Jones Day—wrote on the firm's letterhead. "I've watched you lead as a leader should," the lawyer added, in what sounded like a veiled dig at Brogan. "Your efforts in maintaining interaction and dialogue with each layer of this Firm, lawyer to staff, have made more of an imprint than you likely know."

"No kidding, I'm sitting here with tears in my eyes," a lawyer wrote from Pittsburgh. Another: "This is the saddest day in all my years with the firm." And another: "I am truly devastated."

"I am sad for us and for me," wrote a prominent litigator in the Chicago office. Weber responded: "Somehow something felt different about things here—not as close, not as collegial, whatever, I don't know." Then he dispensed some unsolicited advice: "Try to save the culture."

Some of the writers hinted at their shared frustration with Jones Day's direction under Brogan. "Sad day for the Firm, but I guess I am not surprised," came an email from a Texas partner. "I have sensed your heart not in it since SJB [Stephen J. Brogan] took over."

Weber wrote back and praised the partner for his no-nonsense approach to practicing the law. "Just honest competence and decency. There's just too little of it left here."

It is worth noting that many Jones Day partners, including some who despaired over Weber's departure, disagreed with the sentiment he expressed as he left. These partners told me that Brogan built a culture of shared responsibility, that he looked out for his colleagues and their families, that he was tough but fair.

Brogan "made us personal—committed to one another, no matter our size and reach," one partner, Lizanne Thomas, wrote to me in an email. "No doubt you know from others that he is tough—know too that he is kind. I have direct experience with both, as have many others at this firm."

Others said they thought I was being misled by sources who were nursing long-running grievances against the firm. "Some of your information clearly has been provided by departed partners who fundamentally did not—and do not—agree with our core principles," Chris Kelly wrote. "When they were with the firm, they either sought leadership for themselves because they convinced themselves they were smarter and more deserving than everyone else, or they valued money over everything else. . . . That's okay, there are a lot of different things that drive people, but those former partners' 'frustration with leadership' was really, at bottom, a disagreement with the culture and mission of our firm."

Kelly continued: "The real story is the story of a successful institution with a long history that has only grown stronger in the last twenty years because of a relentless focus, which starts with our managing partner, on our core principles and culture of commitment to each other, our clients, and the firm. This story is even more remarkable because the notion of putting clients and other lawyers before yourself, of making others better, of selflessness, is almost anachronistic in our present-day society."

TWO MONTHS AFTER PURCHASING Gouldens, Jones Day sent word to its new employees in London: They would generally be expected to bill about two thousand hours a year. The Brits reacted with disbelief—not only was that substantially more than what local attorneys typically racked up, but the notion of setting guidelines, even informal ones, for how many hours they billed was out of step with the British legal culture, which was a decade or two behind America's and, with some exceptions, still prized professionalism over profits.

Brogan was exerting similar pressure on other Jones Day offices and practice areas, which were urged to hit more ambitious revenue targets. The combination of Brogan's brook-no-dissent style and the firm's intensifying focus on financial metrics eroded some lawyers' interest in ethics. "It has created opportunities for people to push their professional boundaries a lot," one partner in Texas told me. The urgency to achieve ever-loftier goals began to affect some people's judgment about whether to take on a client with a bad reputation. "You're being consistently pushed in one direction," the partner said.*

That translated into an embrace of clients and assignments that at times conflicted with the firm's values. One small but representative example—set in motion in McCartan's final years as managing partner—involved the Center to Prevent Handgun Violence (later known as the Brady Center to Prevent Gun Violence), which Jones Day had represented on a pro bono basis since at least 1990. Erwin Griswold, who for many years was the firm's most famous partner, had brought the center on as a client, and he had taken great pride in the work. Griswold was a staunch supporter of gun control, and his position carried extra weight given his credentials as a former Harvard Law dean, solicitor general, and prominent Supreme Court advocate.

The gun-control work wasn't especially sexy. It mostly consisted of filing briefs on important court cases involving the Second Amendment and helping to fight legal challenges to federal, state, and local gun-control laws. But especially on the cases when the firm filed briefs in Ohio—for example, in support of assault-weapon bans enacted in Columbus and Cleveland and challenged by gun companies—the prestige of the Jones Day name made a difference.

Then, in 1999, the gunmaker Colt was sued by state and local governments and victims of violence, in large part because of the havoc wreaked by its AR-15 assault rifle. The company wanted a high-profile, no-holds-barred law firm that specialized in bet-the-company litigation. Jones Day was the perfect fit. By early in Brogan's tenure, the gun-control work that Griswold had pioneered was no longer happening—a shift for which some of the firm's lawyers blamed the new managing partner.

When the city of Cincinnati, with the help of the Center to Pre-

* Traci Lovitt, a Jones Day partner, denied that Brogan applied such pressure. She said the firm did not have a 2,000-hour requirement and that Brogan ended a policy that rewarded associates for billing extra hours.

vent Handgun Violence, sued gun manufacturers, seeking to hold them accountable for the harm caused by their firearms, Jones Day showed up in Colt's corner. Among the allegations was that Colt and other gun companies hadn't properly vetted gun dealers. There was no question that the industry had been reckless, but were gunmakers legally liable? Jones Day persuaded jurors that the answer was no. In 2004, the *American Lawyer,* nodding to that work, bestowed upon the firm the title of "Product Liability Department of the Year."

"From handguns to tobacco," the magazine declared, "Jones Day defends the powerfully damned and the damned powerful."

12

ROGUE LAWYERS

At any institution with thousands of employees, there are going to be bad people, bad decisions, and bad luck. None of that necessarily reflects on a place's true character. Yet there is a point at which the occurrence of bad things becomes so regular that it is a pattern, and that *does* reveal something about the soul of the institution.

In the case of Jones Day, sporadic trouble had been bubbling up ever since the mid-1980s, when the combination of the industry's rapidly changing mores, the firm's explosive growth, and the arrival of clients like RJR and Lincoln Savings pushed the staid midwestern firm into an aggressive new phase. The dawn of the Brogan era hastened the firm's transformation into a take-no-prisoners juggernaut.

To understand this shift, which ended up alienating more than a few of the firm's own partners, consider what transpired in Germany and India.

IN HIS LAST MONTHS as managing partner, Pat McCartan had announced plans to open an office in Munich. The city was home to Germany's patent and trademark office, and Jones Day's outpost there would specialize in helping companies from around the world file applications to protect their intellectual property inside Europe's largest economy.

Christian Meister was one of the first people hired to work in the

Munich office. Meister, who was forty-seven at the time, had been a partner in Arthur Andersen's Munich office. Andersen had audited Enron's fraudulent books, and now the accounting firm was unraveling. Meister was among the hordes trying to escape, and Jones Day was among the firms trying to recruit him. The firm flew him to meet partners in Washington, New York, and Cleveland. At every stop, there were fancy dinners, expensive champagnes, the works. Meister felt loved. When the Munich office opened in 2003, he was one of its four inaugural partners.

The partner in charge of Munich was a Jones Day veteran named Ansgar Rempp. Right off the bat, he struck some of the new recruits as a control freak. Before Brogan came to christen the new office, Rempp warned the staff not to speak to the managing partner on their own—and then rushed to halt unsupervised dialogue.* An atmosphere of distrust hung over the office. At one point, an office manager came to Meister in tears. Rempp, she said, was impossible to deal with: He gave contradictory instructions and then lashed out at the lack of consistency. "The leadership style was management by fear," the office manager told me.

Jones Day used a system called Carpe Diem to track the hours lawyers worked for various clients. In Germany, patent and trademark lawyers generally charged flat fees—three hundred euros for this trademark application, a thousand euros for that one—and there was no clear way to enter non-hourly fees into Carpe Diem. At the same time, lawyers throughout the firm felt pressure to bill more hours. The message would often come from Rempp: *You must go the extra mile*. Some lawyers were told that the firm's stars were billing four thousand hours a year—eleven hours a day, every day, all year.

Mathias Ricker was another patent lawyer in the Munich office. He had a small crew of associates working beneath him, and by 2006 they were complaining to other partners that Ricker wasn't giving them credit for the hours they'd logged on his behalf.

---

* Rempp denied that he told staff not to speak to Brogan.

Meister told me that he started sniffing around. He discovered that instead of having the associates enter their hours into Carpe Diem, Ricker had asked them to write down their hours on pieces of paper and give them to him. Ricker would then enter the hours, claiming a lot of them for himself. In the process, Meister concluded, Ricker was inflating how much money certain clients owed Jones Day. (Ricker told me this was "not true" but wouldn't elaborate.)

Meister and another partner took Ricker out to dinner. "You cannot do this," Meister told him. Ricker hemmed and hawed, said he wasn't doing anything wrong, that they needed to meet the firm's billable-hours targets. Meister warned him that overbilling was a crime. After the dinner, they had a few more conversations, but Meister was not confident that his message was getting through.

And so he escalated the matter. In August 2006, he typed a three-page memo, which he sent to Rempp. It excoriated Rempp for creating a toxic workplace, for not tolerating dissent, for humiliating and debasing employees. "Anyone who criticizes you (publicly) will be punished. Anyone who leaves is insulted afterwards," Meister wrote. "Seven professionals have already quit this year, which is more than a quarter of our office. People are dissatisfied, disappointed or displaced, and these feelings are not limited to the seven mentioned. The dissatisfaction extends from the staff to the other professionals and deep into the partners."

Meister's memo also revealed what he suspected Ricker was doing with billings and explained that there was a rebellion brewing among the associates. Meister described the situation as "fraud against clients, fraud against employees, fraud against the system and thus on Jones Day." He warned that as the head of the Munich office, Rempp was responsible for the problems. "The exposure for Jones Day is high," Meister wrote.

Rempp shared the memo with Brogan, who was in Milan. The managing partner summoned Ricker there to see him. A few days later, back in Munich, Ricker approached Meister. "That's what friends are good for," he hissed sarcastically. "They fired me." (In fact, Ricker left voluntarily early in 2007.)

The firm concluded that Ricker had violated its billing policies but that he had done so inadvertently. The solution, from Jones Day's standpoint, was to send letters to some of the companies that Ricker had done work for. "Over the course of the last several years, the Jones Day Intellectual Property Group has experienced tremendous growth," one such letter began. "In view of the tremendous growth in this practice area . . . we conducted a thorough review of all aspects of our intellectual property practice," including "our billing practices for patent prosecution matters emanating from the United States and being handled by our foreign offices with a goal of achieving greater uniformity and predictability for our clients. . . . As a result of this review, we have determined that you should receive a credit of €3,931.22 for work previously performed for you. We will apply the credit to future invoices unless you would prefer a direct reimbursement to you of these sums."

There were quite a few letters like this, though many involved small amounts of money. To Rempp and his allies, this was a fair solution to a problem that stemmed, at least in part, from the idiosyncrasies of the firm's billing system. But when it came time for Meister to sign a letter, as the responsible billing partner for a particular client, in this case a California company that made water-free toilets, he balked. It was great that the firm was making up for the overbilling, but it felt dishonest to not explain to the clients why they were returning thousands of dollars. Eventually, Meister realized he was going to have to sign if he wanted to remain at Jones Day. So he did.

REMPP TOLD ME THAT he viewed Meister as having a "toxic" attitude, a sentiment shared by some other Jones Day partners. Meister's perception was that Rempp began excluding him from office gatherings and urging colleagues not to talk to him, retaliation for having caused such a fuss.

Meister protested to Brogan, who told him that he needed to make peace with Rempp. A few emails went back and forth until, in 2008, Meister was told to come to Washington to see Brogan. Meister had a queasy feeling; he knew the firm's management did not smile upon lawyers making a stink. But he perceived Brogan as a fair, honest man, a little gruff, yes, but really just doing what he thought was in the best interest of his extended family, aka the firm. Meister flew to D.C.

After arriving at Jones Day's imposing building on Capitol Hill, he was ushered into an elegant, wood-paneled conference room that adjoined Brogan's grand office. It reminded Meister of the type of space in which heads of state might sign a treaty. Brogan and another partner, John Normile, were seated at a large table, waiting for him.

As soon as Meister sat down, Brogan told him that he was being fired. He handed Meister an envelope. Inside was a letter detailing the reasons for his termination, which included that he hadn't billed enough hours. (Normile told me that Meister had made unfounded allegations against multiple colleagues and that "it became clear that he was not acting in good faith but was trying to immunize himself against the consequences of his professional failures.") Meister walked out of the room. By the time he exited the building and trudged past the proud, sand-colored griffins, his body was shaking. He was convinced he was being punished for flagging improper activity to his superiors. He took out his BlackBerry to call his girlfriend. His phone was dead; the firm had deactivated the device as soon as Brogan passed him the letter.

Back in Munich, Meister lodged a complaint with the city's public prosecutor, alleging that Jones Day had bilked clients out of hundreds of thousands of dollars. The government opened a preliminary investigation, which was closed in 2010 after the prosecutors did not find evidence of criminal misconduct. The investigators noted in a report that a number of Jones Day lawyers had disputed Meister's version of events. They also said the trail had gone cold, in part because some records were in the U.S.

Meister spent the next several years unsuccessfully battling Brogan and Jones Day over the terms of his termination. Still fuming, he felt like he needed his former colleagues to know what had happened. In 2014, he enlisted the help of an IT pro in his extended family and harvested the email addresses of Jones Day partners from the firm's website. One Sunday that June, he fired off an email to the whole group. "Blowing the internal whistle is dangerous in this firm," the subject line read. Meister recounted a condensed version of what had happened, saying Brogan had fired him in "clear retaliation for my refusal of participating in or covering systematic and substantial overbillings. . . . Are all these secrets in the firm really in the interest of the partners? And do they lead to a better firm? To an 'institution of law'? To fairness?" He went on: "I tried to stand up against overbillings that are financially attractive, but not in the interest of a law firm of utmost 'integrity.'"

The higher-ups at Jones Day set out to paint Meister as unhinged. His email was just angry enough, bordering on hysterical, that it worked. It was easier to accept that this guy was crazy than that there might be something not-quite-right about the law firm to which partners had pledged their undivided loyalty.

THE MESS IN MUNICH was tame compared to Jones Day's self-inflicted fiasco in India.

Growing up in the mountainous state of Himachal Pradesh, Jai and Anand Pathak were taught to love the law. Their father, Raghunandan Pathak, was the chief justice of India's supreme court. When Jai, the eldest of the two brothers, got it in his head to become a lawyer, his father—ever on the lookout for perceived conflicts of interest—told him he was not welcome to practice law in India so long as he, Raghunandan, sat on the high court. So, after receiving his law degree at Oxford, Jai came to America and earned his master's at the University of Virginia School of Law. Jones Day recruited him from there. Jai didn't know much about the firm, but he got the sense that he'd have more opportunities to learn on the job there than at the New York firm that had also made him an offer. Off he went to Cleveland.

It was the mid-1980s, and Jones Day was in a groove, the leading American law firm that wasn't headquartered on a coast. Cleveland, however, was a strange place. It was cold! And not exactly vibrant. One November night, Jai found himself locked out of his apartment. Unable to rouse anyone, and with the city shut down for the night, he slept on a park bench. Still, he loved being in America and working for Jones Day. Three years later, in 1988, his brother Anand joined the firm, too.

In the 1990s, McCartan signed off on a plan to expand into India. It was one of the world's hottest economies and most desirable markets, with countless Western companies (many of them Jones Day clients) setting up shop there to take advantage of the inexpensive labor. Who would lead this new office? Jai was by now a partner, and the Pathak name was invaluable in Indian legal circles. His father had recently stepped down from the Supreme Court of India, and the thirty-five-year-old Jai was soon on his way to his native country.

Unlike the offices that Jones Day had opened in other countries, the Indian setup had to be handled delicately. Indian law barred foreign law firms from having offices, and the country had rigid controls on foreign currency moving across its borders. With the help of Indian attorneys and accountants, Jones Day came up with a work-around. Jai would open an "associate office," with its own name, Pathak & Associates, its own bank accounts, payroll, and the like. Jones Day covered the costs of getting Pathak & Associates up and running. But it had a single owner: Jai. The two firms were separate. When Jones Day announced the venture in November 1995, it said, carefully, that it was "establishing a practice in India."

At first, everything went well. Jai got a rush from participating in the global expansion of this proud firm. McCartan and other leaders traveled to Delhi to see the office, and Jai organized a cocktail party for Indian clients to meet the Jones Day brass. The thinking was that once India liberalized its protectionist laws, which was widely expected to happen within a few years, Jones Day would have a launchpad from which to enter the world's second-most-populous country. In the meantime, some of Pathak & Associates' biggest clients—like Toyota and the auto-parts manufacturer Dana Corporation—were Jones Day customers that needed local representation in India. Soon, Jai opened a second Pathak & Associates office, this one in Mumbai.

Early on, local lawyers accused Pathak & Associates of being a front for a foreign firm. McCartan and Jai, among others, assured Indian authorities that this wasn't true. While both firms were enjoying the fruits of collaboration, they were separate entities.

WITHIN MONTHS OF BECOMING managing partner, Brogan decided to shake things up. "Steve concluded that Jones Day's Indian operations were rudderless and were not on a path to becoming a Jones Day–quality office," one of Brogan's lieutenants, Geoff Stewart, told me. (Jai later left Jones Day amid a bitter dispute with Brogan.)

Brogan asked Anand Pathak, Jai's younger brother, if he would take over India. Anand viewed Jones Day with something approaching reverence. When he had been a summer associate, the firm was moving into new offices in Cleveland, and there was a shortage of desks. He was told to hole up in Dick Pogue's office. It was crammed with legal artifacts, photos, memorabilia. Anand was awestruck; here he was, a twenty-something Indian immigrant, parked in the office of one of America's most renowned antitrust lawyers. Anand saw Jones Day—especially in the Cleveland mothership—as a place of meticulous, honest lawyers who valued their integrity above all else.

Anand's ambition was to follow in Jai's footsteps and make partner. Finally, in 2000, he got the promotion. He took his wife to his first partners' retreat in Palm Springs; he'd been pulling so many eighteen-hour days that they'd hardly seen each other lately. His wife took one look around the resort, jammed with hundreds of partners, and her face betrayed her disappointment. She had figured her husband had been elevated into an elite group. This gathering was too large to be elite. "Anand, what did you really aspire to do?" she asked. "Just be one of so many?"

It was one of those flip remarks that, once you heard it, you couldn't unhear. The more Anand obsessed, the less he was sure that being a partner at a giant corporate law firm was his destiny. He needed to do something with his life that was fulfilling, that was *his*. So, when Brogan suggested that he oversee the Indian operation, Anand agreed. The ownership of Pathak & Associates was transferred into his name.

Jai had been smooth and charming. Anand was not. Some lawyers at Pathak & Associates (it would soon be renamed P&A Law Offices) thought he was difficult; there was no question he was a stickler for rules. At Diwali, the five-day Indian festival of lights, P&A traditionally gave its staff small gifts, generally a box of candies. Anand ended the practice. He said he worried it would violate the Foreign Corrupt Practices Act, the U.S. law that prohibits American companies from bribing foreign officials. "It was a box of sweets!" one P&A lawyer grumbled to me.

But Anand had more substantive concerns, too. There had been a profit-sharing agreement in place between Jones Day and P&A. And Jones Day leaders kept mentioning—sometimes in passing, other times as a boast—that they had offices in India. In Anand's view, all of this was stepping right up to the line, maybe over it. P&A was legally required to be an independent entity, and its finances needed to be walled off. Anand told his American colleagues to stop saying they had Indian offices. He ended the profit-sharing arrangement. To emphasize the separation, he resigned from the Jones Day partnership, reverting to "of counsel" status, which he viewed as akin to being a consultant, not a full-time employee.

This was still a mutually beneficial relationship. Lots of legal work came P&A's way courtesy of Jones Day, and Jones Day could keep its clients happy by referring them to a trusted local partner for whatever they needed in India. Jones Day continued to cover certain expenses for P&A. And while P&A handled work for other law firms, like Ropes & Gray and Goodwin Procter, Anand told the *American Lawyer* in 2004 that "our heart belongs to Jones Day."

Brogan, however, insisted that all of P&A, not just its heart, belonged to Jones Day. He and his team viewed P&A as essentially a subsidiary, even if that wasn't how it had been described to Indian officials in order to comply with the country's laws. "P&A was entirely a Jones Day operation from beginning to end," claimed Geoff Stewart, who joined Jones Day four years after Jai opened Pathak & Associates.

The attitude worried some top Jones Day lawyers. During a meeting of the firm's partnership committee around 2004, someone mentioned the Indian offices' improving financial performance. As the meeting wrapped up, Bob Weber asked about the arrangement. Wasn't P&A supposed to be independent? If so, why were its finances any of Jones Day's business? Brogan cut him off. "Look, Bob, we all know what's going on here," he snapped. The message seemed clear: The supposed independence was a mirage meant to pacify Indian authorities.

BY 2009, P&A'S BANK accounts had what Brogan and his crew regarded as a surplus of cash—money that they argued was the property of Jones Day. The firm instructed Anand "to apply the funds to matters within India that furthered Jones Day's interests." Specifically, Brogan wanted Anand to make a couple of large contributions to charitable organizations: $250,000 to the American India Foundation and $500,000 for the Congregation of Holy Cross, a Catholic group that was planning to open a college in the Indian state of Tripura.

The directive—and especially the money for Holy Cross—disturbed Anand. First of all, what was Jones Day doing ordering him how to use *his* money? More important, India had strict laws governing foreign contributions to charities and other entities inside India. The law was intended, in part, to prevent the financing of terrorist groups. One way to circumvent this law was to have contributions made by someone in India on behalf of an outside party. Anand told me that while he knew the proposed contribution to Holy Cross had nothing to do with financing terrorists, he nonetheless worried it would invite government scrutiny, especially since Tripura was in a restive corner of the country. He consulted with Indian lawyers, who he said confirmed his fears: Brogan's orders were a recipe for trouble. Anand refused to make the contributions. He told his Jones Day contacts that they were asking him to violate the law.

Brogan wasn't accustomed to hearing no. He amped up the pressure. Anand received a series of increasingly angry phone calls and threatening letters from Cleveland and Washington. "This is a directive," Geoff Stewart warned. Brogan himself got on the phone at another point to ram the point home. ("Steve became involved when it became clear that Jones Day had a rogue lawyer who was not complying with the firm's instructions," Stewart told me.)

Anand wouldn't budge. He couldn't believe that the firm he had trusted and admired and regarded as home was now demanding that he do something he feared was illegal. And they were still pressuring him even after he had voiced those concerns.

In August 2011, Brogan escalated things further. He wrote a letter to the Indian Ministry of Home Affairs secretary, seeking his blessing to have P&A make the charitable contributions. A response came back that this sounded like a commercial dispute between private parties.

The next year, having given up on Anand and P&A making the donations, Jones Day's foundation contributed the half million dollars to Holy Cross International (an American legal entity) for "the establishment of a college campus for Holy Cross College." When the campus opened, Brogan and Stewart traveled to Tripura for a ceremony. Shortly thereafter, as Jones Day pitched for a big assignment working for the city of Detroit, the firm highlighted the Holy Cross gift to burnish its credentials as "a civic-minded firm."

That might have been the end of the matter, but Brogan didn't let it go. Perhaps he truly believed that P&A belonged to Jones Day. Perhaps he was worried his authority might crumble if he didn't strike back against this "rogue lawyer." In any case, in April 2014, Jones Day filed a lawsuit in the Cuyahoga County Court of Common Pleas in Ohio. It accused Anand of stealing Jones Day's assets. It also made a number of squishier allegations, such as that Anand delegated too much to his office manager, "a woman with no formal management training."

Anand already knew Brogan was playing hardball, but he was shocked to learn that the firm had sued him. For advice, he turned to some of his former Jones Day colleagues, who told me that they viewed the saga as evidence that Brogan was out of control. "This was as bad conduct as I ever saw at Jones Day," a decades-long veteran of the firm said. "It is a black mark." Jones Day never managed to serve Pathak with the lawsuit, and the firm withdrew it in 2015. ("The only reason the lawsuit didn't proceed was that Anand persistently evaded service of the papers, to the point of refusing to leave his house," Stewart asserted. Anand acknowledged that he was never served but denied that he was hiding. "I'm sick and tired of their lies," he told me.)

Jones Day wasn't done. A partner, Robert Ducatman, filed an ethics complaint against Anand with Ohio's bar association. The complaint accused him of dishonesty, untrustworthiness, and being unfit to practice law. As an associate, Anand had done work for Ducatman and regarded the lawyer as a mentor. This felt like a betrayal.

In his response to the complaint, which Anand drafted with the help of the former Jones Day partners, he explained to the bar association that the relationship between Jones Day and P&A was, by legal necessity, arm's length. It was not Jones Day's law firm or

Jones Day's money. The bar association asked Jones Day for evidence to refute Anand's argument and, having failed to receive anything adequate, informed Ducatman that it was dismissing the complaint. (Anand, who by then had earned a reputation as a distinguished lawyer in India and was registered to practice in California, suspended his bar membership in Ohio anyway.)

While the legal actions were pending, one of the ex-partners advising Anand decided to call Ducatman. The former partner respected Ducatman and figured he could reason with him. The former partner pointed out that when Pathak & Associates was first launched, Pat McCartan had signed documents attesting to the fact that it was legally separate from Jones Day. "Do you really want McCartan deposed on this shit?" the former partner asked.*

"You know what I'm dealing with," Ducatman responded. In other words, the former partner surmised, he was just following orders.

* Ducatman, who died in April 2022, told me that he didn't recall a former partner contacting him about the lawsuit or ethics complaint. He said Brogan was aware of the legal actions but didn't pressure Ducatman to file them.

13

BURNING THE ENVELOPE

On a breezy Monday in April 2008, Megan Surber gave birth to twins at St. Luke's Regional Medical Center in Sioux City, Iowa. She and Troy Kunkel each had kids from previous relationships, but these two were their first together, and they were excited—and a little terrified—to be new parents again. They named the boy James and the girl Jeanine.

Tragedy was about to strike the happy family, and it would reveal the aggressive tactics that Jones Day was willing to employ on behalf of a big-ticket client.

James had jaundice and had to stay in the hospital for a week. Jeanine came home after a couple of days. Megan had struggled to produce enough breast milk for both babies, and so she opted for formula. On the way out of the hospital, she was handed a care package filled with things like wet wipes, diapers, and Similac NeoSure liquid and powdered formula. The loot came in a Similac-branded bag.

Megan and Troy didn't have much money. They lived in a small house, which Troy spruced up with carpet and other materials he procured through his job as a construction worker. Megan poured Jeanine the liquid formula first, since it was what the nurses had been giving her at the hospital. That was gone within a few days. One evening, Megan sanitized a bottle, boiled water, mixed in a couple scoops of the powdered formula, and fed Jeanine. Around that time, James came home from the hospital; he wasn't served the powdered formula.

The following morning, James was peaceful, but Jeanine was crying. She wouldn't eat. By the afternoon she was screaming and running a fever. Soon her yelling intensified into an animalistic wail. "It was like a hyena," Megan told me. The pediatrician told her to bring Jeanine to his office. There, before Megan could even take the infant out of the car seat, the doctor instructed her, with unnerving urgency, to take Jeanine back to St. Luke's, this time to the ER. She was exhibiting signs of meningitis.

Megan sped to the hospital. The staff performed a spinal tap, which confirmed the pediatrician's fear: Jeanine had meningitis. The next several hours were a haze. The hospital determined that Jeanine needed to be transferred to the children's hospital in Omaha, Nebraska, which was better equipped to handle meningitis in a newborn. An ambulance arrived, picked up Jeanine in an incubator, and zoomed off. Megan rushed home to grab a few essentials and then drove the ninety minutes down Interstate 29 to Omaha.

When Megan and Troy arrived, the doctors escorted them into a private room. They explained that Jeanine had contracted a type of meningitis that is caused by a food-borne bacteria, *Enterobacter sakazakii*. They showed the terrified parents images of their daughter's brain, and compared them with images of a normal baby's brain. The two sets of pictures looked very different. The doctors doubted Jeanine would survive the next twenty-four hours.

Megan and Troy peeked in at their daughter. "We named her Peanut because she looked like a peanut in a big old bed with all those wires and tubes," Megan said.

The most common way for a newborn to contract this type of meningitis was through contaminated powdered formula. Theoretically, the bacteria could have been present in other products in Megan and Troy's house, but Jeanine only ate the formula. Plus, James, who was also in the house but wasn't fed the powdered formula, didn't get sick.

Jeanine defied the odds and survived. But the meningitis had severely damaged her brain. She would never walk or talk or eat on her own. After five months at the children's hospital, Megan and Troy brought their daughter home in the fall of 2008. They began trying to adjust to their permanently altered life.

ABOUT TWO YEARS LATER—AROUND the time that German prosecutors were investigating Christian Meister's accusations and that Jones Day was demanding that Anand Pathak give away P&A's money—the phone rang at Megan and Troy's house.

The stress of caring for Jeanine was taking a severe toll on their marriage. Megan and Troy were fighting. Troy in particular was struggling. He'd been so thrilled to have a daughter, to watch her grow up, to help her learn to drive, to meet her first love, to accompany her on life's journey. Now he felt his dreams were shot. The sight of other fathers walking around with their girls on their shoulders felt like getting punched in the gut. Troy slid back into a drug habit. He hooked up with a younger woman. "We were so lost," Troy said. "I had one foot out the door."

Now Megan's mother and aunt were on the phone. They had seen a slick TV ad for a personal injury lawyer named Nick Stein. "For thirty years, my capable staff and I have been helping people just like you," Stein intoned, offering a "no-cost evaluation of your case." Megan's mom had taken the liberty of calling Stein's offices at the number that flashed on her screen. Stein had sounded interested in hearing more about what had happened to Jeanine—it was possible they'd have grounds for a lawsuit. "You need to call this guy right away," Megan's mom instructed her. And so she and Troy phoned Stein. What did they have to lose?

The next thing they knew, Stein, who was based in Indiana, had flown into Sioux City and was sitting on their sofa. Megan and Troy introduced him to Jeanine. It turned out that Stein had worked on a number of other cases in which newborns were brain damaged after consuming bacteria-ridden powdered formula. The first case had walked in the door of his law offices several years earlier, a woman carrying a limp one-year-old who reminded Stein of a rag doll. He'd spent years on that case and ultimately negotiated a sizable settlement. More cases followed, and Stein secured settlements for them, too. The payouts were sometimes in the millions of dollars.

Sitting inside Megan and Troy's home, Stein looked around and found the whole scene—their poverty, their little girl's devastating brain damage—heartbreaking. He could see the family was fraying. "Just hold on a little bit longer, guys," he urged them. The meeting ended with a group hug. For the first time in a long time, Megan and Troy felt hope.

Similac was made by Abbott Laboratories, a multinational company headquartered outside Chicago. Stein had gone up against Abbott in the past; it was not an easy adversary. His firm comprised only himself and a couple of other lawyers, and he was getting older and wasn't sure he had the stamina for another protracted battle. He invited a Minneapolis lawyer at a slightly larger firm to run the case. His name was Stephen Rathke, a former county attorney. After meeting Troy and Megan, Rathke enlisted a Sioux City law firm to act as local counsel.

They all agreed that a lawsuit would be filed on Jeanine's behalf by what's known as a conservator—in this case, Security National Bank in Sioux City. If the suit was successful, the bank would manage whatever money was collected to pay for Jeanine's care. The setup meant nobody would be able to accuse Megan and Troy of trying to get rich off their disabled daughter. And because Megan and Troy wouldn't be the plaintiffs, their personal histories (there were a handful of convictions and some past drug use) were less likely to become an issue.

On February 15, 2011, Security National Bank sued Abbott in federal court, seeking $16 million in compensatory damages to cover the lifetime of costs of caring for the nearly three-year-old girl.

• • •

Abbott was ready. Since 1987, the company had been represented by a team of lawyers in Jones Day's Chicago office. Abbott was an important source of business; in pitch documents seeking new customers, Jones Day cited the company as one of its leading clients. In the past few years alone, the law firm had sued a rival health-care company for infringing on Abbott's patents. It had defended Abbott against claims that one of its prescription drugs, Lupron, had permanently disabled a teenager. And it had battled other lawsuits brought by the parents of children who suffered severe brain damage from meningitis after consuming powdered Similac formula.

The details of those other meningitis cases were remarkably similar to what had happened with Jeanine—right down to the fact that Abbott had provided the formula to hospitals, doctors, and parents as part of promotional campaigns designed to boost sales. In one case in rural North Carolina, a new mother was given a can and ten single-serving packets of Similac powdered formula as she left the hospital. In another, Abbott had sent an unsolicited mailing with four packets of powdered formula to a Louisiana family. In both cases, the infants had contracted meningitis.

Jones Day's tactics in these suits were wide-ranging—but they almost always amounted to the opposite of the firm's recommendation, more than sixty years earlier, that the East Ohio Gas Company accept responsibility for the tragic explosions. Abbott and its lawyers leveled personal attacks.* They waged procedural wars of attrition—filing motions to change venues, filing motions to disqualify lawyers, filing motions for the sake of filing motions—in the hopes of wearing down the plaintiffs. They tried to throw judges

---

* In the North Carolina case, the judge rebuked the Jones Day lawyers for making unfounded accusations about opposing counsel. Jones Day also tried to introduce as evidence a restraining order imposed on a family member years after the baby contracted meningitis—an apparent effort to intimidate the plaintiffs. "Abbott and its attorneys should be ashamed," the family's lawyers wrote in a court filing.

and juries off the scent by arguing that while the deadly bacteria was known to flourish in powdered formula, in theory it could've come from anywhere.

Jones Day's strategy in the Kunkel case would involve a little bit of everything. The firm was not interested in settling. To manage the case, Jones Day fielded a couple of veteran litigators in its Chicago office, Dan Reidy and June Ghezzi. Reidy was the partner responsible for managing the Abbott relationship. Ghezzi had a specialty defending drugmakers accused of harming consumers.

Some Jones Day lawyers regarded Ghezzi as talented but unpleasant. When the Sioux City suit was filed, she phoned an associate who was on parental leave with a two-week-old baby. "When are you coming back from leave?" were the first words out of her mouth. No congratulations, no niceties, just a return-to-work edict in the form of a blunt question. At least one longtime attorney had resigned from Jones Day in part because of what he viewed as the toxic environment Ghezzi created. Reidy, however, didn't see it that way. He liked Ghezzi and regarded her as a gifted litigator. And so she stayed.

EARLY ON A SATURDAY morning in December 2013, a judge named Mark Bennett walked into Sioux City's federal courthouse, in a handsome stone building that occupied most of a block. Bennett had been out of town for a speaking engagement, and he headed into his office to catch up on work. As he entered his chambers, he was surprised to see cardboard boxes stacked everywhere. His immediate thought was that maybe another judge had been assigned to move in. It didn't make much sense, but what other explanation was there for the huge jumble of boxes?

Another judge was not moving in. The boxes contained evidence that Jones Day wanted to be able to introduce at the upcoming trial. Bennett had been on the federal bench for decades, but he had never encountered so much evidence. A couple of days later, he convened a meeting of the lawyers on both sides. As they sat around a table in his chambers, Bennett laced into the Jones Day team for their "incredible obstructionist conduct." This was an Eighth Amendment violation, he told them, tongue-in-cheek: It would be a cruel and unusual punishment to make anyone read even a small fraction of what was contained in the cardboard boxes littering his chambers. The printed list of the exhibits in those boxes was thicker than the Sioux City phone book.

Bennett had been around long enough to suspect what was going on. Jones Day had no intention of using most of this evidence in the trial. No, he reckoned, the firm was trying to snow the plaintiff's lawyers with tens of thousands of pages of paperwork that they would have to sift through. Bennett also noted that the strategy may have reflected the fact that Jones Day had "a lot of associates to keep busy," and preparing all this paperwork was a surefire way to pile up the billable hours.

Bennett prided himself on being a discerning judge with a populist streak. The signature on his email featured Martin Luther King Jr.'s famous quote, "The arc of the moral universe is long, but it bends toward justice," followed by a line of commentary: "But the thing of it is—it does not bend on its own." The judge harbored a deep distrust of lawyers from large corporate firms, having seen them play all manner of barely acceptable games in his courtrooms over the years. (Dan Reidy, the Jones Day litigator, recognized Bennett's predisposition, telling me that the judge was "deeply and irrevocably prejudiced against 'big firms.'")

The mountain of evidence Jones Day had dumped in his chambers was the first indication to Bennett that these lawyers were up to the usual tricks of a big-city firm. (Reidy countered that the plaintiffs were responsible for much of the evidence.) The second sign came soon afterward, when the lawyers submitted transcripts of depositions that had been conducted months earlier. Bennett was in the habit of reviewing deposition transcripts before trials began so that he could rule on any objections that had arisen during the sessions. He started flipping through one of the transcripts. "I was shocked by what I read," he told me.

• • •

To the surprise and irritation of some of her Jones Day colleagues, Ghezzi had insisted on being present for many depositions involving Abbott employees. She did not sit idly by. Time after time, as Stephen Rathke questioned Abbott witnesses, she interrupted with objections. That was poor form, but what really got Bennett steamed as he read the transcripts was his sense that Ghezzi was using her objections to steer the witnesses' testimony. That was potentially a violation of the federal rules of civil procedure, which require objections to be "stated concisely in a nonargumentative and nonsuggestive manner" and warn that "an excessive number of unnecessary objections may itself constitute sanctionable conduct."

In August 2012, Rathke had deposed two Abbott employees, a research scientist specializing in neonatal nutrition and a quality-assurance manager at Abbott's Arizona factory. Over the course of about seven hours, Ghezzi had interrupted 115 times—an average of one objection every three or four minutes. At one point, Rathke asked whether bacteria found in the Arizona facility might be the same bacteria that infected Jeanine. Ghezzi interrupted: "Objection—vague and ambiguous."

"That would be speculation," the witness echoed. Rathke rephrased. Ghezzi interrupted again. "Object to the form of the question. It's a hypothetical; lacks facts."

"Yeah, those are hypotheticals," the witness parroted. Rathke rephrased the question one more time. Ghezzi: "Same objection."

"Not going to answer," the witness stated.

"You're not going to answer?" Rathke asked.

"Yeah, I mean, it's speculation. It would be guessing."

"You don't have to guess," Ghezzi chimed in.

Over and over and over this tag-team routine played out. Sometimes Ghezzi took things a step further, instructing the witness whether and how to answer Rathke's questions—a flagrant violation of deposition rules. Asked if she knew about Abbott's testing procedures, one witness replied: "Very limited knowledge."

"If it's no, then just say no," Ghezzi interjected.

During a break in one deposition, Rathke's cocounsel, a Sioux City lawyer named Tim Bottaro, took Rathke aside. Ghezzi was dominating what was supposed to be the plaintiff's deposition. "Why don't you just let June do the deposition?" Bottaro scolded. "You're getting steamrolled!"* Bottaro told me he never understood why Rathke didn't more strenuously object or complain to the judge about Ghezzi's conduct. (For his part, Rathke told me that complaining would have wasted precious time during the depositions. "I tried to relegate all of this as background noise, because I regarded it as a tactic to distract me," he said.)

Some Jones Day associates on the case privately grumbled about Ghezzi's antics and wondered whether she was going to get in trouble with the court. It was one thing to object, even to do so regularly. That laid the groundwork for the trial judge to block parts of a deposition from being used in court; that was fair game. Once an objection was noted for the record, the witness would still answer the other lawyer's question. What was not fair game was constantly speaking up beyond those objections, especially in a way that influenced how the witness answered the opposing lawyer's questions.

The depositions were important. Even before the trial, Abbott unsuccessfully sought a summary judgment ruling based in part on the depositions. Portions of Abbott witnesses' depositions would be read aloud to jurors during the trial. There was no telling what the witnesses might have said if Ghezzi hadn't been interrupting every few minutes, coaching the Abbott employees and rattling Rathke.

Rathke's inability to control his own depositions was bad enough. But then came Jones Day's depositions of Megan and Troy. Megan's

---

* Rathke said he didn't recall Bottaro making those comments. Bottaro later emailed me to say that Rathke was a skilled lawyer who was well organized and prepared.

lasted more than seven hours. When she and Rathke walked into the conference room where the deposition was taking place, they were met by a row of Jones Day lawyers wearing what looked like tailored suits. Megan was intimidated. The lawyers started with easy questions. How old was she? Where was she from? Then things got tougher. They spent what felt like hours asking and reasking the same set of questions about the ninety-second process of her preparing the fateful formula. "It went from nice to mean to nice to mean to nice to mean," Megan recalled. Rathke at times tried to move the questions along, but the Jones Day lawyers shut him down. He slouched in his seat, looking defeated. ("I was bored," he told me.) The more the Jones Day lawyers asked Megan the same question a different way, the more she tried to use different words to answer the questions. She just wanted this to end. "It was horrible," she said. "They broke me."

Then it was Troy's turn. He had a history of drug use. When he and Megan got together, he'd quit. But after the family returned from Omaha and the reality had started to sink in that their daughter would forever be brain damaged and probably wouldn't live past twenty, drugs had offered an escape. So had his fling with a younger woman. None of it lasted long. Troy got clean, he and the woman split up, Megan knew all about it and had forgiven him, and that was that. Except that now, sitting in that bland conference room, facing a row of Chicago lawyers in their fancy suits, they wanted to talk about this ugly period from years earlier.* It didn't take long for Troy to explode.

At home that evening, Megan and Troy compared notes. They discussed how Rathke had appeared cowed the moment he'd come face-to-face with the Jones Day team. They were disgusted with these hired guns. "I understand they've got a job to do, but at some point you've got to have a heart," Troy said. "They wanted

* Dan Reidy told me Troy's drug use "was potentially quite relevant" to the question of how the bacteria ended up in Jeanine's bottle.

to ruin the credibility of me and Megan so that little girl wouldn't get no help."

AS THE TRIAL APPROACHED in January 2014, Rathke was feeling good. Another meningitis case had recently settled with Abbott, leaving him hopeful that he might be able to score a last-minute deal. Barring that, he was optimistic that he'd win in court. A few weeks earlier, the plaintiff's team held a mock trial in Minneapolis with a focus group of jurors. Bottaro was there, and he warned Rathke that Minneapolis liberals were not good proxies for Sioux City conservatives. The lawyers watched the jury deliberate via a closed-circuit TV. The faux verdict came in: The "jurors" awarded $25 million in damages to the plaintiffs. Rathke embraced the TV screen, Bottaro told me.

Megan and Troy were nervous, unsure whether they'd get justice. Jeanine and James were almost six years old. Jeanine was immobile and mute and had to be fed through a tube. But the family was tough. Megan and Troy had inured themselves to the feeling of having people stare at them—looking at them like they were small, as if they had done something to bring this misfortune upon themselves—as they struggled to get Jeanine and her wheelchair out of a car.

Because they were possible witnesses, Megan and Troy weren't allowed into court to watch the trial. It was just as well. Nobody disputed that Jeanine had been infected by *Enterobacter sakazakii* or that it had caused her brain damage. The question was where the bacteria came from. Rathke and his expert witnesses argued that the lone logical explanation was that it was in the powdered Similac formula. After all, that was the only thing Jeanine had consumed. And powdered formula was a known breeding ground for this exact type of bacteria.

Jones Day's strategy was to raise doubt and to blame the plaintiff—the same playbook that the law firm had mastered when it first took on RJR as a client. Jeanine did not make an inviting target, but her parents did. Reidy used Megan's deposition to impeach her credibility. Why had her answers kept changing? Wasn't it possible that something other than the formula had poisoned Jeanine? The formula that the government had tested didn't contain *Enterobacter sakazakii*. (The bacteria has a tendency to clump together, and it was entirely possible that the portion that Jeanine ate was contaminated even though the tested sample was clean.) What if visitors had brought the bacteria into the house? Maybe it was lurking on the bottle that Megan had used or in the water that she had mixed with the powder. Really, it could have come from anywhere.

"Abbott blames the mom, the dad, the brother, all the other relatives that might have held the baby, the family dog, the kitchen, the city's water, the other food in the refrigerator. They even point a finger at the doctor," Rathke told the jury during his closing arguments.

"We're not trying to blame anybody with respect to this," Reidy responded. "We're trying to show where else it can come from."

After a two-week trial, the jury deliberated for seven hours. Then the verdict was announced: Abbott was not liable. Jones Day's lawyers had managed to sow doubt about the source of the poisonous bacteria. Rathke called Megan and Troy. "I hate to tell you this, but we lost," he said. They had watched plenty of legal dramas on TV, and there always seemed to be another court to appeal to, another angle to pursue. Now Troy realized that wasn't how the real world worked. "There was nothing more we could do," he said. Every part of the process felt like it had been stacked against them. Troy felt foolish for having had faith in the legal system to begin with.*

---

* Scott Stoffel, an Abbott spokesman, said the company's products "undergo rigorous quality checks—from raw ingredients and packaging components through in-process materials to finished products—before release to ensure that they meet both the nutritional and safety needs of infants and children." He added: "We are very sympathetic to the families in these situations," but juries have determined that "Abbott's product was not the cause of the injuries."

• • •

Bennett was not stunned by the verdict—he had been impressed by Reidy and Ghezzi's lawyering during the trial—but he thought it was the wrong outcome. The fact that Jeanine consumed the powdered formula and got meningitis, and James didn't get the formula and didn't get sick, struck him as powerful evidence. (Unlike in criminal cases, where prosecutors must prove the defendant's guilt beyond a reasonable doubt, the threshold in civil trials is lower: The plaintiffs need to show that a "preponderance of the evidence" supports their claim—in other words, that it is more likely than not to be true.) "I thought it should have come out the other way," Bennett told me. "If it had been a bench trial, I would have ruled for the plaintiffs in all likelihood."

The verdict might have been the end of the matter, except that Bennett was still seething about what he'd seen when he'd read the deposition transcripts. At one point during the trial, Bennett had called out Ghezzi for making meritless objections as Rathke questioned a witness on the stand. "Well, I'm sorry, Your Honor," Ghezzi had replied, "but that was my training." Bennett heard that as an admission that Ghezzi had learned her techniques at Jones Day, confirming his suspicions about the underhanded, win-at-all-costs tactics that were rife at corporate law firms. "Their conduct was not pushing the envelope. It was burning up the envelope completely," Bennett told me. "I thought their conduct was appalling. It was the worst by a factor of ten" that he had seen as a judge.

During his two-decade career on the bench, Bennett had only rarely punished lawyers for misbehavior. But he thought Ghezzi's actions warranted sanctions. Normally such a punishment would be in the form of a fine. But Bennett doubted that would do much to deter other lawyers, especially Ghezzi's colleagues at Jones Day, who he figured had been schooled in the same obstructionist tactics.

Bennett wanted to really send a message—to the whole corporate bar. He was sick of these slick, high-priced lawyers prancing into federal courtrooms and then stomping all over attorneys from the government or small firms that weren't bankrolled by multinational companies. So he got creative. He ordered Ghezzi (or another partner at Jones Day) to produce a training video in which she explained the impropriety of her objections and witness-coaching.

The unusual punishment got everyone's attention, just as Bennett had hoped. (A federal appeals court later overturned it on technical grounds without ruling on whether Ghezzi's conduct was sanctionable.*) Bennett soon was fielding emails from lawyers nationwide thanking him for taking a public stand against abusive discovery and deposition practices by big law firms.

In Boston, Dick Daynard, a law professor at Northeastern University, began using the episode as a teaching aid. After discussing the case and Ghezzi's conduct with his students, he'd pose a question: Back when Ghezzi was in law school, had she envisioned a future in which she would use dubious tactics to defend a giant company against a poor family whose child had been brain damaged? Was that her goal as an aspiring lawyer? No? "So how do you keep yourself from doing that?" Daynard would ask.

In each class, Daynard told me, the students would spend time batting around various ideas before eventually arriving at a version of the same answer. The solution, they concluded, was that throughout your career, you had to periodically ask yourself two simple questions: Am I proud of the work I'm doing? Am I the person I want to be?

AT 8:30 ON A brisk Thursday morning, a few days after Jeanine's thirteenth birthday, I connected with Megan and Troy over FaceTime. Megan was in the back, smoking a cigarette. She had just

---

* Ghezzi has since retired, "without any urging whatsoever from the firm," Reidy told me.

returned from an early morning shift—4:30 a.m. to 8:00 a.m.—sanitizing the MidAmerican Energy offices in Sioux City, wiping down phones, toilets, door handles to make the place safe for workers during the pandemic. Troy would be heading there from noon to about 6:00 p.m. to do a general clean and another sanitization. They needed to work these hours so they could take care of Jeanine in between nursing shifts.

The family had moved to a cramped three-bedroom house in a converted army barracks out by the Sioux Gateway Airport. Their walls were decorated with intricate dream catchers that Megan had collected. Two cats, Phoebe and Smokey, stalked the house, and a brown boxer, Scrappy, loafed on a couch.

Jeanine was in bed, which is where she spent most of each day, clutching two Elmo dolls. *Daniel Tiger's Neighborhood* was playing on a small TV. Jeanine was wearing a black and white sweater and had a bow in her hair. A blue glove covered her left hand to discourage her from chewing her fingers. A few stuffed animals dangled from a contraption mounted over her bed; in the mornings, when she woke up, she liked to swat at the toys and watch them move. "She understands cause and effect," Megan told me.

Jeanine was laughing and cooing and gurgling, and her open-mouthed smile illuminated her colorful bedroom. "She's basically in a permanent baby phase," Megan explained. Jeanine couldn't swallow, but sometimes Megan and Troy put small bits of frosting or ice cream into her mouth, causing Jeanine to lift her arms and kick her feet. "That girl gets a sugar high," Troy boasted.

I asked what would be different if they had prevailed in their lawsuit against Abbott. "Well, nothing," Troy said at first. Their daughter would still be brain damaged, their lives would still be hard. He paused. Then he started ticking off the things that, in fact, would be much different.

They would have a medically equipped house designed for someone in a wheelchair.

They could afford to replace their 1998 Chevy's broken wheelchair lift, which had electrical problems and was leaking hydraulic fluid.

They could get Jeanine new wheelchairs as she grew, rather than waiting five years for insurance to pay for one.

They wouldn't have to worry about becoming ineligible for government services if they started earning a little more money.

They could have paid the physical therapists to keep coming. Troy had heard of situations where someone with a terrible injury was never supposed to walk again and then ended up walking again with hard work and a lot of help. "Without that money, she lost that opportunity," he sighed.

As we talked, a nurse was preparing to pour a bottle of PediaSure into Jeanine's feeding tube, one of her six daily meals. PediaSure is made by Abbott. Troy shook his head with disgust. "Every time you have to open one of those bottles," he said, "it's a slap in the face."

14

MAKE IT GO AWAY

In 2013, a decade into his tenure as managing partner, Steve Brogan turned sixty. He still had time left before he reached the obligatory retirement age of sixty-five, but time flies, and neither Brogan nor his allies wanted him to leave anytime soon. That year, Jones Day's advisory committee—a group of about sixty partners handpicked by Brogan—extended his reign through 2020. Not long after, the firm's partners pushed back his mandatory retirement by another two years. The vote was "virtually unanimous," Joe Sims, a partner at the time, told me. He cited this as proof of Brogan's broad support, though others saw it as a sign that few lawyers dared to cross him.

The contract extensions—which put Brogan on track to serve a full twenty years as managing partner—erased any doubts about the scope of his authority, including to shape the firm's culture.

One of Brogan's long-standing cultural priorities had been to make whining taboo. Just about every time he addressed a large group of partners, Brogan made sure to recite his "no whining" mantra. Sometimes he would project onto a screen a slide with the word "whiners" on a bright red stop sign. Other times "WHINING" would appear inside a red circle with a diagonal line slashing through it, like a cigarette in a no-smoking placard. Brogan even had a "no whining" sign, a gift from McCartan, on display in his office.

Brogan's deputies took up his no-whining crusade as their own.

Traci Lovitt, a candidate to one day succeed Brogan, once gave a presentation to Jones Day associates that included a slide featuring images from popular movies of characters rolling their eyes. "*Never* be this person," Lovitt advised. "The 'eye roll' associate. The: I hate the coffee; I hate the tea; I hate that we don't have snacks that I like; I hate the health plan; I really don't like my office. There are a lot of people who love this place. This kind of eye rolling at the firm trickles up and can harm an otherwise successful career because it is a swipe at something we love: this institution."

In addition to grumbling about snacks and offices and health plans, the ban on whining applied most obviously to lawyers' compensation. Even the lowest-paid attorney at Jones Day was earning in the six figures, and the highest-paid were pocketing millions a year. No one was at risk of going hungry. And if they wanted more money, they could always test the waters at a rival firm.

The goal of the "no whining" mandate was to encourage partners to solve problems rather than complain about them, as Lovitt later described it. But the policy had other effects as well. One was that, intentionally or not, it sometimes deterred Jones Day employees from speaking up about issues like racial discrimination. Managers would point to the "no whining" policy to deflect grievances. Those who insisted on escalating their complaints risked paying a heavy price.

DEEPAK PURUSHOTHAMAN WAS AN associate in Jones Day's office in London. With a specialty in the fast-growing world of asset-based lending, he was on track to become a partner, which had made a certain amount of suffering seem worthwhile.

Over the years, he had stood by silently, a forced smile on his lips, as his colleagues made racist jokes. He had gotten into the habit of collecting the remarks, the slights, the off-color "humor," documenting much of it in writing. Purushothaman didn't initially intend to do anything with this growing compendium, but he kept track of it nonetheless, just in case. Sometimes he felt like he was being punished for no reason—like when his mother, who lived in Wales, was dying. Purushothaman started schlepping back and forth between a hospital in Wales and the office in London. On occasion, the long journeys took a little longer than expected, and that caused him to arrive at work late. This didn't seem like a big deal. He was getting his work done, and this was not a long term situation. But Purushothaman's superiors were not sympathetic. They warned that the tardy arrivals might be held against him.

In 2013, Purushothaman complained to one of his bosses about what he felt was a pattern of racism inside Jones Day's London offices. The complaints were escalated; the response boiled down to: *Stop whining*. Purushothaman's managers told him the racist remarks were harmless locker room banter, and what's more, Purushothaman had laughed along with the jokes, which clearly meant he hadn't been bothered. Not long afterward, he was taken aside by his managers, who informed him that he was no longer in the running to make partner, and therefore it didn't make sense for him to stick around. He should look elsewhere for a job.

Purushothaman consulted with outside lawyers, who told him he had a strong case to make that he was the victim of racial discrimination. They advised him to submit a written complaint to the firm about his treatment. So Purushothaman sat down and cataloged the examples of racist behavior he'd endured. Then he compiled examples of women and people of color facing what he viewed as discrimination, calculated the number of racial or ethnic minorities who'd been involuntarily "exited," and amassed other unpleasant statistics about life for women and nonwhite people in Jones Day's London offices. He pulled it all together into a lengthy report, which he emailed to multiple Jones Day lawyers, including some who were named in the document as being responsible for the misconduct. He informed his colleagues, including John Phillips, the head of the London office, that he was considering filing a discrimination complaint with the U.K. Employment Tribunal, which adjudicates such cases.

A day or two later, around lunchtime on an autumn day, Jones Day's local head of litigation burst into Purushothaman's office. "You are leaving," he announced. "You are being exited." The lawyer marched Purushothaman out of the building with whatever he could carry. The rest of his belongings—including paperwork involving his mother's will, which he hadn't had time to gather—would be boxed up and sent to him at some point in the future.

In the days that followed, as Purushothaman's lawyers prepared to file a complaint with the employment tribunal, Jones Day staff searched his computer. On it they found messages that showed that Purushothaman had had a sexual relationship with another associate at the firm. A Jones Day lawyer spoke with Purushothaman's lawyer and informed him that, if the threatened complaint were to materialize, the evidence of Purushothaman's affair would likely become public. Might he prefer to make this whole unpleasant situation quietly disappear with a settlement and a confidentiality agreement?

There was nothing improper about the sexual relationship: It was consensual, and Purushothaman wasn't the woman's boss or above her in the org chart. But Purushothaman was a private person. And so, just as Jones Day had hoped, he chose Option Two: Make it go away.*

"IT WAS A DAILY thing, being told what a piece of shit I was," a former staffer told me. A Cleveland native, he had joined Jones Day's finance department straight out of college. He wasn't a lawyer; his job was to compile lawyers' daily reports on their billable hours, enter them into a spreadsheet, crunch the numbers, make sure clients paid their bills in a timely fashion, and so on.

His boss was in the middle of an acrimonious divorce, and he

* The episode might have remained secret, except that John Phillips described it to another partner, Sebastian Orton, who relayed it to me. Orton is in a long-running dispute with Jones Day, but I confirmed the information with other sources. Phillips told me that this account is "false in material respects" but wouldn't elaborate.

got in the habit of taking out his anger on his subordinates. Sometimes the staffer would make a stupid mistake—adding the wrong column in an Excel spreadsheet, for example—and his boss "would just lose it," he recalled. The employee was on the receiving end of more borderline-violent tirades than he could count.

One day, the eruption was so severe that it wasn't borderline. They were in the boss's office. Very quickly, he went from scowling to ranting to fuming to screaming.

Then the boss swung. He punched the staffer in the chest, hard. The employee was not a small man, but he staggered backward, stunned. He wanted to hit back. He resisted. Then his boss started crying, begging his forgiveness.

It was the staffer's first job. He'd been advised to suck things up, to roll with the punches. He wanted to keep his job. "So," he said, "I didn't tell anyone."

IN 2019, A GROUP of current and former Jones Day associates sued the firm, accusing it of widespread gender discrimination and harassment, of a "fraternity culture," of being a "male brotherhood." The lawsuit ticked off one alleged example after another, many involving the firm's office in Irvine, California. (Jones Day denied most of the allegations.) At a work function at a partner's house, a summer associate in a white dress was shoved into a pool; the man who pushed her allegedly got high fives from Jones Day leadership. Lawyers praised women for being "eye candy." Others were rebuked for having a "stern face" and told to "smile more."

Women who complained were derided. When one lawyer in the New York office threatened to sue, a partner warned her that the firm would "drag you through the mud" and "ruin your reputation." Drunken episodes, by contrast, were sometimes dismissed as mild indiscretions. ("You usually have to knock a partner out cold for it to be a career-ending event," a Jones Day partner once told a reporter.)

The biggest allegation in the lawsuit was that Jones Day systematically discriminated against women when it came to pay and promotions. The firm denied this—and, as it turned out, the plaintiffs didn't have the evidence to support the charge. Jones Day pointed out that many of its senior-most lawyers, including those running practice areas and regions, were women and that the firm compared favorably to many of its peers in its support for and advancement of female employees. Jones Day's confidential compensation data apparently validated the law firm's claims.

But that didn't mean that all or even most of the detailed allegations in the lawsuit were false. The lead plaintiff was Nilab Rahyar Tolton. She had joined the Irvine office as an associate after graduating from Harvard Law, where she'd been a 2010 commencement speaker. She was assigned to work with a partner, Paul Rafferty. Tolton is "smart, committed, and exceptionally hard-working," Rafferty wrote in a 2013 performance review. The next year, he lauded her as "an indispensable cog in my practice [who is] willing to work 24/7 to assist the firm's clients." Another largely positive review followed in 2015. She was rewarded with a coveted invite to the "spa day" that the firm held for female clients and a prominent role recruiting and training lawyers.

Yet the firm's "casual misogyny" made it a difficult place to work, according to the lawsuit. A partner, Eric Landau, kept commenting on Tolton's looks, comparing her and other women to volleyball players. (At another point, in front of the entire Irvine office, Landau referred to his secretary's "banging" body in a bikini.)* Rafferty once noted that Tolton was living with her boyfriend and suggested that made it less likely that her boyfriend would want to get married: "Why buy the cow when you can get the milk for free?" In a limo to a wine-tasting event, men from the office played the game Fuck, Marry, Kill with Tolton and other women in the car. Cary Sullivan, another Jones Day partner, at one point told Tolton to coach

* Landau denied the allegations, though Jones Day acknowledged in a court filing that Landau had referred to his secretary Rollerblading in a bikini.

another female lawyer on not sounding so "ditzy."* (In a court filing, Jones Day denied that "the offensive conduct of a few immature junior associates had any impact on [Tolton's] career at Jones Day or could reasonably be viewed by her or anyone else as representative of the firm's culture.")

In 2016, Tolton had a baby and went on maternity leave. That June, as she was preparing to return to work, she received her annual compensation letter in the mail. She was coming off what she thought was a good year and figured the news inside the envelope would validate that. It didn't. Jones Day informed her that her salary had been frozen. Tolton said in a deposition that she went to two of the top partners in the Irvine office. They initially gave her vague positive feedback. Why, then, had her salary been frozen? The men responded that, um, actually, there had been some complaints about her work. Tolton noted that the only thing that had really changed since her prior performance review was that she'd had a baby.

Tolton soon learned that she was pregnant again. She was determined to work as hard as she could before the second baby arrived. She vowed to herself never to turn down an assignment. Jones Day seemed intent on testing her will. She was given jobs that required all-nighters and frequent travel. Tolton reminded her superiors that she was eventually going to need to stop traveling and then would be on leave. Maybe there was someone better to put on these cases? (Jones Day said Tolton was passing up opportunities and shirking responsibilities, part of a pattern of lackluster performance.)

It was a difficult pregnancy. Tolton worked from home in the early mornings and late evenings, switching off the lights to help deal with the nausea. Her doctor told her she needed to slow down; he wrote a note that Tolton shared with the firm. One of the leaders in the Irvine office, Darren Cottriel, summoned Tolton to a conference room. He admonished her for not working hard enough. Tolton kept up her pace, billing about two hundred hours per

---

* Sullivan told me he was simply passing on feedback from a client.

month from December 2016 through March 2017, when she had her son and went on leave. (Jones Day said it accommodated her as requested by her doctor.)

Tolton was struggling to manage a newborn and a toddler on her own; her partner, a Navy SEAL, was deployed overseas. Jones Day informed her that her salary would again be frozen. When she returned in October, Cottriel and Richard Grabowski, who ran the Irvine office, called her in for a performance review. They told her to "look for other opportunities outside the firm." She had six months to find a new job, they said.

When other lawyers in the office asked what had happened, Tolton said she was being pushed out. Jones Day, up until that point, had been willing to help her find a new job. But a few days later, Grabowski and Cottriel called Tolton. She was at home for her son's birthday party; they were about to sing "Happy Birthday." Tolton took the call outside so that she wouldn't disrupt the singing. The men yelled that she was barred from coming back to the office. Her email account was shut down. Their vitriol was so intense that it took Tolton's breath away.* She'd never received so much as a speeding ticket; she was not accustomed to people in positions of authority going off on her. As the tirade continued, Tolton leaned against the wall of her house for support. She pressed so hard that it left an imprint on her back.

TOLTON AND THE OTHER women dropped their lawsuit in 2021 after concluding that there wasn't evidence to support their claims of systematic pay discrimination. There was no settlement announced, leading to widespread speculation that the plaintiffs had simply given up. "What a royal tease," a Bloomberg colum-

---

* Cottriel told me that he and Grabowski had talked to Tolton about her "subpar performance" before her first pregnancy. He said Tolton was barred from the office after she encouraged colleagues to quit and told them she was being pushed out because she took family leave. Cottriel denied yelling at her.

nist wrote, wondering aloud whether the suit had been "a waste of time." She noted that the case had been poised to "end in bright lights shining on the inner workings of a secretive, powerful law firm. So much for that. It promised so much yet delivered so little."

That wasn't quite right. A number of the partners who were accused of sexist behavior—including Paul Rafferty and Eric Landau—left the firm. (It isn't clear whether their departures were related to the allegations.) Jones Day also agreed to pay the plaintiffs an undisclosed amount.* Brogan issued a confidential memo to the firm's lawyers. He trumpeted the end of the lawsuit as a vindication of the firm's compensation system and of Jones Day's defiance in the face of an assault from disgruntled workers and their allies in the media: "It is precisely because of the firm's prominence, its successes, and its willingness to defend unpopular clients and itself that we will continue to be the subject of occasional attacks for wholly unjustified reasons."

* Terri Chase, a Jones Day partner who represented the firm in the litigation, told me that notwithstanding the payment, the plaintiffs' lawyers "lost their shirts on this case."

15

PSYCHOLOGICAL COMBAT

For millennia, a Native American tribe, the Sippicans, inhabited the area off Buzzards Bay, just west of Cape Cod, where a natural harbor and a wide inlet provided plentiful access to fish, quahogs, oysters, and scallops. Europeans colonized the region in the 1600s and displaced the Sippicans. It wasn't until shortly before the Civil War that residents of what had become a quaint oceanfront village incorporated themselves into a Massachusetts town. They named it in honor of Francis Marion, whose guerrilla tactics during the American Revolution earned him the nickname the "Swamp Fox."

More than 160 years later, the picturesque town of Marion was about to experience another form of asymmetric warfare—one that would illustrate how powerful outside forces, in this case led by Jones Day, can prevent local governments from acting in the interest of their citizens.

OVER THE YEARS, MARION hadn't changed much. Wealthy and with a population of about five thousand, it retained its small-town New England charm. There was the classic white-and-black lighthouse. The inner harbor was crowded with ship masts; nearby, the town kept waterways stocked with shellfish, which residents could catch. (Marion's official seal featured a pair of clamshells and a Native American with a bow and arrow.) The town exhibited the tell-tale signs of a Cape Cod community: roads lined with salt-stunted trees and houses clad in weathered cedar shingles.

Marion prided itself on being inclusive and progressive, and that was part of the reason that Jason Reynolds had decided to move there. A New Hampshire native, he'd scored a job at Boston Children's Hospital as a pediatric oncologist. Spending lots of time in the city convinced Reynolds and his wife that they were not city people. They found a house in Marion near the water. They liked to sail; this was perfect.

In 2016, Reynolds ran for election to the town's board of health. In Massachusetts, the boards wield real power. They are allowed to enact policies to promote the health and welfare of their citizenry—a broad, ill-defined mission that gives ample room to experiment with innovative public health policies. Reynolds saw Marion's board as an underutilized weapon. He campaigned, and won, on a vision of making it more proactive.

Reynolds had a lot of ideas; one thing he felt strongly about was preparing for a pandemic, which his medical training and background reading had convinced him was inevitable. But his first proposal was more focused. As a pediatrician, he abhorred how tobacco companies targeted kids. Their legacy of cartoonish advertising was part of it. But lately cigarette makers had changed tack, introducing flavored products. They made smoking seem fun, and fruit- and candy-flavored tobacco tasted a whole lot better than the traditional variety.

The new flavors were part of the reason that, despite decades of progress at combating smoking, nearly a quarter of American high school students still used tobacco products. It was an acute public health crisis: Tobacco killed hundreds of thousands of Americans annually, more than murders, alcohol, illegal drugs, and car accidents combined.

There were only three members of the Marion Board of Health, and one of them, Betsy Dunn, shared Reynolds's ambitions to activate the board and to make it harder for kids to get into smoking.

The simplest solution, they decided, was to ban the sale of flavored tobacco products at the town's half dozen or so retailers and liquor stores. That would make it at least a little harder for minors to act on their impulses.

There was a wrinkle to consider: Would menthol cigarettes be included as a flavored product for the purposes of the ban? Reynolds consulted with Cheryl Sbarra, an attorney for the Massachusetts Association of Health Boards. Sbarra was a fierce opponent of Big Tobacco, but she was also a realist. She pointed out that very few localities anywhere in the U.S. had banned flavored tobacco, and even fewer had included menthols in those bans. What's more, while federal courts had established the rights of municipalities to restrict flavored tobacco, the courts hadn't weighed in on menthols. From a legal standpoint, Sbarra explained, it was safer to model Marion's ban on what courts had already ruled was acceptable.

But Reynolds wasn't the cautious type. This was what he'd just been elected to do. Menthols were by some measures more dangerous than normal tobacco products: Researchers had found they made it more appealing for people to start smoking and harder for them to stop. "I really wanted to go for menthol," Reynolds recalled. "I wanted to be the first to do it."

The board of health met every couple of weeks at the Marion Town House, an ornate Victorian building constructed in the late 1800s. On a warm evening in August 2016, Reynolds and Dunn floated their idea in public for the first time. The board also called for banning the sale of cigarettes at pharmacies. The local newspaper, *The Wanderer,* briefly mentioned the proposals, but that was it.

The plan was to hold a couple of public hearings and then vote on the measure, which would almost certainly pass, since Reynolds and Dunn constituted a majority. Sbarra warned that the tobacco industry might sue to block the menthols ban and said the board might need a larger venue for future hearings to accommodate protesters. Reynolds doubted it. Marion was a small town. Would anyone even notice? Worst case, he figured, tobacco companies would fight the ban after it was in place. The town could deal with that if and when it happened.

JONES DAY BY NOW had been representing RJR for more than thirty years. The company was one of the law firm's most valued clients. In places like Atlanta, half or more of the firm's litigators were assigned to work full-time on RJR matters. It was steady, profitable, year-in, year-out work, and it was a result, at least in part, of the strong personal bond that lawyers like Bob Weber and John Strauch had forged with men like Chuck Blixt, RJR's general counsel. "We have a relationship that is rare between a corporation and their attorneys," Blixt explained in 2004. "They are as committed to our success as anybody who works at the company."

That might have sounded like hyperbole, but Jones Day's tactics on behalf of its golden goose suggested that the firm was, indeed, deeply committed. Plaintiffs' lawyers got in the habit of telling clients to prepare for the emergence of any skeletons in their closets and to hear from family, friends, neighbors, even old high school classmates after Jones Day's investigators showed up on their doorsteps. Little of this information was likely to make it into the courtroom. The point, it seemed, was to get the would-be plaintiff to think very hard about whether he really wanted to go down this road.

It was psychological combat, and it often worked. Not long ago, a Jones Day lawyer was deposing the widow of a smoker who was suing RJR. The firm had learned that the dead smoker had been having an affair. During the deposition, the Jones Day lawyer asked the widow about it. It was the first she'd heard of the affair. There was no threat to bring it up in the trial, but it was a hint that the family's sad, dirty laundry might be aired in public. The heartbroken widow abandoned the lawsuit.*

---

* Stephanie Parker, the Jones Day partner responsible for RJR litigation, said the firm learned of the affair from the husband's medical records, which the widow's lawyers had access to. She said it was relevant because the husband had human

This work and these tactics didn't appeal to everyone at Jones Day. Some newly arrived lawyers tried to secure guarantees that they wouldn't be placed on tobacco cases. They noted that many leading law firms refused on principle to work with tobacco companies; the fat fees weren't enough to compensate for the costly reputational damage. Sometimes the requests were granted; two former Supreme Court clerks who'd been recruited to Jones Day told me they were exempted from working on tobacco cases. Other times, Jones Day's response was that perhaps such squeamish lawyers would be more comfortable at a different firm. For the most part, though, Jones Day's partners found remarkably similar ways to justify to themselves (and to me) the work that they and their colleagues were doing.

"You can't just pick and choose your clients," a longtime partner, George Manning, asserted. "Moral qualms can be left to the legislators."

"The moral judgments I leave to God," another Jones Day tobacco litigator told me.

"Law firms generally don't draw lines. It becomes a slippery slope," a third partner explained. "Once you start trying to put a moral or ethical screen, it becomes a really hard line to be able to draw. At the end of the day, law firms are profit-maximizing institutions." That, at least, was something that everyone could agree on. And nowhere were there more profits for a tobacco-focused law firm to maximize than in Florida.

In 2006, the state's Supreme Court had issued a landmark decision in *Engle v. R.J. Reynolds Tobacco Co.* It was named for Howard Engle, who, twelve years earlier, had sued RJR for the health problems associated with smoking. The suit became a class action, and the class (similarly situated people who stood to collect damages) included more than a half million smokers and their families. The

---

papilloma virus. HPV infects most sexually active people at some point in their lives. In theory, it could have caused the husband's cancer.

trial was split into two parts. The first found that cigarettes were addictive and deadly and that RJR and other tobacco companies had hidden the health risks and been negligent. The second phase was when jurors had to calculate damages. In July 2000, they returned with an astronomical number: $145 *billion*.

This was a very bad day for the tobacco industry; for a fleeting moment, mass bankruptcy looked like a real possibility. But the companies appealed, and the decision was reversed. Then the plaintiffs appealed, and that was how, in the summer of 2006, the case ended up before the Florida Supreme Court. The court overruled the bulk of the damages that the jurors had awarded, reasoning that it was impossible to figure out how much each plaintiff deserved because everyone's situation was different.

That was disappointing for the plaintiffs, but as part of the decision, the court said that the hundreds of thousands of class members could file their own lawsuits against the tobacco companies. These new lawsuits wouldn't have to establish that cigarettes were addictive and deadly and that the tobacco companies had been deceitful and negligent. Judges in Florida would instruct juries that all of those things were true.

Thousands of lawsuits poured in through the open floodgates. (They were known as "Engle progeny" suits.) This was a pain in the butt for the tobacco companies, but it was a jackpot for their lawyers. There was so much work; even the hundreds of cases that Jones Day resolved via out-of-court settlements devoured thousands of billable hours—not to mention the dozens that went to trial. For years, Jones Day was averaging more than one Engle-related trial a month.

To handle all the work, Jones Day had a rotating cast of associates coming down to Florida. This might not have been the most stimulating gig—the firm had developed templates for deposing witnesses, for example—but trial experience was precious. Getting shipped down to Florida became a prized assignment. Managers encouraged associates to embrace the "work hard, play hard" vibe.

Two female associates told me they got the following advice before going to Florida: *Take advantage of the casual environment. Don't be shy about lounging poolside in a bikini. Don't turn down dinner invitations from the partners.* It was a combination of boot camp and spring break—and it was viewed as a way station on the path to partnership.*

Jones Day's mandate wasn't confined to defending RJR against lawsuits. The firm also was responsible for thwarting regulations that could crimp the industry's profits. That job fell to Jones Day's government regulations practice, which was led by a former Bush administration official, Noel Francisco. Francisco quickly became one of RJR's leading lawyers. Among many other initiatives, he sued the Food and Drug Administration, contesting its authority to require prominent graphic warning labels on cigarette packs.

In some ways, the tobacco work was the cultural glue that kept Jones Day together. So many of the firm's lawyers at one point or another had worked on an RJR matter—and so many had gotten their first courtroom experience on a tobacco case. It was an ideal training ground, and it had the side benefit of desensitizing young lawyers to working for noxious clients.

THE TOBACCO INDUSTRY SOON got wind of the Marion Board of Health's plans to restrict the sale of flavored tobacco.

The first protests were from an entity called the Coalition for Responsible Retailing, which had been created a year earlier in a suburban building that was home to a karate studio and a hair-removal service. The guy in charge of the group was Dennis Lane, the owner of a 7-Eleven store. He'd previously lent his credentials as a small-business owner to powerful corporate interests. He was a

* Stephanie Parker, the Jones Day partner, said she had "never heard anyone suggest that lawyers should 'hang out in a bikini' or go to dinner with partners." She said she wasn't aware of "lawyers going swimming . . . and almost all our meals are taken as a group with food ordered for the entire team."

spokesman for the country's largest retailers—companies like CVS, Target, and Home Depot—in a fight over credit-card fees. He hosted a Republican politician at his store to attack Massachusetts senator Elizabeth Warren for being antibusiness. His coalition claimed to be a grassroots group of stores that wanted to keep tobacco out of the hands of minors. But its real mission was to lobby against tobacco regulations—a fight Lane had been waging since the mid-1990s.

Bald, goateed, and in his sixties, Lane now showed up at a Marion Board of Health meeting. Banning the sale of flavored tobacco would hurt local businesses, Lane said. It would hurt Black smokers, who prefer menthol cigarettes. "Don't discriminate," he huffed. (Betsy Dunn's retort: "You play the race card because then people will be afraid to do the right thing.")

Reynolds and Dunn had expected a certain amount of opposition to their proposal. Now here it was. So far, it felt manageable.

Then, one day in September 2016, a letter arrived by overnight mail at the Marion Town House. It was addressed to the town's board of health and its board of selectmen, which in Massachusetts towns is the equivalent of a mayor-by-committee. The four-page letter was on the cream-colored stationery of Jones Day's D.C. office. Along the bottom was an impressive list of the firm's thirty-seven locations, from Al Khobar and Atlanta to Tokyo and Washington. Noel Francisco had signed the letter in blue ink.

Francisco identified himself as a lawyer for RJR. "It has come to our clients' attention" that Marion was considering a ban of flavored tobacco and of cigarettes being sold at pharmacies and other "health care institutions," he began. "We believe that the flavors ban violates the United States Constitution and that the health-institutions provision contravenes state law. In light of these legal infirmities . . . we urge Marion to refrain from adopting the proposed regulation. If Marion instead chooses to adopt these provisions, we will have no choice but to consider the initiation of litigation challenging the regulation."

The letter was at best a stretch. It claimed that Marion was banning flavored tobacco products, a move that would violate the federal Tobacco Control Act. But of course Marion was simply restricting the sale of the products—a policy that federal courts had previously upheld. The letter also asserted that the prohibition on selling tobacco at pharmacies exceeded the board of health's authority—even though towns and cities in Massachusetts had already imposed such restrictions and were permitted to do so under state law.

But threatening letters from high-priced global law firms are not something to take lightly, which was precisely the point of Jones Day's missive. It cost virtually nothing for a couple of associates to do the research, draft the letter, present it for Francisco's signature, and then send it out in a fancy overnight mail envelope. Sure, maybe the arguments were weak, but this wasn't a court filing, and the lawyers were under no obligation to be forthright in their dealings with some random town. If the letter intimidated town officials, maybe they'd back down. If not, well, nothing much was lost. (Francisco told me the letter was written in good faith and wasn't designed to intimidate. He said his intent "was to represent the interests of my client by advancing credible legal arguments on its behalf, which is, of course, what lawyers do.")

Francisco's letter quickly circulated among Marion's leaders and advisers. Jon Witten, the town's lawyer, informed colleagues that he could not guarantee that Jones Day wouldn't sue. Other Marion officials were as worried by the firm's letterhead as the substance of the letter. They hadn't heard of Jones Day, but they deduced from its list of far-flung offices that this was probably not a firm to mess with.

Someone shared the letter with Sbarra. She took it to Northeastern University's Public Health Advocacy Institute, whose remit included helping local boards of health defend themselves against this kind of corporate onslaught. Chris Banthin, a lawyer at the institute, read the letter and concluded it was "ridiculous and baseless, and thus clearly intended to threaten the town." He told the board of health that he thought it highly unlikely that Jones Day would follow through on the litigation threat, because the firm would probably lose, which would attract attention to the weakness of Big Tobacco's argument and would establish a precedent. The town needed to call Jones Day's bluff.

Banthin offered to have his institute represent Marion for free in the unlikely event that RJR sued. The board of health and Witten, the town's lawyer, welcomed the help. But the board of selectmen also needed to sign off; it was the only body in town that had the power to enter into an agreement with an outside party, in this case the public health institute. That is where things stalled. Francisco's letter was included in a packet of correspondence handed out to selectmen at their meeting on October 4, but they didn't discuss it. (They *did* discuss a one-day alcohol license for a local church's chowder and soup cook-off.) The selectmen, whom Dennis Lane had already lobbied in opposition to the proposed regulations, weren't so sure about picking a fight with a global law firm representing a multinational company. "They felt threatened," Sbarra said.

Jason Reynolds kept pushing to arrange a meeting with the selectmen to get them to sign off, but the selectmen kept deflecting—a remarkable feat in a town of barely five thousand people. Months passed. Reynolds and Dunn were left to publicly wonder what was taking the selectmen so long. "I'm not sure where we're at," Dunn acknowledged at one health board meeting. "All that, I think, was put on the back burner." And until the town had legal representation lined up, it felt reckless to do anything that risked a lawsuit.

By 2017, the tiny health department was getting flooded with emails and phone calls from all sorts of people they had never heard of—another unusual situation in a town of Marion's size. There was record turnout, and a series of increasingly far-fetched arguments, at the health board's meetings that fall. Lane was a constant presence; he would soon send flyers to all of the town's registered voters, urging them to lobby their elected representatives against the proposal. A representative of the Massachusetts

Association of Minority Law Enforcement Officers turned up and claimed that Black smokers would get targeted by police because they were smoking menthols—a hollow argument, since people would remain free to smoke whatever they liked; it was just that retailers could now get dinged for selling flavored tobacco. And a lobbyist from Cumberland Farms, the convenience store chain that had become a leading opponent of tobacco restrictions, showed up, too. "You're essentially shutting us down," the lobbyist hyperventilated. "You might as well ban all tobacco."

The combination of Francisco's letter and the increasingly noisy protests from out-of-towners was grinding down the third member of the board of health, John Howard. At the October meeting, he voiced doubts about whether this really should be a priority. "The town has limited resources," he pointed out. "Our principal job is dealing with urgent health issues. This issue is not." Howard worried that if the town got stuck with a big legal bill—or, even worse, the payment of damages to tobacco companies—he'd get "tarred and feathered." "The town would like us to be very cautious," Howard said.

In reality, with the exception of Cumberland Farms, it was far from clear that the small handful of retail businesses in Marion even opposed the measure. At one point, the owner of the town's general store bumped into Reynolds and asked whether the tobacco restrictions would kick in immediately. He had already procured many cartons of menthol cigarettes, and he didn't want to have to throw them away. Reynolds explained that the rule would be phased in, so the store owner wouldn't waste his inventory. The guy shrugged. What was the big deal?

More months passed. The selectmen refused to meet with Reynolds or sign off on the health institute representing the town. Reynolds and Dunn slowly accepted that this wasn't going to happen. The board's resources were already stretched; there weren't enough hours in the day to wage war against a leading law firm and a deep-pocketed corporation. RJR and Jones Day had won—thanks to one strongly worded letter. "Ultimately, the board voted to table this proposal when it became obvious that any attempt to limit sales of flavored tobacco products would result in a legal challenge," Reynolds wrote in the board's annual report in 2018. The board's meetings returned to their usual fare of things like requested variances for septic systems.

Reynolds was disgusted and deflated. His term on the board of health was up in 2019, and after three years of feeling like "I was banging my head against the wall," he didn't run for reelection. He hadn't fulfilled his ambition of turning the board of health into a model for other towns—or starting a conversation about preparing Marion for a pandemic. Francisco's letter had been the turning point, not just for the proposed regulations but also for Reynolds's appetite for public service. "If it wasn't for the Jones Day threat, we would have continued on our way," he said.

How many times had the threat of costly litigation scared towns into abandoning policies that might have saved lives? Few of these disputes ever spilled into the public domain, but a former Jones Day tobacco lawyer told me that the firm routinely leveled similar threats, often to great effect. "We did this everywhere," she said.

16

DIRTY, DIRTY, DIRTY

If Jones Day's tactics at times seem distasteful, even improper, the firm is hardly alone. In fact, it is not even the worst. The legal industry routinely traffics in borderline behavior designed to maximize profits and shield itself from unwanted scrutiny. It is all in the name of loyally serving even the most compromised clients within the legal profession's ethical confines.

Everyone, the argument goes, has the right to counsel. But the work of elite lawyers and law firms has less and less to do with courtroom representation. Instead, it is geared toward helping clients sidestep regulations, control the media, whitewash their reputations, dodge taxes, and hide their money—tasks that don't fit under even the most expansive definition of work to which clients are constitutionally or ethically entitled.

The results are undeniable. The legal industry mints money. In 1985, when the "AmLaw 50" debuted, only five firms generated more than $100 million in revenue (about $260 million today, adjusted for inflation). In 2020, forty-two law firms rang up more than $1 billion. In 1985, partners at the top ten firms earned, on average, roughly $600,000 ($1.6 million today). In 2020, the figure was well over $4 million. It is not unheard-of for a firm to shell out $15 million annually to a hotshot recruit.

Name a top law firm. Scratch beneath the surface, and you will find evidence of years of exposure to corrosive elements, of the relentless pressure to grow bigger and more profitable. Let's take a brief but representative tour.

BAKER MCKENZIE IS AMERICA'S largest law firm. With 4,700 lawyers in forty-six countries, it is nearly twice the size of Jones Day, itself one of the world's biggest. More than many of its peers, Baker McKenzie, whose roots trace back to 1949 in Chicago, has embraced the fact that it is a business. It publicly discloses its financial results, including *American Lawyer*–created stats like profits per partner. (In 2021, it reported record revenues of more than $3 billion.) Yet Baker McKenzie also expresses pride in its ethical standards. "We don't do business with disreputable characters," the firm's code of business conduct states. "We have legal and professional obligations to know our clients and to refuse to do business with those involved in illegal or corrupt activities or whose source of funds is suspect."

Increasingly, though, Baker McKenzie has become known for using its global network to help clients disguise their assets and avoid taxes. This is a growth industry; plenty of law firms peddle their expertise in the construction of shell companies in offshore tax havens. But Baker McKenzie stands out for the volume of its work and the sketchiness of some of its clients.

A Hong Kong casino magnate, under investigation for tax fraud and ties to organized crime, relied on the firm's services. So did a half dozen state-owned Russian companies under international sanctions. (Even after Russia invaded Ukraine in 2022, Baker McKenzie bragged on its website that it was advising blacklisted companies including Gazprom, Kaspersky Labs, Novatek, and VTB. The firm eventually said it would no longer represent anyone linked to the Kremlin.) And a wide variety of allegedly corrupt public officials and businessmen in South America and other parts of the world. After reviewing a vast trove of leaked documents, the International Consortium of Investigative Journalists branded Baker McKenzie as "an architect and pillar of a shadowy economy . . . that benefits the wealthy at the expense of nations' treasuries and ordinary citizens' wallets."

A Baker McKenzie spokesman, John McGuinness, said the firm complies with sanctions and other laws. "We help our clients assess and meet their tax obligations on a worldwide basis, and navigate highly complex, ever evolving and often conflicting tax rules around the world," he told me. He said Baker McKenzie conducts extensive background checks on clients. "On occasion, we find that clients later engage in activities that are not consistent with our initial due diligence, or new facts or developments come to light which would cause us to terminate our representation of them."

It is hard to square that reasonable-sounding statement with the work Baker McKenzie performed for Jho Low. Prosecutors in the U.S. and Malaysia have accused Low of a multibillion-dollar fraud involving a Malaysian investment fund known as 1MDB. Despite plentiful red flags—Low was using Swiss bank accounts and was politically connected, among many other warning signs—Baker McKenzie and its affiliates helped the Malaysian playboy set up his shell companies, ICIJ found. Low even arranged for a Baker McKenzie employee to work at what would become 1MDB. The law firm later advised the fund on a $1 billion deal, some of whose proceeds allegedly flowed to entities Low controlled. Low used those companies to buy luxury hotels and other assets and to pay kickbacks to Malaysia's then–prime minister, Najib Razak.

Razak, who was sentenced to twelve years in jail for his role in the scandal, blamed Baker McKenzie for giving its imprimatur. "I was comforted that these are big brand-name firms and that they would have alerted me or the board of 1MDB should there be any red flags," he said. Low, who has denied being the fraud's mastermind, remains a fugitive. The Malaysian government remains out billions of dollars.

When a company uncovers or is accused of serious wrongdoing, a standard first step is to hire an outside law firm to investigate. Such reviews allow companies to tell the world that they are taking allegations—of harassment, fraud, other malfeasance—so seriously that they are paying millions to have an eminent law firm get to the bottom of things. But the arrangements also allow companies to control the flow of information. If they choose, they can keep the results of these internal investigations secret, not just from the public but also from other lawyers or government authorities. Why? Because the investigations are conducted under the cloak of attorney-client privilege. If ugly information comes to light, the company can try to keep it under wraps.

These internal reviews at times serve as substitutes for in-depth investigations by regulators or prosecutors. Sometimes, with the company's blessing, a law firm will share its findings with law enforcement. That creates the impression that the company is coming clean, which scores points with the authorities. It also means that, by preemptively handing over certain evidence, the company can establish the scope of what the authorities will examine.

That is what happened when the Swiss bank UBS hired the law firm Gibson, Dunn & Crutcher to figure out whether and to what extent the bank manipulated markets around the time of the global financial crisis. Gibson Dunn's lawyers quickly realized that UBS had a major problem: Scores of bank employees, ranging from mid-level traders to senior executives, had known about or participated in potentially criminal activity. Gibson Dunn approached law enforcement and said UBS was willing to cooperate in exchange for partial immunity. The U.S. accepted the deal and essentially put Gibson Dunn in the investigative driver's seat. The law firm, acting on UBS's behalf, was responsible for sifting through terabytes of data and millions of pages of documents and deciding what did and did not need to be shared with authorities. Gibson Dunn even helped regulators come up with the wording of subpoenas, ostensibly to ensure the Swiss bank's swift compliance.

It was masterful lawyering by Gibson Dunn—not coincidentally, the firm's primary tactician was a former senior Justice Department official—and the outcome was unsurprising. Based on the evidence Gibson Dunn produced, the market manipulation appeared to be largely the work of a handful of rogue traders, nowhere near the executive suites. These were the ones who ended up getting criminally charged. (A Gibson Dunn lawyer testified for the prosecution in at least one trial.) The executives who knew about and at times condoned their subordinates' illegal activity? They were never prosecuted.

THERE IS A CERTAIN element of fear inherent in a plaintiff or witness or journalist going up against a firm that employs thousands of attorneys and is financed by giant multinationals. Firms can bury you in paperwork, subpoena you into submission, bog down the legal process in the hopes of exhausting you emotionally and financially. They draw on virtually infinite resources. Normal people and businesses have to be mindful of how many billable hours and other expenses their lawyers are racking up, and at a certain point, the fight is no longer worth it. The frequent result of this vast power imbalance is a legal system skewed heavily in favor of the world's richest companies and individuals at the expense of everyone else.

That is bad. But sometimes it gets worse: Lawyers at megafirms attempt to frighten opponents into quiescence. Maybe it's a dark-of-night visit from a private investigator. Maybe it's formal letters, sent by certified mail, warning of ruinous litigation in situations where the lawyers know perfectly well that any such suit would be tossed out of court. Maybe it's a veiled threat that embarrassing information might find its way into the public domain.

Some of these tactics bump up against—and sometimes over—the boundaries of ethics and propriety that have historically separated the law profession from any other industry.

Consider the sad story of David Boies, who for many years was America's most celebrated trial lawyer, having faced off against Microsoft and represented Al Gore in the brawl after the 2000 election. In later years, Boies and his firm took on as clients the sexual predator Harvey Weinstein and Theranos, the fraudulent blood-testing startup, and his firm engaged in intimidation and trickery. On Weinstein's behalf, Boies became personally involved in efforts to smear the Hollywood mogul's victims. His firm hired private investigators to derail attempts by reporters to expose Weinstein, in part by unearthing personal information about the journalists. With Theranos, whose board of directors Boies sat on, his firm threatened litigation against employees who spoke with the *Wall Street Journal*'s John Carreyrou. As he did with Weinstein, Boies employed private investigators; this time they surveilled the company's critics and kept tabs on Carreyrou's reporting.*

You could perhaps shrug off Boies's over-the-line tactics as the shameful missteps of a man at the end of a storied career. There was no such excuse for the law firm of Paul, Weiss, Rifkind, Wharton & Garrison, among the world's richest and most powerful.

BRAD KARP, A GREGARIOUS, spiky-haired adviser to many leading CEOs and board members, has long been the chairman of Paul Weiss (the equivalent of managing partner at Jones Day). Karp prided himself on having his law firm stake out left-of-center positions on the legal issues of the day. He also developed a reputation among journalists as a gossip about the internal workings and personalities of his clients. His wager, apparently, was that cozy relationships with the media would serve him, his firm, and his clients well.

One of Paul Weiss's biggest clients was the private equity colossus Apollo Global Management. With more than $400 billion in assets, Apollo's tentacles snaked into just about every nook of the global economy. Paul Weiss was pulling in more than $100 million

* "David's legal career of fifty-plus years extends well beyond these two former representations," his spokeswoman told me. "I think he would be the first to say that he, like all of us, is imperfect."

a year in legal fees from Apollo. Even for a law firm of Paul Weiss's size, that was a lot of money. Keeping this mighty client happy was crucial.

When reporters were chasing tips that Apollo's cofounder, Leon Black, had paid more than $150 million to the sex offender Jeffrey Epstein, Karp threw them off the scent. (The tips turned out to be true, leading Black to step down as Apollo's CEO in 2021.)

And when two reporters approached Paul Weiss for a book they were writing that was likely to cast Apollo in an unflattering light, the law firm went nuclear. The book was about the casino company Caesars Entertainment. Caesars was one of the many companies that Apollo (in this case, in partnership with another private equity firm, TPG) had acquired and then loaded up with debt, a practice that allows private equity firms to juice their profits without putting much of their own money on the line. This particular bet backfired, and Caesars drowned in debt.

As the company went through the bankruptcy process, Apollo plucked choice assets out of the failed company and placed them into entities that Apollo controlled. Paul Weiss was representing multiple parties: Caesars, some of the entities that got assets from Caesars, and Apollo. It struck the two journalists, Sujeet Indap and Max Frumes, as a conflict of interest, given the diverging fortunes between the bankrupt company (and its angry creditors) and its private equity owners. Indap and Frumes planned to delve into this in their book.

In the summer of 2019, after unsuccessful attempts to get other Paul Weiss lawyers to talk, Indap reached out to Karp. Aware of his reputation for chattiness, Indap figured that perhaps he'd be willing to shed some light on his firm's actions and what had happened inside the Caesars boardroom. Karp responded, expressing a willingness to talk. Then a media handler intervened and suggested they all gather at Paul Weiss's offices for a preliminary get-to-know-you meeting.

It took place that September. Indap and Frumes showed up

at the firm's headquarters in a Manhattan skyscraper. Over their months of reporting, they'd visited plenty of law firms, and it was always amusing to see which snack would be wheeled out to visitors. Some served freshly baked cookies. One offered chips and guacamole. Another provided leftover sandwiches. Paul Weiss presented the reporters with cinema-style popcorn. The meeting was cordial but not very productive; it ended with Karp and a veteran litigator, Lew Clayton, saying that perhaps they would answer written questions.

About a month later, Indap sent over twenty-nine detailed queries. "Appreciate the work that went into these questions," Karp replied. "Hope you will have an open mind in considering our point of view."

Two months passed. Then, on a snowy afternoon in December 2019, Indap, on unpaid book leave from the *Financial Times,* was sitting on a sofa at home. An email arrived, with a PDF file attached: It was a letter from Paul Weiss's general counsel, Bruce Birenboim.

"Based on your prior 'reporting' on Caesars, your recent conduct, and your communications with parties you have interviewed, it is clear that you plan a defamatory attack on Paul Weiss and its personnel in order to produce a book that is biased and sensationalistic," Birenboim wrote on Paul Weiss's letterhead, the top half of which was covered with the names of dozens of the firm's partners. He went on to accuse Indap and Frumes of "improper efforts to induce Paul Weiss personnel to breach their confidentiality obligations to the firm's clients and the firm." He noted that the reporters had gotten in touch with Paul Weiss employees and offered to speak confidentially. "Your communications represent an intentional and transparently improper effort to induce Paul Weiss personnel to breach" their obligations to clients.

It was a ridiculous accusation—there is nothing improper about reporters trying to get people to divulge information—made even more so given Karp's penchant for client-related gossip. Birenboim concluded his letter by demanding that the two journalists provide Paul Weiss with their book manuscript and a list of people they'd contacted. He warned that Paul Weiss might "pursue all remedies including compensatory and punitive damages" against the authors. For emphasis, he ordered the reporters to preserve their documents, notes, messages, and the like in case there was litigation.

Letters like this to reporters have become common. There are law firms—like Clare Lock LLP in Virginia, Harder LLP in Beverly Hills, and Schillings in London—that seem to do little other than try to quash legitimate media reporting, often via blunt force. Harder's namesake, Charles Harder, is notorious for dashing off threatening letters to media companies on behalf of aggrieved clients like the Trump family; in 2021, as the *New York Times* investigated Britney Spears's business manager, Harder churned out no fewer than eight cease-and-desist letters demanding that *Times* reporters stop contacting potential sources.

Schillings is even more aggressive. Once, having failed to stop a publisher from releasing the book *Billion Dollar Whale,* about Jho Low and the 1MDB scandal, Schillings sent letters to bookstores around the world, threatening to sue them for libel for simply selling the books. Holding bookstores legally accountable for the contents of the items on their shelves posed a very real threat to free speech. (Would libraries be next?) And at least for a while, Schillings's tactics worked, with some booksellers unwilling to risk litigation for the sake of stocking a single title.

It is less common, though hardly unheard-of, for a major U.S. law firm—whose partners tend to be more sensitive to the ugly optics of censorship and intimidation—to take this route. Paul Weiss partners, however, had penned plenty of these letters in the past, with favorable results: Some recipients had even grudgingly agreed to hand over their manuscripts for the lawyers to inspect. (Journalists don't let the subjects of their reporting review articles or books ahead of publication.)

It was Paul Weiss's right, of course, to defend itself, including by suing people, journalists or otherwise, for defamation. But that wasn't the point of this letter. If Paul Weiss wanted to sue, it could sue. This letter seemed designed to intimidate, to get the reporters and their publisher to consider whether the prudent course might be to soft-pedal any accusations against Paul Weiss or Apollo—especially since the publisher of *The Caesars Palace Coup* was a small independent company, Diversion Books, that lacked the resources to go toe to toe with a firm like Paul Weiss. "I know that these tactics can be effective in softening coverage," said Frumes, who had been on the receiving end of such threats in the past.

In case his letter was too subtle, Birenboim soon amplified its message. In early 2020, he called Indap and asked if the reporters had retained a lawyer to defend them. And he reiterated the importance of them retaining their documents and other materials. "Well," Indap responded, feeling flustered, "I'm writing a book, so of course I'm keeping documents." He told Birenboim that he and Frumes were committed to writing about Apollo and Paul Weiss fairly.

"If you want to report the book fairly, you'll let us review the manuscript," Birenboim barked.

He wasn't done. Weeks later, he FedExed another letter—this one to the CEO of Diversion, Scott Waxman. Birenboim repeated his demand to review a draft of the book and warned Waxman that Diversion, too, must "preserve for evidentiary use" all materials related to the book. "It is critical that you take all of these steps to ensure that the Caesars book does not injure Paul Weiss and its reputation in the legal community," Birenboim wrapped up. "Paul Weiss will vigorously protect the rights of its personnel and clients and reserves the right to pursue all remedies, including compensatory and punitive damages, against you and Diversion for any past or future wrongful conduct."

Birenboim told me that Paul Weiss "had an ethical and professional obligation to protect privileged attorney-client communications, which the reporters were seeking from our associates." He insisted that his letters were purely intended "to ensure that [the authors and publisher] accurately and fairly reported on the firm's work on the Caesars matter. Far from trying to stop publication, we provided written factual material to the authors and met with them." Of course, that didn't explain the repeated threats and the demands to know the reporters' sources, which seemed specifically engineered to instill fear.

In any case, the letter to Waxman endangered the book. "It gave our publisher pause," Frumes said. Waxman informed the authors that Diversion needed to protect itself—the small publisher wasn't equipped to take on a big law firm—and that the reporters therefore would need to hire a lawyer to review their manuscript to make sure it wasn't going to get the publisher sued. Indap and Frumes split the cost, paying thousands of dollars each for the legal review, and they knew they were lucky. Plenty of other journalists wouldn't have been able to spare that kind of money—and their books likely would have died as a result.

The lawyer who reviewed the manuscript concluded it was safe. That was good enough for Waxman, and *The Caesars Palace Coup* was published in 2021. It detailed Paul Weiss's conflicts of interest and painted Apollo in a negative light. Indap and Frumes didn't hear again from Paul Weiss. Still, the episode left them feeling like victims of a schoolyard bully. "They definitely can smell vulnerability," Frumes told me, referring to Paul Weiss and its ilk. "This spoke to just how tilted the power balance is in favor of corporate interests."

JOE FLOM, WHOSE BUCCANEERING legal tactics had attracted the attention of the wide-eyed Steve Brill so many years earlier, had transformed Skadden Arps from a scrappy outsider into one of the world's leading law firms. It was a specialist in tricky mergers and acquisitions—in one particularly frenzied year, the law firm brokered a staggering $1 trillion in mergers—but it was much more than that. These days, it was a hired gun in all sorts of situations that required trigger-happy lawyers and tactics.

In February 2011, Flom died of heart failure. That same year, a world away, the government of Ukraine imprisoned the archrival of President Viktor Yanukovych. Critics, including then-secretary of state Hillary Clinton, decried the prosecution of the former prime minister, Yulia Tymoshenko, as an antidemocratic hit job, designed to kneecap Ukraine's leading opposition party. The international backlash further isolated Ukraine from the West, and so Yanukovych's government went looking for help. Paul Manafort—who would become the chairman of Donald Trump's presidential campaign—was hired to polish the authoritarian government's image. He enlisted Skadden to conduct an ostensibly independent review of the prosecution of Tymoshenko.

Skadden was a natural choice. It had become a go-to law firm for Russian oligarchs and Kremlin-linked conglomerates. One of its most prominent lawyers was Gregory Craig, who had been President Obama's White House counsel. Manafort figured the involvement of the politically connected Craig would imbue the Skadden report with extra credibility in Washington. (Promised millions in fees, Craig went to bat for Manafort, at one point trying to get Skadden to hire his daughter.) The report came out in December 2012. It dispensed some token criticisms of the prosecution, but overall Skadden concluded that Tymoshenko's conviction was just. The firm said it found no evidence that her prosecution or incarceration were driven by politics in such a way that the conviction would have been overturned "under American standards." Coming from an elite American law firm, it was a valuable endorsement. Skadden pocketed more than $5 million in fees.

Alas, the Obama administration didn't buy it. ("Skadden Arps lawyers were obviously not going to find political motivation if they weren't looking for it," a State Department spokeswoman noted.) Nor did other Western governments—or ordinary Ukrainians. By late 2013, hundreds of thousands had taken to the streets of Kyiv to protest Yanukovych's corruption and deepening ties to the Kremlin. The president's government soon collapsed, and he fled to

Russia. Federal prosecutors later investigated Skadden's work for Ukraine, culminating in criminal charges against Craig and a Skadden associate for lying to federal authorities. Craig was acquitted (his colleague pleaded guilty), but Skadden had to pay $4.6 million to settle the Justice Department investigation. And it forked over at least $11 million to Tymoshenko, who emerged from her two-and-a-half-year imprisonment frail, wheelchair bound, and very angry. "It's a pity that such a well-known company like Skadden even considered to take this case," she said. "This is a dirty, dirty, dirty contract."

17

LURCHING TO THE RIGHT

In early 2012, Jones Day lawyers contacted dozens of Catholic organizations. The attorneys posed a version of the same question: Would your diocese or university or church be interested in filing a lawsuit? The law firm was hatching a coordinated national campaign to undercut the new national health care law.

Jones Day by then had a long track record of representing Catholic causes, a tradition that had taken hold under Pat McCartan. A man of faith, McCartan in 1989 had joined the board of trustees of the University of Notre Dame, where he had earned his undergraduate and law degrees. He served as the chairman from 2000 to 2007, and as he stepped down the university awarded him the Laetare Medal, considered the most prestigious honor available to American Catholics. "You have walked the corridors of power while still remaining on the path of the good, the true, and the just in all your pursuits," the citation read.

On McCartan's watch, Jones Day began advising Catholic dioceses and other organizations that faced an existential crisis: For decades, priests had been sexually abusing children; the Church had often tried to bury the evidence, protect the predators, and minimize the public fallout.

In 1997, after a Texas jury awarded a group of former altar boys and their families a $120 million judgment against the Roman Catholic Diocese of Dallas, Jones Day worked to shield the assets of the sixty-six Dallas parishes. At least partly as a result, the plaintiffs ultimately collected about one-fifth of what the jury had awarded.

Four years later, Jones Day represented the Cleveland diocese, whose bishop, Anthony Pilla, was close with McCartan. The Cuyahoga County Prosecutor's Office in Cleveland was conducting an extensive criminal investigation into potential sexual abuse by hundreds of priests and others connected to the Church. The seven-month grand jury inquiry wrapped up in 2002 with indictments of a retired priest and six employees of a diocesan treatment center. The reason there weren't more charges wasn't for lack of evidence. The prosecutors had uncovered allegations against 145 priests. The problem was that so many years—in some cases, decades—had passed since the abuse took place, far exceeding the statute of limitations.

But there still was a chance to hold to account those accused of rape and other crimes as well as those who had buried the allegations and kept the priests on the Church's payroll. The county prosecutor, William Mason, said he planned to open his office's files—which filled several hundred binders—for public consumption. Finally, Clevelanders would get to learn which priests had been accused of abuse—and what if anything the Church had done about it.

Then Jones Day intervened. The lawyer on the case was Stephen Sozio, who had joined the firm two years earlier after a decade as a federal prosecutor pursuing organized crime. Now Sozio tapped out a letter to Mason, warning that the investigative files contained "highly confidential, personal, and intimate information" and therefore needed to remain secret; if they didn't, Jones Day might sue. Rather than fight with Cleveland's highest-powered law firm, Mason backpedaled. The files would never see the light of day. Around that time, Pilla, who was facing calls to resign as bishop, was spotted watching an Indians game from Jones Day's luxury box at Jacobs Field.

• • •

THE FIRM'S WORK FOR Catholic institutions and causes accelerated under Brogan, himself a Notre Dame alum and trustee. Several of Brogan's allies told me that the key to understanding him was through his faith. "Brogan is extremely conservative, hard-core Catholic, and that is the bedrock of who he is," one of his Jones Day confidants, himself a practicing Catholic, explained.

Now this conservatism was seeping into the culture of Jones Day, and the firm began to shed its wariness about overt partisan politics. The landscaped rooftop of the firm's Capitol Hill building had become a regular venue for Republican campaign fundraisers, with top Jones Day partners—including Brogan—playing host to politicians like John Boehner and Mitch McConnell. (There were occasional Democratic events, too, but not with the participation of the firm's top leaders.) While the firm's rank and file may have leaned left, an academic paper around this time found that Jones Day was the most ideologically conservative of the leading national law firms, based on surveys with thousands of lawyers. Brogan didn't feel the need to be discreet with colleagues about his disdain for the Left. Once, on a golf outing in London, a partner, Sebastian Orton, made the mistake of mentioning to Brogan that his wife worked for a local Labour Party group. Orton told me that Brogan started squawking about the evils of socialism.

In the spring of 2012, Mitt Romney was emerging as the Republican nominee to challenge Barack Obama for the White House. Obama's signature legislative achievement—the Affordable Care Act, otherwise known as Obamacare—promised to be a central flashpoint in the general election. Republicans were looking for any vehicle to attack it. One such avenue was the law's requirement that employers' health plans cover the costs of their workers' birth control.

And so Jones Day lawyers were fanning out to Catholic groups, offering to represent them pro bono in lawsuits challenging the contraception mandate. That spring, the firm filed twelve lawsuits on behalf of forty-three different Catholic entities, including

Notre Dame. "It's a firmwide commitment," a Jones Day partner said at the time. "The leadership came from Steve Brogan, who is a trustee of Notre Dame. He feels quite strongly about the issue, as does Jones Day."

THE OBAMACARE LAWSUITS WERE the handiwork of an elite and increasingly powerful group within the firm. It was called Issues & Appeals.

McCartan had established the team in the late 1980s. The idea of a law firm having a practice that handled appeals wasn't new, but McCartan had a bolder vision. This group would be the brain trust for the firm's litigators. Instead of focusing primarily on how to win over a judge and jury, the firm would assemble teams to peer into the future and try to structure arguments that would set the stage for successful appeals, if Jones Day lost the initial trial. Eventually, this troupe would develop expertise in broad areas of the law, enabling its lawyers to take on causes, not just clients.

For most of its first decade of existence, the group was led by a left-of-center lawyer named Tim Dyk. He was surrounded by an impressive crew, including a handful of future federal judges and a prominent Reagan administration lawyer, Don Ayer. The group developed a reputation internally as consisting of the best and the brightest. Lawyers in Issues & Appeals did the toughest strategic thinking and drafted the most important briefs. Dyk himself argued eight cases before the Supreme Court during his decade at Jones Day.

In 2000, President Clinton appointed Dyk to a federal appeals court. Until this point, Jones Day had tolerated—even celebrated—a wide range of political opinions, even if its managing partners almost always were Republicans. Some of the firm's most prominent lawyers, including Herb Hansell, the former Carter aide, were Democratic activists. Now Dyk was gone, and the arrival of a conservative firebrand named Mike Carvin would augur the end of that bipartisan era—for Issues & Appeals and for the firm as a whole.

• • •

CARVIN GREW UP IN a middle-class Catholic family in the New York City suburb of Port Chester, best known, perhaps, as the long-time home of the Life Savers Candy Company. His father was a textile salesman, and his mother was a homemaker. By age twelve, Carvin was a conservative; he viewed liberal politics as irrational and anti-American. By young adulthood, his worldview had hardened. Over beers, he would seek out political fights, his voice thundering through a noisy bar. "Carvin is the guy who you wish the bartender had cut off," one of his colleagues told me.

A history major, Carvin decided to go to law school after realizing "that I had no marketable skills," as he put it. He got his law degree in 1982 and then was hired into the Reagan administration by Chuck Cooper, a deputy assistant attorney general in the Justice Department. At Justice, Carvin met Don Ayer, who was the deputy solicitor general. The men clashed over what to do about racial discrimination. Ayer supported proactive efforts to force public sector employers to hire more minorities. Carvin was dead-set against anything that smacked of quotas. The two men had heated arguments.

One night in 1984, Carvin went to Robert F. Kennedy Memorial Stadium in D.C. for a Michael Jackson concert. A group from Reagan's reelection campaign happened to be there, too, and a young staffer named Mary Matalin spotted Carvin. With a mane of thick hair and an air of bravado, he was holding court between sets, oozing self-confidence. He and Matalin spent the evening talking, and soon they started dating. They'd be together for the next seven years. "If you couldn't have fun with Michael Carvin, go get electric shock therapy," Matalin gushed.

Matalin was a fighter, and she was accustomed to being with men who were fighters, too. As fiery as Carvin was when talking politics, he could be maddeningly calm when it came to personal drama. "I would provoke him all the time, and he'd just laugh,"

Matalin told me. Once, she needled her boyfriend so much that he stalked into their bedroom, picked up the king-sized mattress, hauled it into the living room, then dragged it back. That was it. "He just didn't waste his emotional energy on emotional things." Matalin thought Carvin might end up on the Supreme Court. (She later left him for James Carville.)

As the Reagan administration wound down, a few big law firms tried to hire Carvin and Cooper. One was Jones Day. Cooper told me that the pair flew to Cleveland to meet McCartan, but they ultimately decided to go to another firm. There, they successfully represented Winstar Corporation in a landmark Supreme Court case in 1996.* The victory made Cooper a minor celebrity in Republican legal circles, and he and Carvin decided to create their own conservative law firm, Cooper & Carvin. Its motto was *Vincere aut Mori*—"Victory or Death."

The first associate they hired was a cocky young lawyer named Ted Cruz, fresh off a clerkship for Chief Justice William Rehnquist. In 1998, when Cooper & Carvin was in the market for another associate, Cruz recommended a Scalia clerk named Noel Francisco. (Cruz and Francisco had previously clerked together for Michael Luttig, a conservative icon on the Fourth Circuit federal appeals court.)

Francisco—the same lawyer who, decades later, would write the letter on RJR's behalf to officials in Marion, Massachusetts—was the son of a Filipino immigrant. He credited his Catholic upbringing in Oswego, a working-class city in upstate New York, for shaping his conservative philosophy. Cooper and Carvin set out to hire him. To help win him over, they got Luttig and Scalia to vouch for their upstart firm. If you were an ambitious young conservative like Francisco, there was no way to say no to these two legal lions. Francisco was in.

---

* The court ruled that the government could be held liable for breaching contracts with private parties.

In late 2000, with the presidential election hanging in the balance, Cooper and Carvin dispatched Francisco to Tallahassee to help the Bush campaign on the Florida recount. Ted Cruz was already there, working for the Republican candidate. As the battle went to the courts, Cruz enlisted Carvin to argue *Bush v. Gore* at the Florida Supreme Court, a prelude to the main fight at the U.S. Supreme Court, which delivered Bush the White House.

While Francisco and Cruz joined the new administration, Cooper and Carvin had a falling-out over the direction of their firm. With Steve Brogan's backing, Carvin in 2001 was lured to Jones Day's Washington office as a partner in Issues & Appeals. Some lawyers at the firm had misgivings; Carvin had a reputation as a hothead. During a conversation among top Jones Day partners, one of them voiced concerns about Carvin's "rough edges." Brogan was ready with a response: "We'll smooth those out of him."

Don Ayer groaned when he learned of Carvin's arrival. He remembered the pitched battles in the Reagan administration over what had always struck him as fundamental issues of right and wrong. Ayer, a moderate Republican, worried that Carvin would cause the firm to lurch to the right.

YEAR BY YEAR, CASE by case, hire by hire, Jones Day was growing more ideological. Archconservatives were gravitating to Issues & Appeals like iron filings shimmying toward a magnet. Carvin, for his part, celebrated his freedom to champion polarizing causes. "I've done a lot of controversial cases and not gotten heat" from Jones Day, he told the *American Lawyer,* which cited his work in opposition to gay marriage. "I'm beyond redemption," he smirked.

Carvin liked to tell colleagues how, after the 2000 election, he had bumped into the Democratic lawyer Vernon Jordan. "How does it feel to steal an election?" Jordan asked.

"It feels pretty good!" Carvin gloated, not missing a beat. Some liberal Jones Day lawyers were surprised to hear Carvin telling and retelling the tale, as if it made him look good.*

In 2005, a few years after Carvin joined, Noel Francisco came aboard. Francisco by then was prominent in Washington conservative circles like the Federalist Society. Jones Day's size and stability appealed to him; it didn't hurt that he'd be rejoining his friend Carvin, whom Francisco regarded as one of the country's sharpest lawyers.

Barely a year after Francisco arrived, Jones Day promoted a lawyer in its Columbus, Ohio, office into the partnership and assigned him to Issues & Appeals. His name was Chad Readler, and he was a hard-liner. He had argued against a ban on the death penalty for juveniles. At another point, Readler—whose mother had been an elementary school teacher—called for eliminating language in Ohio's constitution that effectively required the state to provide an adequate system of public education.

Readler, Francisco, and Carvin were already well-known throughout the conservative bar. Now, working together, their stars would soar to new heights.

EACH SPRING, BUNDLES OF envelopes arrive in the chambers of the justices of the Supreme Court. They are addressed to the clerks—four per justice (and one each for retired justices). Inside are letters from the biggest of Washington's law firms, including Jones Day. *Would you please join us for dinner with some of our most esteemed partners?* The invitations are the beginning of an elaborate courtship that often ends with young clerks taking lucrative jobs at corporate law firms. Some firms are in the market for a single clerk. Others, like Gibson Dunn, Kirkland & Ellis, and WilmerHale, are looking to hire a few. Jones Day wants as many as it can get.

---

* When I asked Carvin about this, he replied: "I seriously doubt that any of my colleagues could be so dense as to be surprised at my 'boasting' or misunderstand what was obviously good-natured kidding between people on different sides."

This seasonal mating ritual has been going on for decades, intensifying with each passing year. The allure of hiring clerks was multifaceted. These young men and women, traditionally toting Ivy League diplomas, were smart and ambitious and had gleaned rare insights into the inner workings of the nation's most important judicial body. But the biggest draw was their marketing power. In pitch documents to would-be clients, firms bragged about how many ex-clerks they employed. General counsels of big corporations—the lawyers who handed out assignments to various outside firms—liked nothing more than hiring a firm with a high-profile Supreme Court practice and a passel of former clerks. Why? Because it provided cover if anything went wrong. Who could blame a general counsel for having hired such a gold-plated law firm?

To attract clerks, Jones Day and other firms began dispensing ever-larger signing bonuses. By 2000, the industry standard was about $100,000. Within a decade or so, the bonuses had tripled. (Today they are more than $400,000.)

Jones Day quickly emerged as the leader in this unusual race. From 2011 through 2015, the firm hired a total of about thirty Supreme Court clerks, far eclipsing any of its rivals. Of the ninety clerks I was able to identify Jones Day having hired since 1990, more than 70 percent came from the court's conservative justices.

The outlandish bonuses and the concentration of clerks at a single firm troubled experts. "When the numbers get so high—in terms of the bonus itself and the numbers of hires going to one firm—it unavoidably raises concerns about what is being purchased and the meaning of public service," a Harvard Law professor remarked after Jones Day lured ten Supreme Court clerks in a single year.

But Jones Day lawyers were not the types to care much about criticism from the outside world. Sure, the signing bonuses meant the clerks in their first year were paid more than double what the justices themselves earned, but it was worth it. "It's really not that much money for the return a firm like ours gets," a partner, Glen Nager, said.

Each fall, Jones Day gathered the new recruits on its roof for a group photo, with the Capitol dome as a backdrop. The photo would appear prominently on the firm's website and would be sent to trade publications like the *American Lawyer,* which would dutifully write stories about how Jones Day once again had netted the most clerks. Those articles were as good as gold (or at least as good as paid advertisements) when it came to attracting new corporate clients. "There's going to be a number that's too high, but I haven't gotten there yet," Beth Heifetz, the Jones Day partner in charge of recruiting the clerks (and herself a former clerk), told Reuters in 2014. Here was another surprising repercussion of the long-ago *Bates* decision: What would be the point of snapping up all this expensive young talent if you weren't allowed to boast about it?

The clerks generally were stationed in Issues & Appeals. By the time the hiring bonanza was in full swing, Mike Carvin was scooping up many to work on what he considered the best projects, which often happened to be the ones nearest to his ideological heart. These clerks were told—maybe not in so many words, but the message was clear—that it was okay not to make money for the firm; nobody would be scrutinizing their billable hours. Their mandate was to add value. Promote a cause. It was fine if the work was pro bono—representing a religious institution or an advocacy group, for example. Increasingly, in this rarefied section of the firm, money wasn't what mattered. The mission was.

AROUND THE CORNER FROM Jones Day's Capitol Hill building was the Washington headquarters of Fox News. The law firm and the TV network had a good relationship. When construction was underway on Jones Day's parking garage—part of the project that had been delayed by police concerns about creating a rooftop sniper's nest—Fox let the law firm use its underground lot; Fox and Jones Day employees would share elevators up from the basement. Fox executives and on-air personalities would sometimes go to cocktail parties on Jones Day's roof deck. Adding to the bond, Megyn Kelly, then a Fox News anchor, had been an associate at Jones Day. (The work was so exhausting that Kelly at one point fantasized about crashing her car so that she'd get a break from the eighteen-hour workdays. She soon abandoned the law for a career in TV news.)

Fox News was not just a friend; it was also a client. In the early days of the pandemic, Jones Day successfully defended the network when a nonprofit group sued Fox for claiming that Covid was a hoax, a lie that slowed the government response to the crisis and almost certainly killed people. And the firm shielded Fox and some of its stars when they faced allegations of sexual harassment and defaming victims of assault.

Mike Carvin was among the lawyers representing Fox News. It was one of his ostensibly apolitical clients. Many others were openly ideological. There was the Republican National Committee, which he assisted on redistricting cases. There was the right-wing Free Enterprise Fund, which Carvin and Noel Francisco represented in an unsuccessful attempt to neuter a government-controlled corporate oversight board. And there was the Buckeye Institute in Ohio, funded by the Koch brothers. Carvin paired up with Readler, the partner in Columbus, to file briefs on Buckeye's behalf in support of limiting the scope of the federal Voting Rights Act and in opposition to an Ohio law expanding early voting. Other Jones Day lawyers helped advance Buckeye's argument that the existence of the Consumer Financial Protection Bureau violated the Constitution.

Jones Day was representing Buckeye and the Free Enterprise Fund on a pro bono basis. Some partners found this troubling. The American Bar Association says pro bono work is supposed to be "for the public good . . . with an emphasis that these services be provided to people of limited means or nonprofit organizations that serve the poor." Buckeye and the Free Enterprise Fund had wealthy backers and could easily afford to pay for the time of

Carvin and his colleagues. Classifying such work as pro bono burnished these lawyers' images as public-spirited professionals.*

Jones Day, meanwhile, was increasingly entwined with the Federalist Society—the powerful group Scalia had helped establish before he became a judge, with the goal of implanting more conservatives on the nation's courts. By 2010, dozens of the firm's lawyers were speaking regularly at Federalist Society events. Francisco at times was averaging about one speech a month. ("I always say yes to the Federalist Society," he said at a Federalist Society event.) Jones Day's D.C. offices became a popular venue for the group's gatherings. The law firm's marketing staff, worried that this might spook certain clients, made sure to remove Jones Day's logo before events to avoid it ending up in the Federalist Society's promotional materials.

Lawyers like Francisco viewed their jobs as fitting neatly within their worldview that the government had expanded far beyond what the framers of the Constitution envisioned. Government control—including regulations meant to protect public health or the environment or workers' rights—was often something to fight against. "The government's tentacles invade virtually every aspect of what our clients do," Francisco once said. "The job of a lawyer and the job of courts is to ensure that the federal government lives within the limits that our Constitution sets, and I love making sure that those lines are enforced."

McCartan's vision of the Issues & Appeals practice had made sense. Who could argue with setting up a group that would help trial lawyers lay the groundwork for successful appeals? Now the practice was morphing into something else. Less of its work had much to do with helping longtime clients deal with litigation. It

---

* Carvin said such work qualified as pro bono because it was "designed to benefit the public . . . by enhancing individual freedom." He noted that some of Jones Day's other pro bono work, including for the U.S. Holocaust Memorial Museum, isn't geared toward the poor but is unquestionably for the public good.

was increasingly about championing conservative causes. Jones Day still had many liberal lawyers, but the firm's power center—and the practice area in which its lawyers were most likely to publicly take a political side—was rapidly moving to the right. To some partners in Washington and Cleveland and Columbus, it felt like Jones Day wasn't just representing conservative think tanks; one had been embedded in the heart of the firm.

Some Jones Day leaders claimed to me that the firm was not conservative. "The notion that the ideological heart of the firm is conservative is just not true," Carvin asserted. "We have an incredibly diverse and broad array of lawyers and, I suspect, the majority tend towards the liberal side of the spectrum." He insisted that Jones Day doesn't take on causes. "We represent clients with legal needs, often in conflict with various governmental entities, regardless of the political affiliation of the government's leadership," Carvin said.

There is nothing inherently wrong with a law firm or any other private enterprise leaning heavily to one side or another of the political spectrum. Nobody was forcing liberal lawyers to keep working at Jones Day, and clients that didn't want to be associated with its political work were free to choose another law firm. But asserting that Jones Day wasn't conservative didn't make it true.

In early 2015, a writer named Jessica Shortall was trying to get companies in Texas to sign a pledge promising not to discriminate against people on the basis of their sexual orientation. Shortall had a business degree and had done consulting work for companies, and she believed that most had decent values. If she could get them to publicly articulate those values by vowing not to engage in discriminatory hiring practices, she hoped it would foster a healthier, safer climate for LGBTQ+ people across the state. That, in turn, would help Texas soften its reputation of being inhospitable to people who didn't fit the Lone Star State's macho cowboy vibe. And that ultimately would make Texas a better destination for skilled workers and ambitious companies. Shortall dubbed her initiative "Texas Competes."

The key was to build momentum, and Shortall came up with the idea of allowing companies to sign on to the pledge privately before the effort went public. That way, no individual company would have to worry about being singled out—it would happen as a group or not at all—and anyone that was uncomfortable would have the option to back out if they got cold feet.

Shortall knew a lot of people in the business community, and now she hit them up. One of them was Elizabeth Myers, a partner in Jones Day's Houston office. Myers liked the idea of Texas Competes; she was one of the few openly gay partners at Jones Day, and she figured this was one small way to make things a little less lonely for people like her, at Jones Day and elsewhere. Myers approached her bosses in Texas to get their buy-in. They readily agreed to sign the pledge. It wasn't a hard sell. *Of course we promise not to discriminate!*

Myers told Shortall that Jones Day was in. It was one of a handful of law firms with Texas offices that would be among the founding signatories to Texas Competes.

In April 2015, it came time for the list to be made public. As promised, Shortall gave everyone one last chance to escape. That was when Myers heard from the head of Jones Day's Houston office. There was bad news. The firm would not, after all, be signing the pledge. Word had come from Brogan's office: *We don't sign petitions.* Myers was mortified—and angry. This wasn't even a petition; they were just publicly promising not to discriminate.

Myers broke the news to Shortall, who removed Jones Day from the list. Of the more than fifty companies that had initially agreed to sign the pledge, Jones Day was the only one to pull out. When the initiative was announced, hundreds of companies rushed to add their names. Before long, the list had grown to more than 1,400 companies. Basically every major business with a presence in the state, including a slew of national law firms, had signed the pledge. Except for Jones Day.

• • •

BY THE TIME THE Jones Day lawyers had started lining up Catholic groups to sue over the contraception mandate in the Affordable Care Act, the firm was already leading a multifaceted assault on the health care law. The *American Lawyer,* in an article detailing the firm's willingness to brawl with the government, described Obamacare as "Jones Day's Moby Dick."

In one case, Jones Day submitted a legal brief on behalf of three former Republican attorneys general who wanted to kill the health care law. In another, Carvin represented the National Federation of Independent Business as it sued to invalidate the Affordable Care Act's foundational requirement that all individuals have health insurance. Of the seven cases Carvin had argued before the Supreme Court, this was his first defeat.

Carvin also represented the Competitive Enterprise Institute, another corporate-backed conservative group, as it sought to get Obamacare's insurance exchanges knocked down by the courts, a challenge designed to cripple the program. This case, too, went to the Supreme Court. At oral arguments in 2015, Carvin, in classic form, spoke so fast that justices at times struggled to get a word in. "Take a breath," an exasperated Sonia Sotomayor urged him. Carvin lost again.

The contraception cases were less consequential—unlike the other suits, these didn't threaten to strip millions of Americans of their health insurance—but they had the longest legs. Noel Francisco was in charge of the effort, and he had been deliberate about how the plaintiffs were picked for these lawsuits. They included a group of nuns and "inner city" Catholic schools, he would later explain to an audience at the conservative Heritage Foundation. When plotting constitutional challenges on hot-button social issues, Francisco advised the audience, "focus on the florist, on the baker, the sincere small businessmen under attack."

The contraception lawsuits, filed in federal courts around the U.S., had bounced through the judicial system. Some got thrown out, others advanced, and ultimately they were consolidated into a single case: *Zubik v. Burwell*. David Zubik was the bishop of Pittsburgh. Sylvia Burwell was the U.S. Health and Human Services secretary, whose department was responsible for the health care program. In November 2015, the Supreme Court agreed to hear the case; oral arguments were scheduled for the following March.

About a month before the arguments, history intervened. Justice Scalia had flown to a remote corner of the West Texas desert to attend a small party at the thirty-thousand-acre Cibolo Creek Ranch. After dinner on Friday night, he excused himself and retired to the presidential suite. The following morning, February 13, Scalia didn't show up for breakfast. The ranch's owner went to check on him. He found the seventy-nine-year-old jurist in bed, his hands folded above the sheets, dead.

For many conservatives—not least his former colleagues and clerks at Jones Day—Scalia's sudden death felt like a body blow. "Justice Scalia did not just defend our view of the law, though he did that superbly," Francisco eulogized a short time later, fighting back tears. "He defended our view of the world, and he did it better than anyone else. And that, I believe, is why we were broken, broken to the core, when we heard the terrible news."

Among the many consequences of his death was that the Supreme Court now had only eight justices, allowing for the possibility of deadlock. And that is where it looked like *Zubik v. Burwell* was heading when, on a balmy Wednesday in March, the Supreme Court heard the case. The U.S. solicitor general, representing the Obama administration, pointed out that religious institutions were already partly exempted; those that didn't want to offer birth control were allowed to inform the government or their insurers of their objections, and any contraception costs would be covered by third parties. That didn't do it for Francisco, who still perceived the Obama administration as coercing Catholics to condone contraception and "to violate their sincerely held religious beliefs."

(He also said it wasn't clear "how many women out there actually lack access to contraceptive coverage.") From their questions, it was clear that the court's four liberal justices were skeptical and the four conservatives were not.

The court issued its ruling—if you could call it that—about eight weeks later. There had recently been a few four-to-four ties (in the case of a tie, the lower court's ruling stands, but no precedent is set), and the court in *Zubik* opted for a different route. It released a rare unsigned statement saying it would not decide the case. Instead, it instructed the plaintiffs, the Obama administration, and the lower courts to try to find a compromise that addressed the Catholic groups' concerns while also ensuring that their female employees got adequate health care coverage, including contraception.

And so settlement talks got underway, in the heat of the presidential election. The negotiations immediately proved contentious; there was no love lost between the Obama administration and the Catholic groups' hard-charging attorneys. Mickey Pohl, a Jones Day partner, that summer publicly accused the Obama administration of "assaults on freedom of religion" by pushing the plaintiffs' insurers to provide the disputed coverage. It soon became clear that the case wouldn't be resolved during the Obama administration. The battle would pass to the next president.

PART III

18

THE BLOODY EIGHTH

The Eighth Congressional District of Indiana encompasses the southwest corner of the state, stretching from Evansville up past Terre Haute. It is a land of small cities and smaller towns, of farmland and pockets of industry. While Indiana has long leaned Republican, the district has a history of razor-thin elections. During the 1970s, its voters picked four different congressmen in four straight elections—a sharp break from the long-running national pattern of incumbents almost always winning reelection. Owing to its history of brutal political warfare, the district was nicknamed the "Bloody Eighth."

The 1984 election was the closest ever. A first-term Democrat, Frank McCloskey, initially seemed to beat his Republican challenger, a state representative named Rick McIntyre. But a tabulation error in a single county swung it to the Republican by thirty-four votes out of 233,500 cast. Indiana's Republican secretary of state certified McIntyre as the winner. Congress, however, was controlled by Democrats, and they refused to seat him, citing unspecified voting irregularities. Instead, the House leadership flew a three-member committee—two Democrats and one Republican—to Indiana to oversee a recount.

Both parties rushed resources—money, activists, lawyers—to southwest Indiana. One of them was a young attorney named Ben Ginsberg.

Ginsberg had grown up in Philadelphia, raised by liberal parents. He was liberal, too, at first. By the time he was in college, though, his views were evolving. He was turned off by the Great Society programs of the 1960s, and his politics drifted to the right. To his parents' dismay, Ginsberg registered as a Republican.

Ginsberg had a long face and a stern countenance, which was only slightly softened by a fuzzy, reddish beard. After graduating from the University of Pennsylvania in 1974, he became a journalist. His first real gig was at a weekly paper in New Hampshire, followed by stints at the *Berkshire Eagle* in Massachusetts and then the Riverside *Press-Enterprise* in Southern California. His beat there was the county planning commission. The Inland Empire was growing fast, and the commission was flooded with requests for permits to build. Ginsberg had no idea how to read permit requests, which was an impediment to doing his job properly. He figured a law degree might help. He got into Georgetown Law.

Ginsberg never returned to journalism. Instead, after law school, he joined the legal industry, which in the early 1980s was growing at a wild clip. He landed a job at BakerHostetler, which had been founded in Cleveland in 1916 and now was racing, alongside many others, to become a national firm.

Ginsberg got off to a rough start: He failed the bar exam. Even so, his journalism credentials meant he was a good fit for a group inside BakerHostetler that specialized in representing media companies. Before long, a partner named Jan Baran asked Ginsberg if he was available to lend a hand on political work. Yes, he was. Baran, an authority on federal and state election laws, assigned Ginsberg the task of researching a thin slice of campaign finance law. He was grateful for the ground-level experience, and another assignment soon followed. Baran's clients included the Republican members of the House Administration Committee. When they asked for a report on the laws governing election recounts, Ginsberg did some investigating and typed up a memo, which as far as he could tell nobody read.

And then it was November 1984, and the McCloskey-McIntyre race was basically a tie. The House Administration Committee was supposed to be adjudicating the recount fight. All of a sudden, Ginsberg's newfound expertise was in demand. The day after the election, he was summoned to Capitol Hill to brief leading Republicans on the history of recounts. Then he was sent to Indiana to monitor the three-person congressional squad. For months that winter, Ginsberg traversed seventeen counties, examining individual ballots, making sure they were being properly tabulated. As he watched, his anger grew. The Democrats, led by then-congressman Leon Panetta, excluded some ballots, accepted others, and predictably concluded that the Democrat had won—by four votes. McCloskey was sent back to Washington, where he'd serve another four terms in Congress. The experience radicalized Ginsberg. This was a stolen election.

GINSBERG SPENT THE NEXT eight years in a series of jobs with the Republican Party in Washington. In the early 1990s, the once-a-decade congressional redistricting process got underway. Ginsberg, by now the general counsel at the Republican National Committee, helped cook up a plan to increase the number of both Republicans and racial minorities in Congress. The idea was to cram as many Black voters as possible into the smallest possible number of districts in southern states. In those so-called "majority-minority" districts, Black candidates were encouraged to run; once in office, they had a reliable path to reelection. Meanwhile, the surrounding congressional districts became whiter, and more Republican, than ever.

The result was twofold: There would be more Black representatives in Congress (though not nearly as many as there might have been if districts had been drawn in a straightforward fashion), and the south would be more of a GOP stronghold. (Southern white Democrats became an endangered species in Congress.) Black leaders liked it, and their support diluted Democratic resistance.

Because the initiative deliberately divided the opposition, it came to be known as Project Ratfuck.*

In 1999, Karl Rove got George W. Bush to hire Ginsberg as the chief counsel for his presidential campaign. During the fateful Florida recount, Ginsberg was the field marshal of a small army of lawyers that included Ted Cruz, Mike Carvin, and Noel Francisco. The battle—the culmination of Ginsberg's years in the recount trenches—elevated him to national prominence. (Bush picked Ginsberg to be the top lawyer on his 2004 campaign, too. He stepped down after acknowledging that he had helped the Swift Boat Veterans for Truth plot their attacks on the Democratic nominee, John Kerry.)

Ginsberg worked on both Bush campaigns as part of his full-time job at another law firm, Patton Boggs, which he'd joined in 1993. Patton Boggs was a big name in Washington, renowned for its muscular lobbying. That is where Ginsberg met a young lawyer named Don McGahn.

SHORTLY AFTER LABOR DAY in 1994, McGahn had showed up for a series of job interviews at Patton Boggs. Despite the presence of guys like Ginsberg, the firm at the time was dominated by Democrats. McGahn, who had recently graduated from Widener University's law school in Harrisburg, Pennsylvania, surprised his interviewers by asking what they were going to do if Republicans took control of Congress in that year's midterm elections. His interviewers snickered. This young man clearly had no idea what he was talking about. Democrats had held a majority in the House for the past forty years, and there was no reason to think that was about to change. *That didn't go well,* McGahn thought to himself as he left the firm's offices overlooking Washington's Rock Creek.

Two months later, Republicans stormed into power, led by an ambitious Georgia congressman, Newt Gingrich. (The so-called

* That moniker is often attributed to Ginsberg, though he has denied coining it.

Republican Revolution was partly a byproduct of Ginsberg's success at redrawing congressional maps in his party's favor.) McGahn's phone rang. Patton Boggs wanted to offer him a job. "You're either going to be a really good lawyer or you're going to be a disaster," a partner told him. "It's worth one year's salary to find out."

And so McGahn got a job. He wasn't a natural fit—a continuation of a lifelong pattern. Growing up in New Jersey, members of his extended family had been political royalty, deeply immersed in the state's Democratic Party, but the young McGahn wasn't into politics, and certainly not liberal politics. He was a kicker on the high school football team and the goalie on the hockey team, but he didn't hang with the jocks. And in the status-obsessed legal industry, which valued Ivy League diplomas above almost anything else, McGahn's degree from the largely unknown Widener meant he would have "to work harder than those with the more traditional résumés," as he put it.

At an early age, McGahn had developed "an aversion to concentrated power." That gut-level feeling had hardened into conservatism by college, when he watched the Senate confirmation hearings of Robert Bork. Just as Ginsberg had been animated by the Democrats' theft of a congressional election in the Bloody Eighth, three years later McGahn and a generation of young Republicans were galvanized by what they saw as Democrats' disgraceful treatment of a respected conservative judge.

At Patton Boggs, Ginsberg and McGahn quickly crossed paths. Ginsberg needed help on some election litigation, and McGahn was eager to lend a hand to this fellow Republican. Ginsberg was impressed with his work. McGahn, for his part, was amazed that you could make a year-round career out of working on campaigns. "I ended up latching onto Ben, who was an excellent mentor," McGahn would recall. The more the duo worked together, the more McGahn learned about campaign finance and election law. It wasn't the profession's most prestigious work—being a corporate lawyer was more lucrative, and being a prosecutor was more glamorous—but it was a career, especially for someone who'd come to love politics.

After four years at Patton Boggs, McGahn became an in-house lawyer at the National Republican Congressional Committee. Then, in 2005, he started his own small law firm, McGahn & Associates. One of his first clients was House Majority Leader Tom DeLay, who faced federal indictment for money laundering. A team of lawyers took over a conference room off DeLay's suite in the Capitol, and McGahn became a fixture. He didn't blend in: He wore his hair shoulder length and played guitar in an eighties rock group that billed itself as "one of the Mid-Atlantic region's most exciting and flat-out FUN cover bands." McGahn would perform in spandex pants or a mustard tank top, thrashing on one of his more than thirty guitars.

One of the other lawyers helping DeLay was Richard Cullen, a genteel former attorney general of Virginia. Cullen admired how McGahn didn't seem to take himself too seriously. That said, when President Bush nominated McGahn to the Federal Election Commission in 2008, and the Senate confirmed him by unanimous consent—not even bothering to hold a vote on his elevation into the government—Cullen had trouble believing it. What would this cowboy do as part of the federal bureaucracy?

The answer soon became clear: McGahn would do his level best to destroy it. For all his devil-may-care rock-and-roll vibes, McGahn was driven by a visceral hatred of the "administrative state." Unelected judges, in his eyes, were regularly ruling in favor of unelected bureaucrats, who were trampling the rights of private citizens and companies. "My view had become that the bureaucracy had become its own branch of the government," McGahn would say. "It was extra-Constitutional."

That was the attitude McGahn took with him to the FEC, whose mandate was to enforce campaign finance laws and regulations. His goal was to bring to heel what he saw as an out-of-control agency. He voted to loosen curbs on money in politics. He banded together with the other Republican commissioners to slow the agency's rulemaking. He even pushed to make it harder for staffers to share information about suspected crimes with prosecutors. That caused such an uproar that the FEC's top lawyer resigned.

In 2011, Donald Trump was eyeing a presidential run, and he was accused of violating FEC rules by sending money through the Trump Organization to the ShouldTrumpRun website. The commission's staff recommended that the agency open a formal investigation. McGahn (and his Republican colleagues) voted against the recommendation, blocking the investigation.

McGahn did a good job of handcuffing the FEC. By the end of his tenure in 2013, even routine decision-making had become an immense hassle, and companies and other groups enjoyed greater freedom to spend money however they wanted to sway elections. By now McGahn had become something of a folk hero within Washington's conservative legal circles; Senator Mitch McConnell, a fierce opponent of restrictions on campaign spending, was a particularly enthusiastic fan.

After a nearly fifteen-year hiatus, McGahn returned to Patton Boggs, where he was reunited with Ginsberg—just as the law firm was beginning to implode. Patton Boggs had been hurting ever since the 2008 financial crisis, and now, its revenues plunging and its partners defecting, its leaders were hastily engineering a merger with a Cleveland-based law firm, Squire Sanders. "It was kind of in a death spiral," McGahn would say.

This was no place for prominent Republican attorneys. McGahn, Ginsberg, and a third partner, Bill McGinley, hired a headhunter, who started shopping them around to some of the biggest firms in D.C. The key was to find a shop that would give them something approaching free rein.

THE TRIO PLAYED FOOTSIE with about a dozen firms. Jones Day quickly emerged as the leading contender. It was huge, it had a thriving Washington office and corporate litigation practice, and its leaders were conservative. Plus, the Patton Boggs crew would fill a void. While Jones Day had built up a formidable practice advising companies on how to navigate the federal bureaucracy, the firm didn't have a practice advising politicians on how to navigate election and campaign finance laws. And without the relationships that came from helping people win office, it was harder for Jones Day to wield influence on Capitol Hill and in the White House. For a firm with aspirations like Jones Day's, that constituted a big hole.

It helped that Ginsberg had known Noel Francisco and Mike Carvin for years (dating back to the *Bush v. Gore* days for Francisco and to the Mary Matalin days for Carvin). At the outset, Ginsberg told Francisco that he recognized that Jones Day, despite its conservative reputation, probably employed a lot of Democrats. Would it be a problem to bring in a team of hotshot Republicans? It would not, Francisco assured him.

In May 2014, it became official: Jones Day was hiring Ginsberg, McGahn, McGinley, and their associates to create a new political and election law practice focused on advising Republicans. "The arrival of Ben, Don, and Bill further cements our position as the go-to firm for challenging government overreach and regulation," Francisco cheered to the *Washington Post*.

Jones Day was 121 years old. The hiring of the small Patton Boggs team would turn out to be one of the most consequential decisions in the firm's history.

19

TRUMP'S STALLION

The 2016 presidential election was two years out, but the posturing and preparation were well underway. The Republican Party settled on Cleveland as the location for its national convention, and around the time of Ginsberg and McGahn's arrival, Jones Day agreed to be a leading sponsor, pledging $1.5 million to bankroll the event. The firm's top partner in Cleveland would cochair the convention's host committee.

The next step for Jones Day was to figure out which presidential candidates to work with. There was no shortage of choices—about twenty prominent Republicans were toying with running. In the early stages of the race, the firm didn't need to commit to just one candidate. Ginsberg and McGahn were well-known throughout the Republican establishment, and quite a few wannabe presidents came to them seeking counsel. Soon, Scott Walker, Rick Perry, and Chris Christie would become clients.

These were hardly the only customers the new Jones Day partners were working for. McGahn's roster read like a who's who of GOP power players. He was defending the National Rifle Association, which had been accused of campaign finance violations. He represented a group affiliated with the Koch brothers. He worked for the RNC.

There was at least one other key client: Citizens United. The group, famous for its successful Supreme Court challenge of campaign spending restrictions, was run by Dave Bossie, an influential right-wing activist. Within hours of McGahn's departure from the FEC, Bossie had called him and become his first client upon his return to Patton Boggs. ("Everyone in Washington knows that if you have a problem, Don McGahn is the person to call," Bossie would say.) One day in late 2014, Bossie and McGahn were on the phone, batting around ideas about which presidential campaigns the Jones Day lawyers should work for. "What about Trump?" Bossie asked.

"What about Trump?" McGahn replied, skeptical.

"No, he's really thinking about running."

"He says this every four years. Isn't he a Democrat from New York?"

"He's gotten older, he's conservative," Bossie answered. "I think you guys would hit it off." McGahn trusted Bossie, and the next time he was in New York, McGahn met Donald Trump at his Fifth Avenue skyscraper. At the end of their talk, Trump signed a book for McGahn's son: "You have a wonderful father," he wrote. McGahn thought to himself, *This guy's got a pretty good instinct for how to handle people*.

Long before that first visit, Trump had worked with the McGahn family. In the 1980s, McGahn's uncle, Paddy McGahn, had been Trump's lawyer as he sought to become an Atlantic City casino impresario. Paddy—a power broker in New Jersey's Democratic Party—handled jobs large and small, at one point representing Trump in a fight with a guy hawking hot dogs outside his casino. When Trump bought property from two Mafia-linked brothers, he put it in the name of Paddy's secretary. The Taj Mahal's cocktail lounge, Paddy's Saloon, was named for him. "He gets things done in this town," Trump once remarked. The relationship ultimately disintegrated in typical Trump fashion: He stopped paying Paddy's legal bills and then sued his former lawyer.

At one of his initial meetings with Don McGahn, Trump brought up the work Paddy had done for him decades earlier. He heaped praise on the man. To the extent that McGahn harbored any bitterness on behalf of his long-dead uncle, he was able to subordinate those feelings to the allure of Candidate Trump, who was attacking immigrants and free trade and the establishment. Much of what Trump was saying resonated with McGahn, who was frustrated that Republicans had done so little to stem the growth of the loathsome administrative state. "He and I shared the same view about what was going to matter in 2016," McGahn told me, "and it wasn't what the D.C. consultants thought was going to matter."

IN FEBRUARY 2015, MCGAHN RETURNED to Trump Tower. He took a golden elevator up to the twenty-sixth floor and was led into Trump's office. Trump was sitting behind his cluttered desk. After what seemed like an hour of small talk, Trump got to the point. What do you charge? he asked. "My hourly rate is $800," McGahn replied.

"No shit," Trump exclaimed. "Good for you."

Later that month, Trump began taking steps to show that his easy-to-dismiss candidacy was for real. To underscore his seriousness, he mentioned that he had hired McGahn. "I'm not doing this for enjoyment," Trump said. "I'm doing this because the country is in serious trouble." (In perhaps a more telling sign of his seriousness, Trump also noted that he was holding off on another season of *Celebrity Apprentice,* his NBC reality show.)

Years later, McGahn would insist that he'd guessed early on that Trump might win. The reality, several of McGahn's colleagues told me, was that he and Ginsberg didn't think much of representing the bare-bones Trump campaign. They reckoned he was flirting with a White House bid for publicity's sake and that he'd quickly move on. Most likely, he'd create a super-PAC to throw his money around like any sensible rich guy. By signing on with Trump now, the lawyers would position Jones Day to eventually represent his super-PAC, an easy assignment that paid perfectly good money.

One day in the spring of 2015, McGahn took a Jones Day associate over to Trump Tower. The associate was eager to soak up campaign experience, and McGahn figured the fledgling Trump campaign would be an interesting experience for the young lawyer. The associate would get a firsthand glimpse of how some no-frills campaigns functioned. Also, unlike those with professionally run outfits, the Trump folks wouldn't mind a random lawyer showing up. "I can't take you to Rick Perry's campaign, because they're serious," McGahn told his colleague.

The meeting was with Cory Lewandowski, who was the campaign's manager, and Alan Garten, a longtime Trump Organization executive. After sandwiches at the Trump Grill in the building's lobby, the men moved upstairs to the nerve center of the Trump Organization. They sat in Lewandowski's little office, down the hall from Trump's large one. The meeting was completely unstructured. Lewandowski showed off the campaign's new letterhead, and he asked for the lawyers' input on their talking points on issues like abortion (Trump had previously been pro-choice). Toward the end of the meeting, Lewandowski asked about how to account for the campaign's use of Trump's private jet. The campaign would have to reimburse Trump for flights; was it okay if they just guessed how much each trip cost? McGahn patiently informed them that, no, they could not just guess, there were rules about this, and they needed to be followed.

"These guys are morons," McGahn told the associate afterward.*

ON APRIL 23, 2015, A check for $6,451.38 arrived at Jones Day. It was the first payment from the Trump campaign.

McGahn and his colleagues hadn't done much work for Trump yet, but it was time for him to start paying. Trump's reputation for shortchanging his lawyers (and banks and contractors and custom-

* McGahn disputed the quotes attributed to him, in particular the word "moron." "I certainly have some go-to phrases, but that is not one of them," he said. He added that "many of the folks I met in New York were quite sharp and impressive in their chosen fields—though many of them had little or no political experience."

ers) was well-known. It wasn't just Uncle Paddy. Trump had tried to wriggle out of what he owed one attorney after another, ranging from solo practitioners to partners at big firms. Back in the 1990s, a lawyer at a white-shoe firm had done some work for Trump. The bill came to about $2 million, and Trump refused to pay. After a while, the lawyer lost patience, and he showed up, unannounced, at Trump Tower. Someone sent him up to Trump's office. Trump was initially pleased to see him—he didn't betray any sense of sheepishness—but the lawyer was steaming. "I'm incredibly disappointed," he scolded Trump. "There's no reason you haven't paid us."

Trump made some apologetic noises. Then he said: "I'm not going to pay your bill. I'm going to give you something more valuable." *What on earth is he talking about?* the lawyer wondered. "I have a stallion," Trump continued. "It's worth $5 million." Trump rummaged around in a filing cabinet and pulled out what he said was a deed to a horse. He handed it to the lawyer.

"This isn't the 1800s," the lawyer stammered once he regained the capacity for speech. "You can't pay me with a horse." After the lawyer threatened to sue, Trump eventually coughed up at least a portion of what he owed.

Jones Day, too, wanted to be paid with money. So a decision was made that Trump would pay a regular retainer. In addition, there would be a strict schedule for disbursing any other fees or reimbursements.* Even after that timetable was established, Jones Day lawyers—including some working for the Trump campaign—doubted it would hold. "We figured he wouldn't pay, and that would be the end of it," one told me. But against all odds, Trump paid and paid again. Within a few months, he'd forked over tens of thousands of dollars—including more than $29,000 on June 16.

That same day, McGahn was back at Trump Tower. He stood on the mezzanine level of the lobby as Donald and Melania Trump

---

* McGahn said there was not an unusual payment schedule. "The Trump campaign was billed in regular order and paid regularly," he told me.

descended on an escalator to a makeshift, flag-studded stage, where Trump formally launched his candidacy. McGahn watched the small crowd go nuts. Then he listened as his client laced into immigrants and the Beltway establishment. Outside, storm clouds gathered, and a light rain began to fall.

IN THE YEARS TO come, as the firm came under fire for its Trump work, Jones Day would proudly declare that it stuck with clients, no matter how unpopular they might be. This was how good lawyers operated. It was the ethical—the American—thing to do.

That argument was not nearly as bulletproof as Jones Day liked to make it sound. The principle made sense in a criminal context where a defendant couldn't afford or wouldn't be able to find alternate legal services. But those were rarely the circumstances in which the loyalty obligation was invoked—more often these were civil, not criminal, situations, and the rich clients had many other options at their disposal.

But even if the principle were universal and inviolable, the logic didn't apply to a brand-new client. That was the point of the "Independence Principle" that Frank Ginn—Jones Day's first managing partner—had articulated a century earlier when he turned down a lucrative but problematic assignment working on a corporate transaction. It was the reason Jones Day still liked to boast about its refusal to take on Nixon as a client, even though Chappie Rose had already been advising him informally. Nothing had obligated Jones Day to accept Donald Trump's money. This was not an instance of a law firm feeling an ethical or moral duty to defend a client under assault by the government or other powerful interests. This was a political and financial choice. And by making the decision to accept Trump as a client, and then to stand by him and to help him, Jones Day would bear some responsibility for what he wrought.

As with the choice to represent RJR thirty years earlier, not a whole lot of thought went into this fateful decision. The Trump campaign was run through Jones Day's standard client-onboarding process, which was primarily focused on business considerations. Were there conflicts of interest between the Trump campaign and other clients? None were apparent. "It looked like it was a fairly anodyne political engagement," one partner recalled.

There had been some internal grumbling about the firm's hiring of Ginsberg and McGahn—here was final confirmation, as if any more were needed, that Jones Day was a Republican law firm—and now there was more grumbling about working for Trump. Jones Day prided itself on its devotion to the rule of law. How could a firm like that get in bed with a client like Trump? "It was culturally weird," another partner told me.

But many Jones Day lawyers weren't yet aware that the firm was representing Trump, and the complaining was mild, even among liberals. "To be a partner, you need to accept that you're not going to love every client," one said. In any case, Brogan was supportive, and that was all that mattered.

As it became clear that Trump was a viable candidate—polls showed him at the front of the Republican pack—it also became clear that Jones Day's workload would grow. In the fall of 2015, McGahn beat back an effort to keep Trump off New Hampshire's primary ballot. Similar attempts had to be defeated in other states. Jones Day had to set up Trump campaign committees that adhered to FEC rules. The firm would be handling the selection and wrangling of delegates to the 2016 convention. And it had to fend off lawsuits. In one case, someone at the campaign had grabbed a photo of a bald eagle from a search engine and then plastered it on Trump merchandise. When the two wildlife photographers who'd snapped the photo sued for copyright infringement, Jones Day arranged for a swift settlement.

By the time the first Republican primaries rolled around in early 2016, the Trump campaign had paid Jones Day nearly $600,000. Millions more would soon pour in.

20

YOU CAN COUNT ME IN

"*You say you want a revolution,*" the loudspeakers screech, as a sea of cellphones, held aloft by cheering fans, record the scene. Donald Trump, in a dark suit and shiny tie, strides onstage. He waves, gives a thumbs-up, a grin spreading across his face.

It is Tuesday, February 9, 2016. Trump has just won the New Hampshire primary, buoying his candidacy after a second-place finish a week earlier in Iowa. He is here to address supporters—and a nationwide TV audience—from his campaign office in Manchester. *"Well, you know, we all want to change the world . . . ,"* sings the voice of John Lennon. *"But when you talk about destruction—"* And then the music stops, and Trump begins to speak.

He is surrounded by his family: Melania, whose diamond-studded belt buckle sparkles on her all-black outfit, to his right; Ivanka and Jared to his left; lesser relatives arranged on either side. Behind Trump, a small band of advisers shuffles onto the platform, taking their places between the Trump clan and a row of six American and New Hampshire flags at the rear of the stage. It was Trump's idea to get his inner circle up here, to make it look more like a professional operation. As Don McGahn moves into position—behind and slightly to Trump's right—he bumps one of the gold-tasseled flags, causing it to sway.

Klieg lights shine on Trump, and his shadow partly darkens his lawyer's visage. McGahn stands, hands clasped in front of him, and alternates between licking his lips, swiveling his head back and forth, and staring straight ahead with what might be a grimace.

Lies spill from Trump's mouth. Federal economic data is bogus. France's gun control laws make it a haven for terrorists. A wan smile is on McGahn's half-shadowed face. "Political hacks" negotiate American trade deals, Trump declares. McGahn swallows, looks down at his feet. "We're going to build a wall," Trump promises. McGahn grins, his teeth bared, appearing uncomfortable.

Trump complains about how much money is sloshing around campaigns, how candidates are beholden to special interests. It is a phenomenon that his lawyer helped perpetuate, and now McGahn's smile vanishes behind pursed lips. Trump bemoans the opioid epidemic ravaging New Hampshire, attributes it to drugs coming across the Mexican border. McGahn, whose employer represents Purdue Pharma, which caused this epidemic, applauds politely.

"I am going to be the greatest jobs president that God ever created," Trump bellows, wagging his index finger, and McGahn seems almost to laugh, like he can't decide whether to take this guy seriously.

Then the speech ends, and "Revolution" comes back on, and this time the song plays through. As Trump steps off the stage, Lennon sings: *"But when you talk about destruction, don't you know that you can count me out."* McGahn is still up there as the cameras stop recording.

AT THIS POINT, UNLESS you were a senior partner at Jones Day, or a political junkie, it was possible to work at the firm and not realize it was working for Donald Trump—the representation wasn't something the firm had been bragging about. A couple of partners told me they'd been watching Trump's raucous New Hampshire victory speech, and out of the corner of their eyes they spotted something familiar. They looked, did a double take, and sure enough, their colleague was up onstage. To some, this was the moment it became clear that the firm had hitched its wagon to Trump. Even if he lost—which everyone expected—Jones Day was staking its reputation on this unpredictable character. These lawyers were apoplectic, even as they grasped for silver linings of McGahn's onstage appearance. "This is where you find Jones Day partners—at the front of things," one partner said, half-heartedly.

Folks inside the Trump campaign were puzzling over McGahn. He had become a fixture, traveling with the candidate, advising him on matters beyond the law. It wasn't normal to have an outside lawyer occupy such a central position. Then again, there was nothing normal about the Trump campaign. It had a skeleton staff, practically zero national operation. Some dyed-in-the-wool Trumpies initially viewed McGahn, with his long history in D.C. and his job at a giant law firm, as the embodiment of the corporate sleaze that oozed through the swampy capital. But as time passed, and McGahn remained devoted to the cause, their views shifted. They could tell McGahn was enduring dirty looks from his colleagues in the legal profession. Yet he was toughing it out. Most important, Trump himself was chummy with McGahn. And in the Trump orbit—much like inside Jones Day—everything hinged on what the top guy thought of you.

McGahn by now had his eyes on a very big prize. Trump was emerging as the front-runner for the Republican nomination, and he was not burdened by strong views on many of the major issues of the day. One of the blank spots on the Trump canvas involved the appointment of federal judges. This was a topic dear to McGahn—and his tabula rasa candidate offered a rare chance for the lawyer to stamp his own beliefs onto the agenda of a leading presidential contender.

McGahn's judicial philosophy consisted of a preference for smart, young, conservative judges who would rigidly hew to the letter of the law and the Constitution as it was written in the late eighteenth century. He was completely in synch with the views of the Federalist Society, and this was not an accident. McGahn had been a member of the society since his time as the president of

Widener law school's chapter. At Patton Boggs, he'd hung a framed Federalist Society certificate on his office wall—quite the conversation starter with the firm's liberal lawyers.

In January 2016, McGahn had traveled with the Trump team to Iowa for its caucuses. Word reached McGahn that Jonathan Bunch, the Federalist Society's head of external relations, was looking to speak to someone at the campaign. McGahn called Bunch from his hotel room overlooking downtown Des Moines. Bunch explained that the group was surveying the major candidates and wanted to know if the Trump camp had given much thought to the sorts of judges he might nominate if elected.

"We actually have someone on the campaign who's going to help us out, with a lot of experience on this," McGahn replied. He was about to unspool a practical joke that showed how well he understood the psychology of conservative activists—and how his role was much more than counseling the campaign on mundane matters of election law.

Who? Bunch asked.

"It's John Sununu," McGahn deadpanned. Sununu had been George H. W. Bush's chief of staff, and he was widely viewed as responsible for Bush having nominated David Souter to the Supreme Court. Souter had turned out to be a centrist, and conservatives had never forgiven Sununu. Bunch gasped, then went silent. "Well, it's good that you have someone helping," he eventually managed.

McGahn kept going. The campaign, he said, had asked Sununu to come up with a list of moderate pragmatists with no paper trail, "the kind of folks who will get through the Senate"—judges like Souter, in other words.

Another long pause.

McGahn finally told Bunch he was kidding. Someone like Sununu wouldn't get anywhere near the Trump operation, McGahn said. "You have nothing to worry about with us."

• • •

On a brisk Monday in March 2016, several dozen Republicans showed up at Jones Day's Capitol Hill office for lunch. Senators Jeff Sessions and Tom Cotton were there. So were a clutch of congressmen—and their old leader, Newt Gingrich. The Federalist Society's Leonard Leo came, as did the president of the Heritage Foundation and a handful of lobbyists. McGahn had organized the meeting, getting Jones Day's approval to use the building as the venue for a political event. He instructed everyone to enter through the underground parking garage, where reporters wouldn't see them. Gingrich disobeyed, walking up the wide stone steps, past the rough-to-the-touch limestone griffins, and entering through the ceremonial front door, "to assure he would be seen by the media," as the *Washington Post* put it.

McGahn had convened this session to help Washington's conservative establishment gain comfort with the Republican Party's unorthodox front-runner. The idea was that Trump would deliver brief remarks and then open it up to questions. Because the gathering was private, there would be no need for grandstanding.

It had been only a few weeks since Justice Scalia's sudden death. Mitch McConnell had made clear that the Senate would not hold a vote on anyone Obama nominated to replace him. The next president, therefore, would get an immediate vacancy to fill on the Supreme Court. McGahn and Trump had plotted about how to use this unforeseen development to shore up conservative support for his candidacy. Today they would roll out the first phase of their strategy.

After Trump spoke for a few minutes, Leonard Leo invited him to talk about judges. "Why don't I put out a list publicly of people who could be the sort of people I would put on the Supreme Court?" Trump suggested. The room—and Leo in particular—reacted with joy. If Trump would publicly commit, in writing, to selecting Scalia's replacement from a preapproved list, well, that would do a lot to assuage conservatives' concerns about a guy who had previously supported abortion rights. Leo and others started throwing out names of judges who would receive the Federalist Society's unqualified backing. "The List" was born.*

The meeting lasted a bit more than an hour. Afterward, Republicans marched out the front entrance of Jones Day's building onto Louisiana Avenue. Reporters were waiting. "It was all about making America great again," a Republican congressman, Chris Collins, explained, with Jones Day's logo and façade serving as a backdrop. Trump headed down Pennsylvania Avenue to the Old Post Office building, which his company was transforming into a hotel. At a press conference there, he discussed the Jones Day gathering. "It was a beginning meeting with a lot of the most respected people in Washington," Trump said. "They can't believe how far we've come. A lot of people wouldn't have predicted that."

The final list of potential Supreme Court picks would take months to come together—a team led by McGahn and Leo obsessively read all of the candidates' court opinions—but it would become a crucial turning point for Trump's campaign. "The list reassured a whole lot of Republicans . . . that, OK, maybe he was doing fundraisers for Schumer four years ago, but looks like he may be OK on something that's really important to us," Mitch McConnell would explain years later. The creation of The List, he added, "became the single biggest issue bringing our side in line behind him."

It was thanks, in no small part, to Jones Day.

---

* McGahn and Leo have told multiple versions of this story. In one, McGahn instructed Leo to come with a list of Federalist Society–approved names, which was presented to Trump after the lunch.

21

A LAWLESS HOBBESIAN NIGHTMARE

Within hours of the Trump event wrapping up, news articles about the meeting ensured that everyone inside Jones Day soon knew about the firm's role on this incendiary campaign. The reaction was explosive. "Cringeworthy," one lawyer vented to the popular legal website Above the Law. "Many people in the firm are upset by it and concerned about the negative implications that representing a sexist, racist demagogue could have on our client base." Another lawyer: "shameful and embarrassing." A third: "Trump's bigotry doesn't speak for us all, and many (if not the majority) of us are ashamed to have learned this today."

In Jones Day's Manhattan office, the partner in charge, Wesley Johnson, convened an all-hands meeting in part to address employees' concerns. "I don't like this any more than you do," Johnson acknowledged to the lawyers assembled in a top-floor conference room. "Nobody expects you to want to build a wall."

Steve Brogan didn't generally care much about what other people thought, but the internal uproar was beginning to spill into public view, which he hated. That spring, Brogan tried to get people to stop whining. He sent out a memo to partners noting that the firm had a history of representing controversial clients. *Everyone deserves representation. And we are not budging.*

At times like this, Brogan and other leaders liked to invoke how

Jones Day had stood by Art Modell when he moved the Browns out of Cleveland. The firm had persevered through attacks on its lawyers and staff. Twenty years later, the "Judas Day" moniker remained a rallying cry.

This was a self-serving act of revisionism. The honor Jones Day derived from sticking with Modell was because the firm had *stuck* with him—he was an existing client. That wasn't the case with Trump. Some convenient misinformation had spread inside the firm and among its diaspora about the genesis of the relationship. Supposedly when McGahn arrived from Patton Boggs, he had brought Trump with him as a client. If that had been the case, Jones Day could argue that the work that followed fit under the rubric of standing by an existing client. But, of course, that wasn't what had actually happened.

IN MAY, JONES DAY notified its staff in Cleveland that its offices would be shut for regular business the week of the GOP convention. The official explanation was that the city would be crowded with delegates and media; there were also plans for protests outside Jones Day's offices, given its role in helping Trump get this far. But there was another reason that the lakefront office was closed for most employees: It was doubling as a venue for political gatherings.

The firm hosted a slew of events at its offices and around town. (At one Jones Day cocktail party, guests ate cupcakes with tiny edible elephants perched on the frosting.) The Cleveland office offered a large menu of panel discussions at which the firm's partners were paired with high-ranking Republicans. There was Newt Gingrich, blasting away at Obama. There were Scott Pruitt, the future EPA administrator, and Jeff Sessions, the future attorney general, lashing out at Democrats. And there was the Jones Day logo splashed behind each of them.

This was almost certainly not an accident. Brogan scrutinized Jones Day's branding with an intensity that most lawyers would reserve for reviewing sensitive settlement documents. Once, the firm's marketing staff was told that Brogan did not want tables at law-school recruiting events to display the Jones Day logo because it would be "brand-dilutive" for it to appear among so many other logos. Another time, when someone proposed handing out Jones Day umbrellas—a staple giveaway from law firms—the idea was vetoed from on high: It would be bad for the brand to have rain on it. So it was a safe bet that the firm's leadership had signed off on the decision to so closely associate Jones Day's brand with the Republican events.

At one panel discussion, McGahn, Mike Carvin, and Chris Kelly, the partner in charge of the Cleveland office, appeared alongside Sessions. The event was held in one of the firm's lecture halls, and there were about one hundred people in the audience. Onstage, sitting before a blue Jones Day–branded backdrop, the lawyers made no effort to maintain the pretense of calm, sober professionalism. "Not to put too fine a point on it, but if Hillary Clinton is elected, we will descend into a lawless Hobbesian nightmare that we will not emerge from for at least two decades," Carvin declared. "Everybody knows about the kinds of activist things the judiciary has done that she's endorsed, like same-sex marriage and *Roe v. Wade* and that sort of stuff. The parade of horribles is not simply limited to inventing constitutional rights. The notion that there are moderate appointees that could come out of the Clinton administration is like saying there are moderate Iranians to deal with on the nuclear front. It's something that doesn't exist in nature."

Inside the convention hall, a beaming, shaggy-haired McGahn was holding court. "It's a great day," he intoned to a reporter for the fringe One America News Network as a speaker onstage trashed Clinton. "It's not just a campaign, it's a movement, and we're really excited to be here."

The TV reporter gazed at McGahn with a transfixed smile, and catchphrases tumbled from the Jones Day lawyer's mouth:

"Make America Great Again."

"Making America safe again."

"'America' is going to be okay to say again. We're going to be putting America first and not going to be embarrassed to say it."

"Which we all hope," the reporter chimed in.

FOR HIS WHOLE LIFE, Don Ayer had been a Republican. He grew up in a family of small-government conservatives, the types who thought FDR was a disaster. When he was fourteen, Ayer had volunteered for Barry Goldwater's campaign. As a young man, he remained true to his conservative upbringing, believing in fiscal responsibility, limited government, and the transformative power of free enterprise.

After law school, Ayer was cruising upward on a well-trodden path in Republican legal circles. There was a job as a federal prosecutor, then the years as a deputy solicitor general in the Reagan administration. Even as Ayer's politics were moderating—he was turned off by the Republican Party's social conservatism and its embrace of a tax code that rewarded the rich—he still considered himself a conservative.

Ayer had been recruited from the Reagan administration to run the first iteration of Jones Day's Issues & Appeals practice. At the time, he had two kids under the age of ten. *It's time to go make some money,* Ayer had told himself. Plus, he liked Jones Day's structure: total power vested in a managing partner in pursuit of collegiality and teamwork in the interest of clients. Months after arriving, though, he was approached by the new Bush administration: Would he serve as the deputy to Attorney General Dick Thornburgh? Ayer felt he couldn't say no to such a senior job. So back he went to Justice in late 1989.

It didn't go well. In February 1990, Ayer wrote a letter to the U.S. Sentencing Commission, which issues guidelines to help courts mete out consistent punishments for criminals. Ayer expressed the Bush administration's "strong support" for tough mandatory minimum sentences for corporations convicted of crimes like fraud or dumping toxic waste. The letter infuriated the business lobby, which did not help Ayer's standing in the Republican administration.

The bigger problem was that Thornburgh had told Ayer to investigate a rival inside the Justice Department. Ayer did as asked—and, to Thornburgh's immense frustration, the investigation cleared the rival of wrongdoing. When Ayer said as much publicly, Thornburgh ordered him to take it back. Ayer, forty-one at the time, believed in sticking to his principles. Rather than recant, he resigned—after six months as deputy attorney general. ("The guy thought he was an independent player and that he was not part of a team," a top Thornburgh aide sniffed.*) Ayer returned to Jones Day in May 1990. That was where he'd spend the next twenty-eight years.

In addition to helping build Issues & Appeals into a force, Ayer became a mentor to many young lawyers. He invited former Supreme Court clerks to guest-teach classes with him at Georgetown Law; some would come to his house to have dinner with him and his wife. I haven't spoken to a single Jones Day lawyer who has had anything negative to say about Don Ayer. And until Jones Day took on Donald Trump as a client, Ayer didn't seem to have anything negative to say about his firm.

Then Ayer made a couple of missteps. The first one might not even have been reasonably described as such, since everything went exactly as planned. Ayer was appalled by Trump, and he was dismayed that Jones Day was representing him. Ayer felt obliged to speak out. In the fall of 2016, he and a Republican friend got former Justice Department officials to sign an open letter. It was published less than a month before Election Day. "We believe that Donald Trump's impulsive temperament, flair for controversy, vindictive approach to his opponents, and alarming views outside the constitutional mainstream, ill suit him to oversee the execution of

* Ayer's replacement as deputy attorney general was an up-and-coming lawyer named Bill Barr.

the laws in a fair and even-handed manner," the letter said. It went on like that, before concluding that Trump "must be decisively rejected in November." Ayer's signature came first and was followed by those of twenty-two other senior DOJ officials from Republican administrations. (Among them was Jonathan Rose, Chappie's son.)

Ayer didn't bother giving anyone at Jones Day a heads-up about the letter, which might not have been a big deal, except that there was another mistake, too.

Trevor Potter, a former John McCain aide and FEC chairman, ran a nonprofit called the Campaign Legal Center. The center promoted voter rights and limits on money in politics, among other things. Potter invited Ayer to join a team that would look at legal strategies for protecting people's democratic rights. "I'd love to," Ayer replied. His plan was to work for the group on a volunteer basis.

The problem (or one of them, anyway) was that in June 2016, the center had filed a complaint with the FEC accusing the Trump campaign of illegally soliciting campaign donations from foreign politicians. The center followed up a month later by asking the Justice Department to investigate.

Ayer's error wasn't agreeing to work with the center. His mistake was that, even though he wasn't proposing to take on the Campaign Legal Center as a client, or to bill any hours, he decided it would be prudent to let Jones Day know that he intended to lend his considerable credibility to this group. He figured it would sail through the firm's conflict-vetting process. This was the same process that, without much hassle, had cleared the Trump campaign to be a client.

But when McGahn learned of Ayer's plan, he objected. A Jones Day partner shouldn't be permitted to work with a group that had filed a legal action against one of Jones Day's most prominent clients, McGahn argued. His protests were heeded. Glen Nager—a member of Brogan's inner ring—let Ayer know that he would not be allowed to work with the center. "There is no suggestion that the firm's interests would be advanced in ANY way by the proposed work," Nager argued to me in an email, while saying he didn't recall the specific incident. "On the other hand, there is a suggestion that the firm would face ethical, legal, branding, and/or revenue risk from the proposed work."

Ayer was flabbergasted and furious. On a couple of subsequent occasions, he tried to get clearance to do different projects at the Campaign Legal Center, to no avail. McGahn had asked for this work to be blocked, and Brogan's power structure had done the blocking. It was not up for negotiation.

Ayer expressed his grievances to quite a few people at the firm. Some—maybe most?—privately agreed with him. While Ayer still loved Jones Day, he came to be viewed as a lonely, proud voice of dissent about the toxicity of the Trump relationship. His colleagues admired the stand he was taking, but they sensed that he had fallen out of favor with the firm's leaders. Ayer retired in 2018; now he was free to publicly warn about what he saw as America's dangerous descent under his former employer's client. One of his first phone calls was to Trevor Potter, volunteering, again, to help.

I first spoke with Ayer in January 2021, the day before Joe Biden was sworn in as president. The insurrection that Trump had helped stir up two weeks earlier remained a raw wound. "I am disappointed that the firm made the judgment ever to represent Trump," Ayer said, sounding sad. "At some point they should have gotten off the wagon, because he is a scoundrel."

22

A NICE LITTLE CUSHION

In the weeks before the 2016 election, Trump, down in the polls, repeatedly warned about the election being rigged. He urged his supporters not only to vote but also to be on the lookout for fraud (which, the candidate neglected to mention, is vanishingly rare). "You've got to get everybody to go out and watch, and go out and vote," Trump bellowed at a rally in Akron. "And when I say 'watch,' you know what I'm talking about, right?" It was just the type of inflammatory rhetoric that would come to define Trump's presidency. His supporters heeded his call to action. The provocateur Roger Stone recruited volunteers to loiter outside polling places in Ohio and elsewhere.

The state's Democratic Party sued the Trump campaign in federal court in Cleveland, seeking a restraining order blocking these "poll watchers" from intimidating voters. The lawyer for the Democrats said Trump was using "racially charged calls for actions by people who will act like vigilantes." The Trump campaign's defense lawyer was Chad Readler, the Jones Day partner who had argued that kids should be eligible for the death penalty. Now he asserted that Trump was innocently urging citizens to take advantage of their constitutionally protected rights—he wasn't inciting anyone. Candidates like Trump, Readler wrote in a court filing, "are perfectly within their rights to encourage their supporters to serve as poll watchers." That was hard to dispute, but was it what Trump was really encouraging?

The funny thing was that, at about the same time, a number of associates in Jones Day's Washington office had sought clearance to serve as outside lawyers or poll watchers for Democratic campaigns. Historically, these requests had been a formality. There was a long tradition of lawyers volunteering their time to do things like this for candidates from both parties. This time, though, at least a few were told to stand down. (One lawyer told me she decided to risk her job for the sake of volunteering in Clinton's war room. She spent election night fretting about what would happen if Jones Day found out she was there.)

Back in Cleveland, a federal judge called a hearing on the lawsuit against the Trump campaign. Readler again protested that Trump's rhetoric about the dangers of voter fraud—unfounded and in bad faith as it might have been—was constitutionally protected speech. The judge, James Gwin, seemed to smell bullshit. Did Readler truly believe, "as an officer of the court, that there is such a thing as voter fraud that impacts elections?" Readler hemmed and hawed before eventually mustering a reply. "Your honor," he said, "I don't know. I'm not a political scientist."

Judge Gwin issued a restraining order. The next day, at Readler's urging, a federal appeals court in Cincinnati voided it. Roger Stone's activists were free to stand sentry outside polling stations. In the end, it was only the principle and the precedent that would matter. Trump carried Ohio by more than 400,000 votes.

ON ELECTION NIGHT, BEN Ginsberg was at MSNBC's studios at 30 Rockefeller Center. The newsroom was a buzzing blur of caffeinated energy. Ginsberg was on standby to go on-air to discuss the results. He and Bob Bauer, who had been Obama's White House counsel, were paired together, and they sat waiting at desks outside a glass-walled studio.

The two men had known each other for years. During the 2012

election, Ginsberg had represented Romney, and Bauer was working for Obama. Even as the two campaigns warred, things had remained cordial enough that Ginsberg agreed to share a stage with Bauer at a retreat for Perkins Coie, the liberal law firm where Bauer was a partner. Onstage in a hotel ballroom in downtown D.C., the two had chatted amicably about what it's like representing a presidential campaign. At one point, in response to a question, Ginsberg said something that surprised the Perkins partners. *There might not be political law practices at big law firms in the future,* he predicted. Representing politicians tended to spoil relationships with more lucrative clients, namely companies. What was the upside to attaching your firm's name to a politician that half the country would dislike?

Yet four years later, here Ginsberg was, working at a firm that had staked so much on the most polarizing major-party nominee in recent memory. As Ginsberg and Bauer sat together in the MSNBC hive, producers and data guys, in a state of increasing agitation, kept coming by to warn that Trump might pull it off. Some were cursing, others were crying, and Ginsberg, deep in liberal territory, did his best to keep a poker face.

Late that night, he dialed McGahn. He was at Trump Tower, trying to keep in touch with lawyers who were stationed all over the country, monitoring results and preparing to fight recounts in a few states. By the time he and Ginsberg connected, Trump had been declared the winner. McGahn sounded overwhelmed—like the rational, analytical side of his brain was fighting a losing battle to regain control from the emotional side, which was in hyperdrive. Ginsberg, too, felt a bit disoriented. Nobody had expected this outcome.

The next day, the world began coming to terms with what had just happened. In Jones Day's Washington office—home to plenty of liberals, notwithstanding the firm's embrace of conservative causes—some associates were in tears. It wasn't just that they were upset Trump had won. They were mortified by their employer's role in helping him. They felt complicit. It undercut their faith in Jones Day—and maybe, if they dared to admit it, in themselves, too.

The reality was that in the twenty-four preceding hours, nothing had changed about the nature of Jones Day's work for Trump. If he had lost, as everyone had anticipated, these idealistic attorneys wouldn't have been enduring the same moral and ethical reckoning. They would have done their best to forget this unpleasant episode, and they would have prayed that it didn't hurt the reputation of the firm to which they had yoked their own reputations, and then they would have gotten back to their day jobs, fending off threats to big companies' profits.

But Trump hadn't lost, and it was in no small part a result of Jones Day's work. The firm had helped professionalize a fly-by-night operation. It had plugged Trump into the Republican establishment. It had stabilized an unbalanced campaign by helping devise and create The List. It had neutralized lawsuits and ballot-access challenges. Would Trump have won absent Jones Day's assistance? Perhaps. But the long odds would have been even longer.

These doleful associates didn't know it at the time, but the orbits of Trump and Jones Day were about to achieve greater synchronicity than ever. The law firm had helped Trump seize the White House; soon it would help him govern.

That same Wednesday in November, Ginsberg's phone began ringing. He was getting call after call from people who hoped to position themselves for jobs in the Trump administration. Rather than trying to get the attention of folks inside the campaign madhouse, they figured it would be simpler to go straight to a well-connected lawyer at Jones Day.

IN THE WEEKS AHEAD, McGahn's phone kept buzzing, too. He would step into a hallway or excuse himself from a meeting to field questions or instructions from the incoming commander in chief. Then, one day around Thanksgiving, Trump was on the line, and he didn't have a question or an instruction. He had an announcement. "You're coming to the White House," the president-elect informed his lawyer. "You're White House counsel."

Here it was: McGahn's reward for nearly two years of loyal service to a man whom many would have long since abandoned. McGahn was prepared. He told Trump that he would be honored to take the job, on one condition: He needed to have complete control over the process of selecting federal judges. That would be a break from the tradition in previous administrations, where a committee of experts tended to debate the merits, substantively and politically, of various judicial candidates.

The bargain had been Mitch McConnell's idea. About a week after the election, the Senate majority leader had phoned McGahn to plot strategy; there were more than one hundred judicial vacancies, because McConnell had been refusing to hold votes on Obama's nominees. (When Obama entered office, there had been half as many unfilled judgeships.) "Just do this yourself," McConnell advised McGahn. "Don't have a committee. Don't get in all this bureaucracy."

Not one to be hemmed in by tradition, Trump agreed. Now McGahn was poised to wield immense power, and his law firm was positioned to reap the spoils.

THE TRUMP CAMPAIGN HADN'T done much to prepare for governing. For a brief spell, the hapless Chris Christie oversaw the presidential transition. Christie, the former New Jersey governor, had not long ago nurtured his own White House ambitions, hiring Jones Day to represent his campaign and blowing nearly $50,000 on legal fees. Now he was in the awkward position of working for a man whom he had fiercely opposed. It didn't take long for Jared Kushner, Trump's son-in-law, to plant a knife in his back. With Christie gone, the task of preparing for a new administration fell in part to Jones Day.

The firm's lawyers were responsible for identifying and scrubbing candidates for many positions in the White House and Justice

Department. The work was unpaid. Why was Jones Day willing to do it? For bragging rights, in part. But it also provided the firm with a unique opportunity to seed a new administration with its own staff.

About a month after the election, a Jones Day lawyer named John Gore contacted a bunch of associates. Gore was a recently minted partner in the Issues & Appeals group. He needed to enlist a small army of associates to work on filling federal jobs. It was largely grunt work: running background checks and scouring resumés and public filings for all the people in contention for the political posts.

To the surprise of some associates, Gore told them that the assignment was pro bono. The Trump campaign and the Republican National Committee both had money, and the presidential transition had a government budget; pro bono work was usually reserved for clients that couldn't easily afford to pay. More than one associate complained to a partner who helped oversee pro bono work at the firm. She agreed that this was inappropriate; it certainly wasn't consistent with the American Bar Association's definition of pro bono work.* It also felt overtly political. The partner flagged the issue to her boss, who flagged it to D.C. leadership. The answer came back: *Stop whining.*

TO BE SURE, THERE were other large law firms that also lent their credibility to Trump—sometimes with embarrassing results. Morgan Lewis, for example, was hired to devise a plan to isolate the president-elect from his businesses once he took office. In January 2017, a Morgan Lewis partner, Sheri Dillon, joined Trump at a press conference in the flag-festooned lobby of Trump Tower and assured everyone that there was nothing to worry about. Next to the lectern was a table stacked with what Dillon implied were doc-

* Gore said he didn't recall emailing associates about doing pro bono transition work. He and others also noted that the ABA guidelines are nonbinding and that Jones Day lawyers had volunteered to work on the transitions of previous administrations.

uments related to Trump's businesses. Reporters at the event noticed that the papers all appeared to be blank.

But Jones Day had done more than any other firm to help form the new administration, lining up dozens of people to assume senior positions. And lo and behold, many of those people came from the same place: Jones Day.

In the White House counsel's office, McGahn would be surrounded with his colleagues. Greg Katsas, a Jones Day partner who helped lead the Justice Department's transition planning, would be his deputy. Annie Donaldson, who had followed McGahn from Patton Boggs, would be his chief of staff. Three other Jones Day employees—James Burnham, David Morrell, and Blake Delaplane—would be heading there, too. Bill McGinley landed the White House job of cabinet secretary.

The Justice Department would also be jammed with Jones Day lawyers, including Noel Francisco, John Gore, and Chad Readler. Readler soon brought on Brinton Lucas, a Jones Day associate. Mike Murray, a Jones Day partner in Chicago, became counsel to the deputy attorney general. The crucial job of running the department's civil rights division would go to Eric Dreiband, who recently had helped defend Abercrombie & Fitch's refusal to hire a seventeen-year-old Muslim whose head scarf violated the company's "classic East Coast collegiate style," as Jones Day put it.

There were more. At the Commerce Department, a Jones Day lawyer, James Uthmeier, became a special adviser to the secretary, Wilbur Ross, whose company was a Jones Day client. (Uthmeier would later become chief of staff to Florida governor Ron DeSantis.) Stephen Vaden, who also had joined Jones Day from Patton Boggs, became a special assistant to the secretary of the Department of Agriculture.

Any new presidential administration draws heavily from the partnerships of major corporate law firms, and Jones Day attorneys had previously served under Obama and other presidents. But what transpired at the dawn of the Trump era was an extraordinary transfer of talent from a single law firm to a new administration. “I don’t know of a precedent,” Ted Olson, who’d served as George W. Bush’s solicitor general, said. For Jones Day, it marked the moment the firm achieved a position of unique, historical dominance in Washington, after decades of swelling ambition. Sixteen years earlier, Jones Day had proudly announced that a grand total of three partners had been tapped to join the Bush administration. Now there were more than a dozen—and the ranks would soon grow.

Brogan made it financially worthwhile for his lawyers to join the new administration. Jones Day generally didn’t award bonuses—lawyers’ compensation was set a year in advance, based on their and the firm’s expected performance. Now, though, Brogan handed out special payments to at least some of the lawyers who were entering the government. Greg Katsas received a bonus—“at the discretion of its managing partner,” as he explained in a government filing—that brought his compensation to nearly $4 million for the year. Francisco reported getting an “earnings supplement” that inflated his pay to $4.6 million. And James Burnham, an associate, received a bonus that roughly doubled his pay to $810,000.

Jones Day’s partnership agreement permitted Brogan to make these payments. But as word of them trickled out, some Jones Day lawyers were agog. “Oh, I don’t think that’s true,” one said to colleagues who mentioned Burnham’s payday.

“Yeah, it’s true,” a partner replied. When some lawyers went into the government, “the firm, meaning Brogan,” handed out bonuses.

“The firm sees it as prestigious for those people to move into the administration, so they all got a bump,” another partner explained. Brogan was “making their transition from the law firm life to the public life easier. . . . That was just a nice little cushion.”

A DAY OR TWO after Jones Day hosted the rooftop going-away party for McGahn and others headed into the administration, the incoming White House counsel took his seat on a black folding chair on the main platform of the inauguration stage. Nearly a year had passed since McGahn had stood behind Trump at the New Hampshire victory speech. Now he was among Trump's family members, past and future cabinet officers, former presidents, and bigwigs from both parties and the military. As Trump delivered his "American Carnage" speech, a drizzle dampened McGahn's bare head.

A quarter of a mile away, Jones Day hosted another reception. Every four years, the firm threw an inauguration event on the roof terrace. This time, a memo had gone out to Jones Day lawyers in D.C.: *There are a limited number of spots, let us know if you want to bring a client*. A couple of weeks passed, and another memo came, reminding folks to put their names on the list. A week later, another reminder. It turned out that not many people in the office were excited to witness Trump's inauguration.

Jones Day instead partnered with a women's networking group, Ellevate, to hold an "open house." "Light meals and refreshments"—including mimosas and Bloody Marys—were available from 9:00 a.m. to 4:00 p.m. Fewer than a hundred people showed up (not counting the black-clad Secret Service agents who prowled the roof with guns and long-lensed binoculars). Ellevate members mixed with a smattering of Jones Day lawyers and clients, including Mike Carvin and Noel Francisco and some energy executives from Texas.*

On this wet, gray day, the outdoor terrace wasn't enticing. People mostly clumped at tables inside a room named for Welch Pogue, who had so abhorred influence peddling in Washington. It was a genteel crowd, not a MAGA hat in sight. "It felt like a Georgetown cocktail party," one guest told me. Shortly after Trump finished his speech, a marine helicopter carrying the Obamas thundered over the subdued party on its way out of town.

* Carvin denied that attendance was sparse. "I remember a lot of people," he told me.

23

RICH, PISSED OFF, AND WRONG

The solicitor general of the United States is responsible for representing the federal government before the Supreme Court. Since its creation in 1870, the position has been one of the highest-ranking legal jobs in the U.S. government, subordinate only to the attorney general and the nine Supreme Court justices. The role has been a stepping-stone to seats on the high court (and, in the case of William Howard Taft, who became solicitor general in 1890, a way station before the White House). Aside from Scalia, Jones Day's most prominent alum may well have been Erwin Griswold—the thirty-fourth man to serve as solicitor general.* So it was remarkable that, as Trump prepared to take office, there were two Jones Day lawyers rumored to be on the short list for the prestigious post.

One was Mike Carvin. He was a leading Supreme Court litigator and a reliable conservative. Carvin insisted to me that, while he'd heard whispers of being in contention, he "was not interested" in becoming solicitor general. But he also must have known he wasn't cut out for the position. He lacked the managerial chops; one of the solicitor general's jobs is to oversee a fleet of deputies and as-

---

* Only two women, the Obama administration's Elena Kagan and the Biden administration's Elizabeth Prelogar, have held the job.

sistants. And he was too much of a bomb thrower for this dignified role, sometimes referred to as the "tenth justice."

The other candidate was Noel Francisco. He, too, was a talented advocate and a reliable conservative with an impressive track record before the Supreme Court. Unlike Carvin, Francisco was mellow. Everyone seemed to like him, even if they loathed his politics.

Alas, Trump was gravitating toward another familiar figure: Chuck Cooper. Cooper was the Reagan administration veteran who had started his own firm with Carvin and, on the recommendation of Ted Cruz, plucked Francisco out of his Scalia clerkship. Trump's nominee for attorney general, Jeff Sessions, offered Cooper the job, and Cooper in turn offered Francisco the role of his principal deputy. It wasn't a hard sell; Francisco jumped at the opportunity to summit the legal profession. "He was excited," Cooper told me.

Once he was formally nominated, Cooper would need to be approved by the Senate. Francisco, in a lower-ranking job, wouldn't. While the solicitor general's office sat vacant, Trump named Francisco to fill it in a temporary capacity.

Cooper helped prepare Jeff Sessions for his Senate confirmation hearings as attorney general. They were rough, which was not surprising given Sessions's hardline views. Cooper knew he'd be in for an equally bumpy ride—he had left a long paper trail as a conservative lawyer. That prospect so unnerved Cooper that he told Sessions he was withdrawing from consideration.

The White House mulled a number of other replacement candidates—George Conway and Brett Kavanaugh were reportedly in the running—but by March 2017, the president had settled on Francisco. It surely helped that he was already serving as acting solicitor general—and that McGahn had recommended him to Trump. Trump announced the nomination with little fanfare in a press release about a few other appointees. Among those who praised the pick was Ted Cruz. "Noel and I have been close friends for over two decades, and I know him personally to be a brilliant lawyer and a principled conservative," the Texas senator clapped.

This was a wonderful, historic occasion for Francisco, the immigrant's son, the pride of Oswego. He would later compare his role representing the Trump administration to his work for RJR. "Frankly the most interesting law practice is where you're representing clients that are not particularly popular," he told Catholic University students in 2018. "We had a partner at Jones Day who always described the perfect client as someone who was rich, pissed off, and wrong."

Almost as much as for Francisco, this was also a seminal moment for Jones Day. The firm would have its representatives implanted in two of the most powerful legal jobs in the U.S. government: solicitor general and White House counsel. The key was to make sure that Francisco got confirmed, which was not a given. There was the hyper-partisan climate in Washington, of course, as well as the fact that Francisco had taken on a series of high-profile conservative causes, including the *Zubik* contraception case.

In the spring of 2017, an email went out to Jones Day partners. Its message was that they were expected to sign a public letter endorsing Francisco. This was too much for some Jones Day lawyers, appalled by the Trump administration's first two months of norm-shattering shock and awe, including an executive order banning people from Muslim countries from entering the U.S. (Jones Day was among a number of law firms that filed Supreme Court briefs on behalf of clients opposing the travel ban.) One partner told me this was the moment she began looking for a new job. "I felt like I was being conscripted into supporting an administration I didn't believe in," she said.

That September, the Senate voted along party lines to confirm Francisco as solicitor general.

• • •

ONE DAY IN 2017, the phone rang in Kevin McIntyre's office at Jones Day. Warm and outgoing, with a head of curly orange hair, McIntyre had been at the firm for a quarter century and was the co-head of its energy practice. On the line was a White House staffer. "Kevin," he asked, "can you come over and explain how FERC works?"

FERC was the Federal Energy Regulatory Commission, which oversees the transmission and sale of electricity, oil, and natural gas. McIntyre probably knew as much about FERC as anyone outside the agency—he had represented countless companies before the commission and had even written a book about energy policy. He was also a Republican, and he dutifully traipsed over to the White House. He sat down in a small room and briefed the staffers on FERC, its powers, and energy regulation more broadly.

At the end of the meeting, a White House aide popped a surprising question: "Would you like to be the agency's chairman?" McIntyre later told a Jones Day colleague that he readily agreed; he considered it his dream job. That summer, though, McIntyre was diagnosed with a brain tumor. Trump nominated him anyway, and, following surgery and treatment, he took up the chairmanship in December 2017.

McIntyre's conservative reputation and history of representing energy companies raised the hackles of environmental groups, which unsuccessfully opposed his nomination. But as chairman, he steered FERC on what even environmentalists regarded as a sensible, middle-of-the-road path. Notably, he shot down a push by the White House to help coal and nuclear companies—a plan that appeared designed in part to aid a mining company whose CEO was a big Trump backer.

McIntyre would be at FERC for barely a year. He died, age fifty-eight, at his home in the Virginia suburbs on January 2, 2019, killed by the brain cancer. "We salute his high civic calling," a lawyer at Natural Resources Defense Council, a leading environmental group, told the *Washington Post*, lauding McIntyre's "fairness and evenhandedness."

• • •

TO FILL A VACANCY on the Consumer Product Safety Commission, Trump nominated another Jones Day partner, Dana Baiocco. The CPSC has a vital role: It oversees more than fifteen thousand types of products, from baby toys to garage openers, and it can issue public warnings about faulty products or sue companies to force them to recall those products. Since its creation in 1972—a response to Ralph Nader's movement for corporate responsibility and consumer rights—the CPSC has served as a last line of defense for people who unwittingly buy things that turn out to be deadly.

Baiocco, who got a journalism degree in college but opted for a career in the law, was not a natural choice for an agency whose duty was to protect people against powerful companies. Over nearly two decades at Jones Day, she had developed a specialty in, among other things, assisting companies that faced CPSC recalls. She represented Mattel when it got in trouble for knowingly selling toys that contained lead. She represented Yamaha Motor when its Rhino off-road vehicles revealed a tendency to flip, killing and maiming riders. She represented Honeywell when its face masks turned out not to protect workers against harmful substances like asbestos. And, like so many of her Jones Day colleagues, she represented RJR, whose products were the rare breed that, when used as directed, often had the predictable result of killing their user.

It wasn't just Baiocco. Jones Day, like many other giant firms, was known for impeding aggressive enforcement of consumer protection laws. A reflexive pro-corporate attitude was part of the firm's DNA. In a booklet for clients accused of selling defective products, Jones Day lamented how the CPSC and others had embraced the notion that companies "should be viewed as insurers of their products, for indefinite periods of time and regardless of how their products have been used." (That was a distortion of what most consumer advocates wanted, which was for companies to promptly pull unsafe products and for people harmed by those products to have legal recourse against those at fault.) "Companies need to be well armed and well prepared to defend against this trend," the booklet advised. "If your company has the misfortune to come under attack, give us a chance to be your lawyers."

The Senate confirmed Baiocco, fifty to forty-five. Her arrival, along with the elevation of another Republican as the CPSC's chairman, gave Republicans the upper hand. (This wasn't automatic, since commissioners serve staggered seven-year terms.)

Until then, the commission had been turning up the heat on companies that made dangerous merchandise. Penalties and product recalls were on the rise. Now, with the commission in GOP hands, that trend reversed. The number of CPSC-forced recalls soon sank to its lowest level in sixteen years. The commission's public warnings—traditionally a key method of spreading the word about perilous products—declined, too, as if the "mute" button had been pushed on the agency's audio. In 2019, the CPSC didn't penalize a single company for violating federal safety rules. It was unlikely that products across the board had suddenly become safer. A more plausible explanation was that Baiocco was helping erode the CPSC's core powers, ceding ground to the types of companies she had spent years representing at Jones Day.

Not surprisingly, Baiocco took issue with that characterization. She told me that since she arrived at the CPSC, commissioners had voted four times on whether to impose financial penalties on companies; she voted yes all four times. "I am and always have been firmly committed to following the governing statutes and to the important mission of the agency," she said.

But voting on penalties is a small part of the power that the commissioners wield. Consider the case of a popular three-wheel jogging stroller made by a company called Britax. The strollers, which sold under the brand name BOB (short for "Beast of Burden"), had a problem: Their front wheels kept falling off while they were in motion. Grown-ups who were pushing the strollers broke bones.

Kids who were riding in them lost teeth. The CPSC staff concluded that nearly 500,000 of the BOBs should be recalled.

Britax refused, claiming that customers were at fault and that the CPSC had previously signed off on the bicycle-style quick-release feature that was at issue. It was the rare company to defy the agency, whose power to name and shame dangerous products and their makers often scared businesses into submission. In early 2018, the CPSC sued Britax to force it to recall the strollers.

Not long after, Baiocco joined the commission. A *Washington Post* investigation in 2019 found that her arrival decisively shifted the balance of power. She and another Republican commissioner, Ann Marie Buerkle, blocked the agency from subpoenaing former Britax employees to testify, a crucial blow to the CPSC's case.* Months later, the agency dropped its lawsuit altogether and reached a settlement with Britax. The company produced a public-safety video and offered replacement bolts to certain customers. It was a far cry from the full recall that the safety experts on the commission's staff had concluded was necessary.

"I think it was good for consumers," Baiocco said.

For a lawyer like her, with great experience representing companies in similar situations, the postscript should not have come as a surprise: Britax failed to notify retailers about its safety campaign, as the settlement required, and some of its replacement bolts proved defective and themselves had to be recalled.

THE PROCESSION OF JONES Day appointments in the young administration was causing bitterness in Trump World. Some of the president's loyalists blamed McGahn for stocking the upper ranks of the government with corporate lawyers, the exact opposite of the Make America Great Again populists who might really shake things up in Washington. It looked like the Trumpies' initial in-

* Baiocco told me that the proposed subpoena "did not satisfy the agency's governing rules."

stincts about McGahn being a swamp creature were well-founded after all. Thanks in large part to him and his Jones Day crew, this presidency was shaping up to be just as corporatist as any other Republican administration. Maybe more so.

This was obviously not a concern to Jones Day's leaders. They set out to capitalize on their golden opportunity.

A group of about two dozen lawyers were sent on a "road show," traveling the country to meet with companies that either were or might become Jones Day accounts and to explain what to expect from the Trump administration. They talked about regulations and law enforcement and the new personalities and the power dynamics. This was the kind of promotional tour that plenty of law firms might schedule when there was a change in governments, and Jones Day had done similar events in the past. This time, though, the firm had the advantage of knowing what it was talking about. "We saw it as a client development opportunity," one participant told me. "The fact that we had represented the campaign was certainly a calling card." So was the fact that the administration—including some of the federal agencies where big companies were most likely to encounter flak—was occupied by Jones Day alumni.

The firm even began running ads touting its expertise—not something it did lightly. Glen Nager was generally required to sign off all ads, and he was a stickler. Once, the San Francisco Symphony hosted a charitable event, and Jones Day, as a sponsor, got space for an ad in the evening's program. The firm had a basket of preapproved taglines and images to use in situations like this: pictures of people rowing, phrases like "collaborating for clients." The marketing department produced an ad with a photo of three women performing in an orchestra. When Nager reviewed the ad, he flipped out. The image, while apropos of the evening's event, had not been authorized to be paired with the slogan that was being used; it was only permitted to go along with a line about "formidable multidisciplinary services."

The ads that began appearing online in 2017 featured a photo of the White House and were headlined "Insights on the New Administration." At the bottom was Jones Day's logo and motto, *One Firm Worldwide*. The ads trumpeted the firm's expertise in areas such as trade policy, energy, and so on.

Was it a coincidence that James Uthmeier was a top Commerce official and that Kevin McIntyre was headed to FERC—not to mention the hordes of Jones Day veterans in the White House and at the Justice Department? Perhaps. But there was no getting around the appearance, intended or not: The law firm was using its web of federal connections to trawl for clients. One legal scribe derided the promotional campaign as "tacky, tasteless, bush league."

The ads ran almost exactly forty years after the Supreme Court's decision in *Bates v. State Bar of Arizona*.

24

SUBSIDIZING TRUMP

On Inauguration Day, Trump's aides filed the paperwork to formally launch his 2020 reelection campaign. The candidate was the same, but the campaign was different. At least in theory, it was an opportunity, if Jones Day had wanted to find one, to disembark from the Trump Train with the firm's never-abandon-a-client principle intact. Jones Day wouldn't be abandoning a client. It just wouldn't be taking on a new one.

That might sound like an exercise in splitting hairs, and maybe it was, but Jones Day's leaders—Brogan and a small group of lieutenants—did discuss whether they would accept the assignment of working for Trump 2020. It didn't take them long to decide: Yes, they would. In some ways, this choice was nearly as momentous as the initial decision, two years earlier, to work for the first Trump campaign; the knot tying the firm to its client was now cinched even tighter.

Within weeks, Jones Day's political law practice—missing some of its key players, who had moved into the administration—again had its hands full. There were endless meetings and conference calls and paperwork to set up the legal infrastructure for the campaign to reelect the president.

At the same time, while the ugly 2016 election was history, the lawyering associated with it was not. A presidential campaign, one of the Jones Day partners working on this told me, is like a billion-dollar startup that goes belly up. As it winds down, there is a backlog—often years—of humdrum work to do. And that is the way things work in a normal campaign, which Trump's was not.

First and foremost, there were the various investigations into Russian interference in the election. The special counsel, Robert Mueller, as well as investigators on Capitol Hill, demanded that the campaign hand over millions of pages of emails and other documents. Before the campaign complied with these subpoenas, someone had to read all the stuff. This drudgery fell to Jones Day. The firm hired a consulting firm that had a secure facility capable of handling classified documents. A horde of associates and paralegals were given the thankless task of sitting in a windowless storage room and perusing documents on computers that were disconnected from the internet to ensure security. Jones Day also would handle investigators' requests to interview campaign staffers. (And it would defend Trump in cases such as the FEC's investigation into his campaign's relationship with Cambridge Analytica, the controversial British consulting firm bankrolled by Robert Mercer.)

With McGahn gone, Ben Ginsberg became Jones Day's point person for the Trump campaign. Ginsberg liked to tell people that he was hardly involved with anything Trump related, and it was true that he had a couple of associates to handle much of the day-to-day. But from the time McGahn joined the White House, Trump campaign aides were regularly talking to Ginsberg, who helped them strategize about how to respond to government investigators and to keep the searches for emails as narrow as possible. Brogan, too, took part in devising plans to help Trump, his campaign, and the White House foil the various investigations—or at least get them to end as quickly and painlessly as possible.

Jones Day could have left it at that. The firm was already irrevocably enmeshed with this unusual president—more than it ever had been, by orders of magnitude, with any president at any time in Jones Day's long history. It was already collecting many hundreds of thousands of dollars a year in fees from the campaign, making it by far the largest law-firm recipient of Trump money. But Brogan soon made a play for more work.

It had been McGahn's idea, one of his confidants told me. He wanted to be spending his time in the White House filling the judiciary with Federalist Society judges and, to a lesser extent, dismantling the "administrative state." Thanks to the legwork that he and his colleagues had already done vetting judicial candidates, McGahn had gotten off to a fast start. He had arranged for Trump to nominate Neil Gorsuch to replace Scalia on the Supreme Court and also had presented the president with nominees for various appeals courts. But what McGahn increasingly found himself and his team spending time on was Trump's personal legal problems.

McGahn wanted the president to have his own, competent counsel. The investigations into Russian interference in the election and, more recently, Trump's firing of FBI director Jim Comey were sure to drag on for a long time. (Recognizing this, White House lawyers waived ethics rules and allowed McGahn and five other ex–Jones Dayers to communicate with their former firm as they defended the president.) McGahn had zero interest in this being part of his remit. He and Brogan discussed whether Jones Day could be brought in to run legal strategy for the White House. Brogan would play quarterback, directing the different lawyers and plotting legal strategy on the president's behalf. Brogan was game. He met at least twice with Trump in the Oval Office to pitch Jones Day's services.

If Brogan scored this high-profile gig, Jones Day would be representing not just the Trump campaign but also Trump himself. Even some of Brogan's close allies told me they worried that the firm was fast approaching a point at which this would become a problem for clients. Big companies, after all, had been getting increasingly vocal about their opposition to Trump's most extreme policies and rhetoric. Brogan's advisers suggested that he pull back. He forged ahead. A team of Jones Day lawyers in D.C. was assigned the task of researching and tracking every angle of the Mueller investigation in anticipation of possibly getting the job. One partner, Geoff

Stewart, was roped in because he had worked with Mueller in the early 1990s at a law firm that later became WilmerHale. Stewart advised his colleagues on what strategies and evidence the special prosecutor might be pursuing.

In the end, Brogan didn't get the job. (It went instead to John Dowd.) The feeling among some senior Jones Day partners was that Trump wanted someone a bit more bombastic than Brogan as his defender-in-chief.

AT FIRST, WORKING IN the White House had been a goose-bump-inducing thrill for McGahn. He was one of a handful of staff with all-access privileges. It was an opportunity for him to give behind-the-scenes tours to friends, to show acquaintances from high school, where he'd felt a bit like an outsider, that he was now the ultimate insider. "It's kind of a cool thing, like I've kind of made something of myself," McGahn would say. Plenty of staffers could take guests on a tour; very few could escort them behind the velvet ropes that cordoned off the Oval Office. "I rated the ability to just take the rope down and say, 'Go on in,'" McGahn marveled. He found himself in the unusual—if not unpleasant—situation of noticing strangers in airports scrolling through pictures of him on their phones, before mustering the courage to approach him for a photo. (The bad news was that he was once mistaken for Sean Spicer.)

But when McGahn was interacting with his boss, he was a lot less happy. He and Trump had gotten along during the campaign, but it didn't last. Now McGahn was one of the few White House staffers who dared stand up to the president, which didn't go over well. "Their clashes were primal," Michael Schmidt wrote in *Donald Trump v. The United States*. Trump would insult McGahn to his face. Behind Trump's back, McGahn referred to the unpredictable president as "King Kong" or just "fucking Kong."*

* McGahn told me he'd always known the job would be grueling and that he never saw it as "something to enjoy."

The bigger problem was that McGahn was growing worried about his own potential legal exposure—especially when Trump pushed him to fire Mueller. McGahn refused and contemplated quitting. He called Brogan. The president was crazy, McGahn fumed. Maybe, he ventured, he should cut his losses and return to Jones Day.

Brogan's response was essentially: *Stop whining*. Being unhappy is "not a good enough reason to quit," he said. If McGahn threw in the towel, especially so soon after joining the White House, it would look bad not just for McGahn but also for Jones Day. McGahn, who had gotten as far as packing up his office, heeded Brogan's advice and stayed put.

MOST OF JONES DAY'S leaders were outwardly supportive of continuing to work for Trump. It was oh-so-easy to fall back on the platitude that the courageous American law firm must never abandon a client. "We're proud to have represented the campaign," Glen Nager told the *American Lawyer* in the spring of 2017. "Once a client is a client of this firm, we stand with them. That's what lawyers do. At least good lawyers." Plus, it was what Brogan wanted, and what Brogan wanted, Brogan got.

But there was no masking the awkwardness—in part because Jones Day, for all its work for corporate lawbreakers, also had many lawyers devoted to helping those in need. The firm had a strong tradition of encouraging its attorneys to undertake ambitious community service endeavors. The most powerful example of this was a remarkable pro bono project that Brogan initiated along the U.S.-Mexico border. The firm would send lawyers down to Texas and other states to help undocumented immigrants as they awaited deportation hearings. Until Jones Day arrived in 2014, very few of the migrants had real legal representation. The firm's attorneys would spend a week or two on the border, assessing whether the migrants had valid asylum claims and, for those who did, representing them in the chaotic immigration courts.

In early 2017—just as Trump was taking office—Jones Day

broadened this effort into what became the Laredo Project. The city of Laredo, Texas, was home to private detention centers where women and unaccompanied minors were locked up. Jones Day booked a block of rooms on the top floor of the boutique La Posada Hotel, and scores of lawyers cycled through, representing hundreds of women and children and giving "Know Your Rights" presentations to thousands of inmates. There were often ten Jones Day lawyers down there simultaneously—a huge investment of the firm's time and money. (Jones Day says its lawyers have dedicated nearly $200 million worth of billable hours to the project.) The law firm even hired investigators and lawyers in Central America to look for evidence to corroborate clients' asylum claims. So impressive was the initiative that some Jones Day clients sent their in-house lawyers down to Laredo to participate.

It was an inspiring sight: elite lawyers standing shoulder to shoulder with frightened immigrants on the cusp of being deported back to the lands from which they'd fled violence and persecution—and regularly securing their freedom. In dozens of cases where Jones Day lawyers won asylum for clients, the firm would buy them clothes and food and pay for their travel anywhere in the U.S. to be reunited with family members. "Those moments are etched in the minds and hearts of all of us who were there," said Laura Tuell, who oversees pro bono projects at Jones Day. "Each of us who were fortunate enough to have the privilege of representing these clients are unbelievably proud to be a part of the firm that created and supported this extraordinary initiative." One hardened litigator was so taken by the experience of working in Laredo that he cried as he described it to me.

But it was hard to miss the dissonance of a law firm simultaneously helping refugees and helping Trump. The migration crisis pre-dated Trump, but he exacerbated it through violent language and cruel policies. This directly undermined the lifesaving work that Jones Day lawyers had been performing in Laredo. And now, in the upper echelons of the Trump administration, it was former

Jones Day lawyers who were getting up in court to defend the president's actions.

For more than a few lawyers at the firm, it was heartbreaking. They were so proud of the Laredo Project, yet they felt that their firm—through its support for the Trump campaign and now their former colleagues' work for the administration—was hacksawing what Jones Day stood for and had achieved on the Mexican border. Jones Day has a "split personality," one lawyer in the D.C. office seethed to me. "We do good things [like Laredo] that are in direct opposition to the bad things we do."

Some of the firm's best-known lawyers began tiptoeing away from Trump. In a 2018 interview with a *Plain Dealer* columnist, Dick Pogue said, carefully, that while he supported many of the administration's policies, "I worry about his commitment to the rule of law." The columnist noted that, in private conversations, Pogue was considerably less charitable. Around this time, Kevyn Orr, the head of the Washington office and the firm's most prominent Democrat, vented to numerous colleagues that he was deeply uncomfortable with the work Jones Day was doing for Trump.*

Even so, the firm trundled on. In 2018, Ginsberg met with a small group of Trump staffers. In the past, Republican and Democratic campaigns had used specially created companies to cover certain expenses, such as TV ads. Ginsberg now suggested to Brad Parscale, the 2020 campaign chief, that Jones Day arrange a supersized setup for Trump. The advantage was secrecy. Private companies don't have to disclose their finances. If the Trump campaign routed its spending through this shell, which then doled out money for ads

* Orr told me that "the firm has always encouraged our partners, particularly our leaders, to express their thoughts on firm matters with each other." He said he had "no problem" with the initial decision to represent the Trump campaign. "We are a large institution whose attorneys have views that run across the ideological spectrum and political landscape. Our ability to practice together despite our personal views or opinions on certain issues or persons is one of the many strengths of our partnership."

and whatever else it wanted, the flow of money would be largely invisible to the outside world.

Jared Kushner soon signed off on the plan, and Jones Day helped file the paperwork to incorporate American Made Media Consultants. Nearly $800 million of hard-to-track spending would soon gush through the company.

WHY DID BROGAN EVEN want to be working with Trump? Sure, Brogan was a Republican, and the lower taxes and conservative judges that the administration was spawning must have appealed. So did the Justice Department's full-throated backing for greater religious freedoms. (Jeff Sessions unveiled his "Place to Worship" initiative—in which the department would sue localities that blocked the construction or expansion of houses of worship—at an event at Jones Day's D.C. offices.)

But Brogan was supposed to be looking out for Jones Day. How did the Trump representation further the firm's interests?

The money was, at most, part of the equation. Through the end of 2018, Jones Day had collected a total of $7.5 million from various Trump campaign committees, a sum that would continue growing over the next two years. That was a lot more than the firm had previously earned on federal campaigns—prior to the 2016 cycle, Jones Day hadn't pocketed more than $1 million in a year—but it still worked out to somewhere in the vicinity of one-tenth of 1 percent of the firm's total revenue during that period.

Virtually every time the Trump campaign issued a quarterly financial statement, there would be news articles mentioning that Jones Day had received hundreds of thousands of dollars, more than any other law firm, and it created the vague impression that the firm was raking in megabucks. But to anyone who worked in the industry, the figures revealed the opposite. Jones Day was throwing many high-priced lawyers at this work, and they were each racking up hundreds of billable hours. In terms of the workload, this was the equivalent of a large corporate client, except that a large corporate client could easily generate tens of millions of dollars in annual billings.

Jones Day lawyers—conservatives and liberals alike—told me they puzzled over the relatively small payments disclosed in the Trump campaigns' quarterly spending disclosures. Some became convinced that the firm was doing lots of this work basically for free. And for what? To sabotage their reputation? To scare away clients? "We were subsidizing Trump!" barked a partner who was close to Brogan. "I told everyone who would listen: 'We are fools. We are taking partnership money and subsidizing him!'"*

What, then, was the draw? Some of Brogan's confidants told me they suspected that the more criticism Jones Day got for its Trump work, the more Brogan wanted to keep doing it. There were few things he relished more than thumbing his nose—or his firm's nose—at Beltway snobs. "He loves to give prissy establishmentarians a kick in the balls," another longtime ally told me. (The irony was that the main focus of Brogan's firm was assisting corporate America—the very establishment he claimed to detest.)

But maybe there was another rationale at play. Perhaps the proximity to Trump increased the odds that Jones Day and its clients would get their way with his administration. And whether by design or by luck, that is what sometimes ended up happening.

* Joe Sims, a retired partner, told me that speculation about the firm having subsidized Trump was "almost certainly wrong. I have been told that all time for legal services provided to the campaign was appropriately billed and collected."

25

BIZARRE COINCIDENCES

The revolving door between the private and public sectors—lawyers, accountants, consultants, and bankers bouncing back and forth between their corporate jobs and the government—is by now a well-known phenomenon. There are certain benefits to the system. The government gets people who possess real-world experience and are acquainted with the ways in which well-intentioned regulations can have unexpected consequences. Private law (and accounting and consulting and Wall Street) firms, meanwhile, glean expertise about the inner workings of the government, which they can use to help themselves and their clients comply with complex laws and regulations.

But the downsides are insidious. There is a pronounced pattern of industry insiders arriving in Washington and continuing to advance their clients' interests—and then returning to the private sector, where they are rewarded with promotions and hefty pay raises. "Lawyers who come from the private sector need to learn who their new client is, and it's not their former clients. It's the American public," Stephen Shay, a retired partner at Ropes & Gray who served in the Reagan and Obama administrations, told the *New York Times* in 2021. "A certain percentage of people never make that switch. It's really hard to make that switch when you know where you are going back in two years, and it's to your old clients. The incentives are bad."

The incentives are similarly bad for public servants who hope one day to land a lucrative job with a major law or accounting firm. What better way to win favor with would-be employers than to make decisions that benefit them or their clients? And even if that calculus never enters officials' mind, even if there is no trace of a quid pro quo, the fast-spinning revolving door can erode fragile public confidence that government officials are acting in the best interests of taxpayers. In some ways, the perception of a tilted playing field is just as bad as the reality.

ON OCTOBER 13, 2017, FOUR Jones Day lawyers signed their names to an important agreement they had spent months negotiating with the U.S. government. More than a year had passed since the Supreme Court punted on *Zubik v. Burwell*, the case in which Jones Day, representing dozens of Catholic organizations, had sued to invalidate the Affordable Care Act's requirement that employer health plans cover workers' contraception. The deadlocked court had urged Jones Day, the Catholic groups, and the government to hash out a compromise.

That had proved impossible with Obama in the White House. But the Trump administration—staffed with Jones Day lawyers like Noel Francisco, who had brought the cases in the first place—was a much more conciliatory negotiating partner.

Early on, Trump signaled that he would abandon the contraception fight. "For too long, the federal government has used the power of the state as a weapon against people of faith, bullying and even punishing Americans for following their religious beliefs," he had said in a Rose Garden ceremony in May. In early October, the administration formally caved. The Department of Health and Human Services issued a rule saying that employers with religious objections to birth control could exclude contraceptive coverage from their health plans. The litigation—having meandered through the courts for five years—was moot.

The wrinkle was that something still needed to be done with the lawsuits. They had to be disposed of, closed out in the federal court system. And so the parties agreed on a simple settlement: The litigation would be terminated, and the government would promise not to force the plaintiffs to provide contraceptive coverage. Jones Day lawyers handled the talks. While the firm had said it was donating its services to the Catholic groups, the settlement included a provision to pay Jones Day $3 million to cover costs it incurred during the litigation.

The settlement was formally signed on a mild, foggy fall Friday in Washington. In addition to the four Jones Day attorneys, the signature of a single representative of the U.S. government was affixed to the settlement. His name was Brett Shumate. He was a deputy assistant attorney general in the Justice Department's civil division. Chad Readler—until recently a Jones Day partner—was his boss. Less than two years later, Shumate would leave the Justice Department and be hired as a partner in the Washington offices of . . . Jones Day.*

THIS WOULD BECOME A pattern.

In January 2019, Shamoil Shipchandler resigned from the Securities and Exchange Commission. A former federal prosecutor, he had spent the past three-plus years as the head of the agency's office in Fort Worth, Texas. While there, Shipchandler had made a name for himself as a leader in the regulation of cryptocurrencies. He was young and bright and had an active social media presence. Praise rolled in when he announced he was stepping down. "Shamoil was an energetic leader who wasn't afraid to try the unconventional," said the previous head of the SEC's Forth Worth office, a lawyer

* Matthew Kairis, a Jones Day partner who helped negotiate the settlement, told me he was not aware of Shumate being involved in the negotiations and that it was "silly" to connect this to his hiring. He said the $3 million payment was less than 10 percent of the costs Jones Day incurred in the litigation.

named David Woodcock. "He was well-liked in the office, and they will no doubt miss him."

Woodcock now worked in Jones Day's Dallas office, where his practice involved helping companies deal with the agency he had recently left. It wasn't public yet, but Shipchandler was preparing to make the exact same leap. He was in talks to become a partner with Jones Day in Dallas.

This might not have been noteworthy except for one thing. Toward the end of the Obama administration, the SEC had opened an investigation into ExxonMobil. The agency was looking into whether the company had accurately disclosed the value of its assets in light of climate change, which posed an existential threat to, among many others, enormous energy companies like Exxon. Was the company downplaying the risks of climate change and sugarcoating its financial condition to investors?

In addition to the SEC, state prosecutors in Massachusetts and New York were conducting similar investigations. Exxon had been trying to derail those state inquiries by asserting that the SEC was the only authority with jurisdiction over the matter. It was an odd argument for Exxon to make; what gave the company such confidence that the SEC case would be resolved more favorably than the state ones? As it turned out, though, the bet proved prescient.

The SEC investigation was being handled out of Shipchandler's Fort Worth office. In August 2018, the investigation was declared over. Shipchandler wrote a four-sentence letter delivering the good news to Exxon's lawyer: none other than David Woodcock at Jones Day. "We have concluded the investigation," Shipchandler wrote, and "we do not intend to recommend an enforcement action by the Commission against Exxon." This was a relief for Exxon. The company trumpeted the letter to the media, noting that the SEC was moving on "after a thorough investigation," which included a review of more than four million pages of documents that Exxon had graciously provided.

Now, months after Jones Day's client had notched a big win, Shipchandler was leaving the SEC, and Jones Day was quietly in the process of bringing him on as its newest recruit.

As one Jones Day lawyer acknowledged to me, the optics of this were not great. A person familiar with Shipchandler's version of events told me that everything was aboveboard. He hadn't started talking to Jones Day about a job until two months after the Exxon investigation was closed. There was no quid pro quo. Yes, Woodcock (aka Exxon's lawyer at Jones Day) was one of two people who had recruited him to the firm, but the other was someone whom Shipchandler had known for years. What's more, this person said, Shipchandler had disclosed his job discussions with Jones Day and other law firms to SEC officials.

Take all of that at face value. Shipchandler's hiring—on the heels of him overseeing an investigation that ended as favorably as could be for a key Jones Day client—was nothing more than a bizarre coincidence.* It reminded me of the time, nearly thirty years earlier, that Jones Day was getting raked over the coals for its work for fraudulent savings and loans. In the midst of the federal investigations into the firm's actions, Jones Day had hired a senior official at a federal agency that was conducting one of the investigations. That, too, had been innocuous, Steve Brogan asserted at the time. ("This type of thing happens all the time in Washington.")

After the S&L debacle, Jones Day had grown shyer about overtly wielding political influence. Now the firm was coming full circle—and an idealistic Texas lawyer named Josh Russ was about to experience it firsthand.

---

* In 2020, Woodcock left Jones Day for a job at—you guessed it—Exxon. Shipchandler left to go to Charles Schwab.

26

REDEFINING SHAMEFULNESS

Josh Russ grew up in tiny Robertson County, halfway between Dallas and Houston. His grandfather was a longtime prosecutor; his portrait still hangs in the county courthouse in the farming town of Franklin. Russ's father, a judge, would adjudicate sibling spats by holding "court" in his home office. Russ was raised to have faith that honest lawyers and courts and juries—the American justice system, in short—could make the world a better, fairer place.

When Russ was a kid, his dad would tell him how he'd look forward to facing off against lawyers from big-city firms who'd occasionally show up in Franklin. These hotshots tended to overestimate themselves—and to underestimate him. Yes, they got paid big bucks and wore nice suits and had prestigious clients, but they didn't have the faintest notion of how to work a Robertson County courtroom. They would calibrate wrong, and they would lose. Russ loved hearing those stories, and he decided that he, too, wanted to be a Texas lawyer. It was something he could feel good about. "I like to be able to sleep well at night," he would tell the *Texas Lawbook*.

After getting his law degree from Berkeley in 2010, and following an unsatisfying job at a large firm, Russ joined a smaller outfit, Reese Marketos, in Dallas. He worked on fraud and contracts cases. Then came his big break. The United States attorney for the Eastern District of Texas was hiring. Part of the Justice Department, the ninety-three U.S. attorney's offices nationwide serve as the primary investigators and prosecutors of federal crimes on a local level. In 2015, Russ, thirty years old, got the job. "I liked that Josh had East Texas values," his boss explained.

This particular U.S. attorney's office had a half-dozen outposts around East Texas; Russ worked out of one in a boxy, black-glass tower in Plano. It had both criminal and civil prosecutors. Russ worked mostly on the civil side, suing companies and individuals for misdeeds like fraud and false advertising. Russ was built like a basketball player, tall and fit, and he kept his light brown hair cut short, gelled, and combed back from his high forehead. He was good at his job, and after three years he was promoted to run East Texas's civil division. Sometimes he couldn't quite believe that he'd managed to land this dream gig at such a young age.

Not long after Russ had arrived in the U.S. attorney's office, its criminal side teamed up with the federal Drug Enforcement Administration to investigate the illegal prescriptions and sales of opioids. Opioid addiction and overdoses had become one of the country's most pressing public-health crises, thanks in large part to the successful sales and marketing of Purdue Pharma's OxyContin painkillers. As the prosecutors and DEA agents chased down leads involving doctors who were churning out thousands of bogus prescriptions, they were led to a Walmart in McKinney, fifteen miles north of the U.S. attorney's office in Plano. The pharmacy inside the sprawling Supercenter had become an opioid dispensary of choice for local pill pushers.

The more the investigators dug, the more they concluded that this particular Supercenter wasn't the problem. Or, to be more precise, it was only a small part of a big problem: Walmart pharmacies in numerous states had for years been filling opioid prescriptions that didn't appear to have any legitimate medical purpose.

The prosecutors soon discovered that Walmart's legions of local pharmacists had repeatedly warned corporate brass about doctors who individually wrote tens of thousands of OxyContin prescriptions—a sign of being part of a "pill mill." The response from headquarters was always the same: The pharmacists could refuse to fill particular prescriptions, but they were not permitted to cut off doctors altogether. In fact, they were pressured to keep dispensing drugs as quickly as possible. At one point, a Walmart compliance manager told colleagues that they should focus on "driving sales" rather than policing doctors. Meanwhile, the compliance unit didn't alert pharmacists to evidence it had collected pointing to doctors who were writing preposterous numbers of opioid prescriptions. And so thousands upon thousands of scripts for dangerous narcotics kept getting filled at Walmart stores nationwide, long after other pharmacy chains had cut off the offending doctors.*

To the prosecutors, the evidence was clear: One of the country's largest pharmacy chains was fueling the opioid epidemic by, at best, turning a blind eye to illegal activity. What's more, the DEA had repeatedly reprimanded Walmart for this kind of stuff in the past, and the government's sundry wrist-slaps had had approximately zero discernible impact on the company's behavior.

Walmart executives and their lawyers soon realized the feds were onto them. The company had long been represented by Jones Day. The partner in charge of the Walmart account was Karen Hewitt. Among other recent feats, she had defused a years-long federal investigation into the company's alleged violation of antibribery laws in countries like Mexico.

In May 2017, Hewitt asked the Texas prosecutors to meet with her and other lawyers for Walmart. They told the prosecutors that Walmart's pharmacists couldn't just refuse to fill prescriptions; that would hurt patients with legitimate needs. It was up to the DEA, they argued, to go after the prescribing doctors and the drug dealers who were taking advantage of Walmart. There was no criminal

* These are the facts as outlined by the U.S. Justice Department in public court filings. Walmart has denied wrongdoing.

wrongdoing, they asserted; if anything, this was a civil matter, to be resolved with a financial settlement.

The prosecutors in the room didn't buy that this wasn't criminal. Their view was that Walmart was acting like a giant drug dealer. There was no question how prosecutors would treat a drug kingpin: They'd aggressively build and prosecute a criminal case against him. That was the approach they should use with Walmart.

Even so, Walmart's argument that this was a civil matter led Russ to open a parallel investigation of his own—one that had the potential to culminate in the U.S. government suing Walmart, creating a public record of the company's alleged wrongdoing, and collecting damages.

Not long after, Russ came across a book that shaped his perspective on being a federal prosecutor. It was Jesse Eisinger's *The Chickenshit Club,* an exposé of how Justice Department honchos had lost the nerve to criminally charge powerful corporations and their senior executives. Eisinger, a Pulitzer Prize–winning journalist for ProPublica, argued that many federal prosecutors were so scared of losing high-profile cases that they took the easy route: reaching monetary settlements in which companies didn't admit wrongdoing. (Even penalties in the hundreds of millions of dollars barely dented large companies' quarterly profits.)

The book, which Russ checked out from a local library, enraged him. Why was it okay for a giant company to skate when normal people's lives got ruined for lesser crimes? He had not been brought up to believe in a system of unequal justice. The Walmart case represented an opportunity to challenge and hopefully overcome the Justice Department's timidity.

THE U.S. ATTORNEY FOR East Texas—this was Russ's boss—was a former county prosecutor named Joe Brown, whom Trump had appointed. In the spring of 2018, Brown instructed his prosecutors to inform Walmart that they were preparing to indict the company for violating the federal Controlled Substances Act.

Hewitt responded by seeking another meeting with the prosecutors. The marathon gathering, which took place over two days in May 2018, was in a large conference room in the U.S. attorney's office. Legal volumes and Texas-themed artwork adorned the walls. The prosecutors made coffee for the Walmart team, hoping to impart a little civility before things got combative.

Russ and his civil team by then were well on their way toward assembling a lawsuit. Walmart hoped to resolve the two cases, criminal and civil, at once. Hewitt and the Walmart lawyers spent six hours outlining the results of an internal investigation Jones Day had conducted into Walmart's opioid-dispensing practices. Hewitt acknowledged that the company could have done more to combat this crisis, but there was no evidence, she insisted again, of any crimes. Her team floated the idea of Walmart shelling out a settlement in the low nine figures, on the condition that no lawsuit ever be filed and that most of the evidence of the company's alleged misconduct stay out of the public domain

This was a nonstarter for Russ and his colleagues—especially the stipulation that the evidence would be swept under the rug. On the second day of the meeting, the prosecutors said they wouldn't accept anything less than $1 billion to resolve the civil investigation. A Walmart lawyer shot back that this was an unethical attempt to use the threat of an indictment to strong-arm Walmart into a massive settlement. Offended, Russ stomped out of the room.

A Jones Day lawyer, Jason Varnado, followed him into the hallway. Varnado had spent a decade in the U.S. attorney's office for the Southern District of Texas. The same year that Russ joined the Eastern District, Varnado had taken a job at Jones Day. Now, outside the conference room, Varnado tried to patch things up. "Josh, look, you've got a record settlement on the table," Varnado urged. "You can put your name on it. Come on!" It struck Russ as a clumsy and patronizing effort to butter him up. The two-day meeting ended with no resolution.

Russ, however, soon started getting the feeling that Jones Day's involvement might pose problems. A couple of months after the meeting with Hewitt and Varnado, he flew to Columbia, South Carolina, for a conference at the National Advocacy Center, a training facility the Justice Department runs for its prosecutors. A top DOJ official, Jesse Panuccio, gave a speech in which he said that attacking opioids was a priority for the department. Russ, pumped that folks in Washington shared his enthusiasm, approached Panuccio outside the lecture hall afterward. Russ mentioned that his office was preparing to sue Walmart. Panuccio asked him who was representing the company. Russ replied: Jones Day.

Panuccio arched his eyebrows. "Well, there goes half the department leadership," he said. "They're going to have to recuse themselves." As it turned out, that would not be happening.

Before joining Jones Day in 2010, Karen Hewitt had spent eighteen years at the Justice Department, including as the U.S. attorney for Southern California. She liked to boast about Jones Day's bare-knuckled strategy when it came to fighting the government. "We are not about self-protection," she crowed in 2015. "We will go adversarial."

After the unsuccessful settlement talks in Plano, Hewitt wrote a letter to the deputy U.S. attorney general, Rod Rosenstein. She claimed the Texas prosecutors had said they wanted to "embarrass" and inflict gratuitous pain on Walmart—in other words, they were acting unethically. "Walmart is a responsible corporate citizen and stands ready to engage in a principled and reasoned dialogue concerning any potential conduct of its employees that merits a civil penalty," Hewitt sweet-talked in a subsequent letter to DOJ. She asserted again that the prosecutors were unethically threatening indictment to coerce Walmart into paying an outrageously large penalty.

Russ took it personally. It was normal for defense lawyers to cast aspersions on prosecutors. That was part of the game, and sometimes it was even legitimate; there *was* such a thing as a prosecutor who abused his power. But Russ perceived Hewitt as taking things to a new level. She was making false allegations to a Justice Department led in part by her recent Jones Day colleagues. In a normal investigation in normal times, Russ might have laughed this off. But in the Trump era, when the president was fanning outlandish conspiracy theories about federal prosecutors, it wasn't remotely funny.

Hewitt's offensive worked. Rosenstein instructed his deputies to look into the matter; they concluded that the Texans didn't have the goods to justify an indictment. Officials in Washington called Joe Brown, the U.S. attorney, and instructed him to halt the criminal investigation.

While the Texans were irate, the edict didn't apply to Russ's civil investigation. By August 2018, a lawsuit was ready. The U.S. attorney's office organized a press conference to unveil the complaint. And Russ held meetings with the families of people who had died of overdoses from opioids they procured from Walmart. At one point, a widower sobbed as he described having to raise his daughters alone. "We can never repair your loss," Russ told the families, but he promised that he and his colleagues would hold accountable those responsible for their loved ones' deaths.

On a Friday in late August, a couple of days before the suit was to be filed, Russ got a phone call from Gus Eyler, a Justice Department official in Washington. Eyler had bad news: He'd been instructed to tell Russ not to file the complaint. Eyler sounded apologetic; Russ's takeaway was that higher-ups at Main Justice, as DOJ headquarters is known, had directed Eyler to run interference on Walmart's behalf.

Eyler, as it turned out, had recently gotten a new boss: James Burnham. Burnham was the former Jones Day associate who had received an extra year's salary on his way to the White House. From there, he'd jumped to Justice, and in the summer of 2018 he was named deputy assistant attorney general with responsibility for

Eyler's consumer-protection group. Now the division that Burnham oversaw was helping an important Jones Day client.*

Nor was Burnham the only Jones Day alum in the vicinity. The man right above him on the department's org chart was Chad Readler. Readler had remained in touch with his Jones Day colleagues. For example, he helped the firm line up a senior DOJ official to speak at a conference Jones Day was hosting. (That official was Rachel Brand, who months later would decamp for a top job at Walmart, where she, too, would try to thwart the Texans' investigation.) Readler was also working with Mike Carvin and other Jones Day lawyers on defending Trump in a lawsuit filed by protesters who'd been roughed up at a Trump rally. Given that ongoing contact, it was hard to imagine Readler turning a deaf ear to Jones Day's pleas for help with Walmart.

In any case, to Russ's fury, his hands were tied by political appointees in Washington. The civil investigation was still alive, with Gus Eyler now riding shotgun. But month after month, word came from Washington not to file the lawsuit.

JONES DAY WAS WELL acquainted with opioids. The firm was one of many working for Purdue Pharma. Jones Day's role was narrow but important: It was responsible for protecting Purdue's patents on its blockbuster painkiller, OxyContin. Over the years, more than a dozen Jones Day lawyers had helped Purdue either sue rivals for alleged patent infringement or fend off intellectual property claims filed by others.

Reasonable people might disagree about whether lawyers can ever ethically represent a company as sinister as Purdue—one that ignited a public health crisis for the sake of its founding family's fortune. "Not that there isn't room to represent corporations; that's worthy work," the Massachusetts attorney general, Maura

* Burnham told me that neither he nor Eyler had the power to forbid a U.S. attorney's office from filing a lawsuit.

Healey, told Patrick Radden Keefe, the author of *Empire of Pain*, about the Sackler family that owned Purdue. "But this corporation? These people? It's no different from representing a drug cartel, in my mind."

Jones Day was proud of its representation. Purdue was one of the clients that the firm boasted about as it sought jobs with prospective customers. The online bios of quite a few of the firm's lawyers—including John Normile, the partner who'd been involved in Christian Meister's firing years earlier—mentioned their roles protecting OxyContin. In some cases, these lawyers told themselves a feel-good story to justify their well-paid work. Some of the firm's recent assignments involved defending patents for a version of Oxy that was supposed to be tamper-proof. In theory, such a product couldn't be easily ground into powder and would be harder for people to snort or inject. Purdue even provided placebo pills to Jones Day lawyers so they could see for themselves that the newfangled product was indestructible. The lawyers viewed this as something akin to God's work. After all, absent patent protections, what incentive would Purdue have to produce a safer pill?

Not surprisingly, this turned out to be a distorted version of reality. The new patents allowed Purdue to market its pills as "abuse deterrents," but regulators would later conclude that there was no evidence that they deterred abuse. Arguably these tamper-proof pills were more dangerous, not less. Researchers found that they lulled users into a false sense of security, even though they were just as addictive as ever. Indeed, a study later found that the reformulated pills *increased* overdose rates. And, researchers discovered, already-hooked users who wanted to snort or inject opioids now turned instead to black-market drugs like heroin. There was not much for Jones Day to feel good about here.

THE ORDER FROM WASHINGTON to halt the criminal investigation into Walmart didn't preclude charges being filed against Walmart employees. Joe Brown's crew had someone in its sights:

the compliance manager who had seemed to urge a focus on sales over safety.

When Jones Day got wind of this, Hewitt shifted her focus to protecting the manager—and to using him as a cudgel to bash the Texas prosecutors. In September 2019, she wrote a twenty-three-page letter to Gus Eyler. She asserted that the Texas prosecutors had threatened the manager and had falsely told him that Walmart was trying to make him a scapegoat, apparently in an attempt to get him to turn against the company. As a result, Hewitt concluded, Walmart had decided to stop complying with the Justice Department's subpoena for the company's records.

Copies of Hewitt's letter also went to thirteen other DOJ officials. The highest-ranking was David Morrell. Morrell had replaced James Burnham, who had moved on to another role in the Justice Department. So now Morrell was Eyler's boss. Morrell, too, came from Jones Day. After clerking for Clarence Thomas in 2013, he'd been recruited to the firm, hitched himself to Don McGahn, migrated to the White House, and then hopped over to Justice, where he'd nabbed the career-making title of deputy assistant attorney general. Now his recent colleague, Hewitt, was seeking his help protecting one of the biggest clients of his once-and-future employer.

Russ wasn't the only DOJ lawyer taken aback by Walmart's aggression; some officials at Main Justice were, too. They saw it as part of a worrisome recent pattern of corporate defense lawyers leveling flimsy ethical allegations to advance their clients' interests. "These are like brushback pitches that cause a lot of folks to pull back from pursuing matters aggressively," one senior DOJ lawyer in Washington told me. He said the attacks have become increasingly common from national law firms, whose lawyers typically aren't all that worried about damaging relationships with outside-of-Washington prosecutors, who they're unlikely to encounter again. Even by those standards, he said, Jones Day's actions on behalf of Walmart stood out as extreme.

The Trump appointees at Main Justice summoned the warring

parties to Washington. This was itself a minor victory for Walmart. The senior DOJ official told me that all the Jones Day lawyers at Justice and the White House, plus the arrival of Rachel Brand at Walmart, were a potent combination—and that Karen Hewitt and her team played it to perfection. "There was a lot of sensitivity to not treating Walmart unfairly," the official said, and not all of it was grounded in the facts and law of the case.

At Justice, Morrell attended at least one meeting between the Texas prosecutors and Hewitt and her Walmart colleagues. So did Burnham. (Burnham's colleagues on occasion saw him in the hallway exchanging warm greetings with his former Jones Day coworkers.) Russ recalled Panuccio's comment in South Carolina about how half the department would have to recuse itself because of Jones Day's involvement. Now here he was, locked in what felt like existential battle with Walmart, which not only was leveling career-damaging personal allegations but was also flaunting its refusal to comply with a lawful subpoena. And the guys who were supposed to be on Russ's side were sitting across the large wooden table from their former colleague.*

Russ told his superiors that he thought they should go to court to force Walmart to comply with their subpoena. What else were they supposed to do when a company refused to do what it was legally bound to do? The response came back: no. Russ asked again: no. He pleaded. He was told to stand down.

THE NASTY SURPRISES KEPT coming, like Russ was stuck in a nightmare that wouldn't end. At one point, Ivanka Trump visited a Walmart near Plano to showcase the company's efforts to train workers. It was a vivid and perhaps intentional reminder of Walmart's cozy ties to the Trump administration.

Another time, a lawyer in a different U.S. attorney's office alerted

* Morrell and Burnham told me that nobody complained to them about their presence at the meetings.

Russ that Walmart had invited federal prosecutors from all over the country to come to its headquarters in Arkansas to hear about the great things the company was doing to alleviate the scourge of opioids—an apparent effort to curry favor with the Justice Department and pit prosecutors against each other. Russ raised such a stink that the gathering got canceled, but the fact that it almost happened without his or Joe Brown's knowledge left him feeling like he'd narrowly survived a lethal backstabbing.

Russ remembered how his father used to say that he loved when big-city lawyers came to small-town Texas. It might have been true, as his dad had always said, that these hotshots generally weren't all that good at lawyering. But Russ was beginning to realize that lawyering wasn't all that mattered. In fact, that's not even what Walmart's gunslingers were really attempting. They were playing a different game, whose essence was politics and connections and power. Russ didn't begrudge lawyers who zealously represented clients, but he resented what felt to him like Jones Day's underhanded tactics.

What was most infuriating was that the politicos at Main Justice seemed to keep falling for it, pressing Russ to negotiate with Jones Day to resolve the civil investigation. (Some of those officials told me they viewed Russ and his Texas colleagues as well-intentioned but overeager.) They set deadlines for Walmart to come to the table with a productive offer. The deadlines passed. And yet Washington kept giving Walmart more time.

This was too much for Russ. For the past year, he had been working around the clock. He was frequently traveling to Washington, taking him away from his wife and two young sons. He hadn't even told his wife what he was so busy working on—it was supposed to be confidential. Now, though, he had reached his limit. He told her what he needed to do. She agreed.

On a cold, stormy Thursday in October 2019, Russ drove an hour through a downpour. He had hardly slept the night before;

he faced the most gut-wrenching decision of his life. He walked into the U.S. attorney's outpost in Sherman, in a squat brick building with tinted windows. Brown was there, and Russ delivered the news: He was resigning.

The next day, Russ sent his colleagues a farewell letter. Walmart, he wrote, "has abused the department's fairness, largely ignored our subpoena, and scoffed at our larger work on behalf of all Americans." Russ recounted how, at that tearful meeting with those who had lost family members to Walmart's opioids, he had vowed justice. "I failed to make good on that promise, and I will carry that with me always. Now, cognizant of the many deaths it has caused, [Walmart] redefines shamefulness by claiming it is a victim." He went on: "Corporations cannot poison Americans with impunity. Good sense dictates stern and swift action when Americans die."

Russ also FedExed a complaint to the Justice Department's inspector general. It said DOJ's political appointees had improperly interfered in the investigation on Walmart's behalf. (Some DEA investigators on the case soon quit, too, furious that their years of work were flicked away by Walmart's lawyers and their sympathizers in D.C.)

In March 2020, Eisinger, the *Chickenshit Club* author, cowrote an article for ProPublica that revealed how the Texas investigation had been thwarted. Joe Brown went on the record to defend his office's work: "Walmart chooses now to attack the investigators, a tried and true method to avoid oversight. We are confident that once all of the facts in this matter are public, the hollowness of this criticism will be apparent." Two months later, Brown was out as U.S. attorney.

As he left, Brown issued a public statement, which alluded to his frustration with not being able to indict or sue Walmart. "We must win the fight against opioid abuse in order to save our country," he said. "But in order to be effective, we must be willing to prosecute all facets of the expansive network that feeds these destructive drugs into our communities. Players both big and small must meet equal justice under the law."

By the fall of 2020, many of the Jones Day lawyers that had populated the Justice Department had moved on to other jobs. Walmart's clout inside the agency was diminished.

Even Karen Hewitt had thrown up her hands. That October, a bunch of former U.S. attorneys who had been appointed by Republican presidents began talking. They decided to band together to write an open letter denouncing Trump's politicization of the Justice Department and endorsing Joe Biden for president. A couple of drafts circulated, and about twenty former federal prosecutors added their signatures. Hewitt's name was on at least three drafts, including one dated October 23. Other signatories were surprised to see her on there. Not only was Jones Day representing the Trump campaign, not only had the administration been filled with Jones Day veterans, but Hewitt had only recently been tapping those connections inside the administration.

The letter was publicly released in late October. "The President has clearly conveyed that he expects his Justice Department appointees and prosecutors to serve his personal and political interests," the former prosecutors wrote. By then, Hewitt's name had been deleted.*

Hewitt at that point knew the threat from the Justice Department had intensified. Gus Eyler and his colleagues at Main Justice were putting the finishing touches on a version of the lawsuit that Russ's crew had crafted two years earlier. It was hard to avoid the impression that Russ's noisy resignation—which had sparked not only media coverage but also angry letters from lawmakers about political meddling in a federal investigation—had forced the department's hand.

That October, the deputy attorney general, Jeffrey Rosen, con-

* Hewitt said that after thinking about the letter, "I decided against signing it."

vened a conference call with DOJ and Walmart lawyers. He urged the company to make a "serious" settlement offer to forestall the filing of the lawsuit; senior Justice Department officials were looking for something in the billions. A couple of weeks later, Hewitt delivered a lowball offer in the tens of millions of dollars, roughly half of what Varnado had previously pushed Russ to accept. Justice Department officials told Walmart to forget about settlement talks; they planned to sue. Now it was Jones Day's turn to be alarmed. Mike Carvin happened to know Rosen, and he arranged to come to Main Justice in a last-ditch effort to broker a compromise.

Carvin failed. When the Jones Day lawyers and their client realized there would be no deal, they resorted to a desperate tactic, one that showed they had run out of cards to play inside the Trump administration. In late October, Walmart sued the Justice Department and the DEA, asking a federal judge to preemptively find that the company hadn't done anything wrong. "Congress entrusted DEA—not pharmacists and pharmacies—with the responsibility, tools, and legal authority to strip unscrupulous doctors of their prescribing privileges," the suit maintained. "DOJ and DEA should not be allowed to outsource to pharmacists and pharmacies the job DEA has failed to do." (The suit was dismissed. Jones Day appealed.)

Then, three days before Christmas, the Justice Department filed its civil lawsuit against Walmart. "As a nationwide dispenser and distributor of opioids, and given the sheer number of pharmacies it operates, Walmart was uniquely well positioned to prevent the illegal diversion of opioids," the 160-page suit stated. "Yet, for years, as the prescription drug abuse epidemic ravaged the country, Walmart abdicated those responsibilities."

The lawsuit was teeming with the evidence that the Texas prosecutors had hoped, years earlier, to use to criminally charge the company. Thanks to Jones Day, that wouldn't be happening. The civil litigation, already delayed, was likely to spend years drifting through the judicial system, awaiting a trial or settlement. In the meantime, Walmart could continue to operate as usual.

27

NO VACANCY LEFT BEHIND

One day in August 2018, Don McGahn was in his spartan corner office on the second floor of the West Wing—he would tell folks that he kept it bare in case he ever had to leave in a hurry—when John Kelly, the president's chief of staff, rushed in. "I can't believe you didn't tell me you had decided to go," Kelly exclaimed. McGahn asked what he was talking about. "The president just tweeted that you're leaving once Kavanaugh is done," Kelly said.

McGahn, who had drawn Trump's ire for cooperating with the special counsel's investigation, stuck around another two months, by which time he had accomplished his mission. The Senate had just confirmed Brett Kavanaugh to the Supreme Court, the second justice that McGahn had chosen, Trump had nominated, and Mitch McConnell's Senate had confirmed. That was only part of the story, though. With McGahn in charge of selecting judicial nominees, the White House had placed more than 150 judges on the federal courts. Fully one-quarter of the appellate bench had turned over. It was a testament to McGahn's nearly single-minded devotion to the cause of reconstituting the federal judiciary—a planning process that had started years earlier when Trump huddled with Leonard Leo and others inside Jones Day's D.C. offices.

Back then, McGahn had assured the Federalist Society that they had nothing to worry about with Trump, and he had been true to his word. After he left the White House, McGahn liked to say how much it bugged him when Democrats groused that Trump had outsourced the judge-picking process to the Federalist Society. "We didn't outsource it," McGahn would recite, building to the punch line. "We in-sourced it!" He noted that his underlings in the White House counsel's office were all members of the group. At a Federalist Society event at the Reagan Presidential Library in California, he declared: "I am you. You are me."

This would be one of Jones Day's great legacies during the Brogan era. Through its successful representation of Trump and the installation of its lawyers in the White House, the firm played a crucial role in a once-in-a-generation remaking of the federal judiciary that would long outlast Trump. "Why the Left is triggered by Trump is because they understand they're in a Kafkaesque nightmare, that Donald Trump is going to be in their personal lives, ten, twenty, and thirty years from now," a gleeful Steve Bannon explained in 2019. "And the reason is Don McGahn."

Right before McGahn left the White House, Trump sat down with him in the Oval Office and offered to write him a letter of recommendation. McGahn didn't need Trump's help. Multiple law firms had already approached him with job offers. McGahn considered other fields, too; some of his predecessors had gone into finance, or run trade associations, or joined the paid-speaking circuit, or written books. But McGahn liked being a lawyer, and he liked Brogan, and he liked working at Jones Day. And so, he told me, "it was an easy decision." He would return.

The decision was made even easier when Brogan agreed to give McGahn, who had reported earning $2.4 million when he left for the White House, a seven-figure raise. Instead of being in the election law practice, he would now run the larger government-regulation group. (Jones Day permitted McGahn to keep advising McConnell on judicial nominations.) On a gusty Monday in March 2019, a few days after being interviewed by Robert Mueller's team of investigators for the final time, McGahn walked into Jones Day's offices as the firm's newest—and most famous—partner.

INSIDE AND OUTSIDE THE government, Jones Day had arguably done as much as any private institution to help Trump and his administration. It wasn't just defending the campaign against the Mueller investigation, which ended with a whimper. And it wasn't just McGahn's herculean efforts to protect the president and pack the courts. Once-and-future Jones Day lawyers had helped reshape a smorgasbord of federal bodies: the agriculture, commerce, and labor departments, the CPSC, and of course the Justice Department, which had been transformed into a political appendage of the White House.

Now Jones Day was poised to become a refuge for battle-scarred veterans of the Trump administration, who, given the president's toxicity, would be unwelcome at many law firms. The ensuing two-year exodus from the administration to Jones Day would further alter the identity of the 126-year-old firm.

Right on McGahn's heels came Rob Luther. He had been one of McGahn's assistants in the White House counsel's office, a crucial cog in the judge-selecting machine that McGahn had assembled. (While in that post, Luther also helped Jones Day lawyers get jobs in the administration, passing on their résumés to the firm's alums in senior government posts.) Luther wasn't a big gun, but he still swaggered. A Jones Day lawyer bumped into him at a cocktail party shortly after Luther joined the firm. The lawyer asked Luther what it had been like to work in the White House. It was just small talk, an icebreaker. Luther missed the cue. "We did it," he raved, eyes wide. "We reshaped the judiciary. We changed the country."

In June 2019, Schuyler Schouten joined from the White House. Then came Brett Shumate from Justice. He was the lawyer who had signed off on the government's settlement of the Obamacare contraception lawsuit. "The insights and understanding he brings to regulatory matters will immeasurably benefit our clients," McGahn said.

A few months later, John Gore returned. He was the lawyer who, following Trump's victory in 2016, had raised eyebrows inside Jones Day by inviting associates to work on the transition on a pro bono basis. His stint in the government had raised even more eyebrows. The Trump administration had tried to add to the 2020 Census a question about people's citizenship. It seemed like an attempt to deter immigrants in Democrat-heavy parts of the country from participating in the census, and when lawsuits challenged the inclusion of the question, the administration scrambled to find apolitical rationales. One came from Gore. He claimed that knowing people's citizenship would help the Justice Department enforce the Voting Rights Act—a hard-to-keep-a-straight-face argument given the president's general disinterest in voting rights. Gore was accused in court of covering up the raw political motive and of providing false testimony. In the end, federal courts blocked the inclusion of the question, finding that the voting-rights rationale was a pretext. The courts didn't reach a conclusion on whether Gore had lied, which a federal judge emphasized was different from finding that he did not lie.*

Rounding out this first wave was Noel Francisco. He announced his departure as solicitor general in June 2020. By then he had argued seventeen cases before the Supreme Court. He'd defended Trump's ban on travelers from Muslim countries. He'd eroded the power of labor unions. He'd protected a Colorado baker's right to not make a wedding cake for a gay couple. He'd beaten back an injunction that would have blocked funding for a wall along the Mexican border. The month after stepping down as solicitor general, he rejoined Jones Day. Like McGahn, he'd entertained other

---

* Gore told me: "I did not cover up anything and never provided false testimony. The accusations to that effect are false, baseless, and represent the worst of divisive politics."

offers, but he loved the firm. Another factor in returning, he told me, was that he admired "the way the firm stands by its clients even when some of them are unpopular and subject to unfair attacks from the press and others."

Having the most recent solicitor general and White House counsel on staff—not to mention all the others—afforded undeniable bragging rights to Jones Day. But it also deepened the growing cultural chasm inside the firm. Quite a few lawyers told me this influx from Team Trump was a breaking point. They'd been willing to swallow the fact that their firm worked for the Trump campaign. They had managed to wave that away as an unfortunate accident. But welcoming back the men who had been entwined with what felt like a poisonous, lawless administration? "That is the firm giving its imprimatur," a lawyer in the D.C. office said, echoing others. "It's not an accident. It's an endorsement."

WHILE MCGAHN WAS IN the White House, there had been a saying among some Republicans at Jones Day: *No vacancy left behind.* It was a nod, of course, to how many conservatives McGahn was embedding in the judiciary. But it had a more specific, close-to-home meaning, too: Jones Day lawyers were among those ending up on the bench.

Greg Katsas had been first. Trump nominated him to the powerful D.C. federal appeals court in September 2017. Katsas, a longtime Jones Day partner who had also worked in George W. Bush's Justice Department, had gone with McGahn to the White House counsel's office. Now he was getting a lifetime appointment to the country's second-highest court.

Nine months later, Trump nominated two men to the federal appeals court in Cincinnati: Eric Murphy and Chad Readler. Murphy was the state solicitor of Ohio; before that, he'd worked in Jones Day's Columbus office, alongside Readler. They were now joining the same Cincinnati appeals court that Readler in 2016 had persuaded to overturn an injunction against Trump and his "poll watchers." (They'd sit on the Sixth Circuit with a third Jones Day alum, Jeffrey Sutton, who'd been there for fifteen years.) Katsas swore Readler in as a judge in a Justice Department conference room in Washington. "We're very proud," Jones Day cheered in a press release.

Then there was Stephen Vaden, who'd followed Ginsberg and McGahn from Patton Boggs to Jones Day. As an associate at Jones Day, he'd distinguished himself by defending state voter-ID laws. Vaden landed at the Department of Agriculture, and after a few weeks as an adviser, he was promoted by McGahn to general counsel. ("I am honored to serve and to have Don's and your confidence," Vaden chirped in a thank-you note after Rob Luther delivered the good news.) Vaden was unpopular inside the USDA, its employees resenting his far-right ideology and antipathy to the unionized workforce. In 2020, the White House came through with another promotion for Vaden. This time, it was a lifetime appointment to the U.S. Court of International Trade.

Finally, Kathryn Mizelle. She'd been lured to Jones Day (and its $400,000 signing bonuses) after clerking for Clarence Thomas in 2019. "I selected Jones Day in large part because I wanted to do high-caliber appellate work with excellent attorneys," Mizelle explained in a promotional video. She was sitting in a wood-paneled room, a string of pearls around her neck. "Jones Day's reputation precedes itself as being one of the premier appellate practices, both here in D.C. but importantly for me in many areas of the country. And I hope to get back to Florida where I'm from, and I wanted to be able to have that same high caliber of work regardless of keeping a D.C.-centric practice."

Mizelle soon got her wish to return to Florida. In 2020, Trump nominated her to be a federal judge in Tampa. She was thirty-three years old, and the American Bar Association deemed her "not qualified" because of her lack of experience, noting, among other deficits, that she had never tried a case as lead or even co-counsel. The Senate confirmed her anyway. (In April 2022, Mizelle would make national headlines by striking down the Biden administration's requirement that people wear masks on planes and other transportation.)

Mizelle's husband, Chad, had worked in Trump's White House and Department of Homeland Security. A few months after Kathryn got her lifetime judgeship, Jones Day hired Chad to work in its Miami office.

28

FEARMONGERING

Ben Ginsberg's office at Jones Day was like a shrine to the old Republican Party. Its walls and shelves were crowded with campaign artifacts that he had collected on the trail with Bush and Romney. There were campaign buttons and convention placards and old political posters. In the summer of 2020, with the neoclassical building largely deserted because of Covid, Ginsberg started boxing the stuff up.

Week by week, Ginsberg had been feeling worse about his work on the Trump campaign. The president was intensifying his rhetoric about the risk of a rigged election, and he and his Republican Party had essentially declared war on mail-in voting and other policies that might encourage democratic participation at a time when large swaths of the country were under lockdown. At one point, Ginsberg flagged his discomfort to Brogan, describing Trump's rhetoric as "beyond the pale." Brogan nodded and said he agreed. Another time he complained to Michael Glassner, a senior Trump campaign aide. Not only did Ginsberg object to what Trump was saying, but it was just stupid politics, he noted. Why oppose mail-in voting in the middle of a pandemic? (Glassner dismissed Ginsberg as an elitist and a prima donna.)

Other Jones Day lawyers, too, were getting anxious that Trump was laying the groundwork to try to overturn the election results if they didn't go his way—and that Jones Day would end up getting sucked into the ensuing disaster. What would happen if Trump or his allies asked the firm to take on a case to challenge the election results? To sow doubts about the integrity of those results or the vote-counting process? To defend Trump if he refused to leave the White House? These were crucial questions for Jones Day, the culmination of five years of having stood by an increasingly radical leader. For how long would the firm invoke its obligation to remain loyal to even the most dangerous clients?

In conversations with other partners, Ginsberg argued that Jones Day should preemptively draw a series of bright lines: It would not take cases that called into question the fairness of the election. It would not take cases in which it argued for voting restrictions, such as by banning ballot drop-boxes or discouraging the use of absentee voting. It would not participate in the further erosion of democratic norms.

Ginsberg, of course, was no political pacifist. This was the guy who, decades earlier, had launched Project Ratfuck to divide Democrats. He had helped attack John Kerry's decorated record in Vietnam. But this felt like a dangerous, decisive moment. The way Ginsberg saw it, no believer in the rule of law—and certainly no respectable law firm—should flirt with the antidemocratic notions that Trump and more than a few of his backers were peddling. Ginsberg was sixty-nine years old, and he didn't want his last presidential campaign to involve helping a demagogue destroy democracy. It was time to take a stand.

That summer, Ginsberg, his neatly trimmed reddish beard long since having faded to white, told Brogan he was leaving the firm. The process of extracting someone from the Jones Day partnership normally took many months; Ginsberg wanted to accelerate it so that he could leave by Labor Day—and well before the November election. Brogan didn't try to talk Ginsberg out of retiring. When Ginsberg told McGahn, McGahn laughed it off. "You'll be back in January when you get bored," he predicted.

Ginsberg doubted it. He left the office for the final time the last week of August. Days later, he was booked to appear on NBC's *Meet the Press* to discuss the homestretch of the presidential race. Ginsberg would be on with the Democratic lawyer Marc Elias. Beforehand, Ginsberg reached out to Elias and asked him to please not paint him as a pro-Trump vote suppressor. Elias didn't know what to make of this, but he had enough respect for Ginsberg that he agreed to pull his punches.

"So, Ben, welcome to retirement, I guess," Chuck Todd, the *Meet the Press* host, said as he introduced Ginsberg on TV. Viewers were treated to twelve parched minutes of discourse about the minutiae of state laws governing the counting of votes. When Todd asked Ginsberg whether Trump was inviting fraud by encouraging his supporters to try to vote twice, Ginsberg dodged, referring to Trump's "mangled syntax." ("What's new?" Elias snarked in the background, and Ginsberg chuckled. It was the closest the show got to drama.) Ginsberg didn't condone Trump's efforts to question the integrity of the election, but he didn't denounce them either.

Todd looked bored. "Ben, good luck with retirement," he said, wrapping things up. "It'll suck you back in, my friend."

"It may," Ginsberg allowed.

Two days later, it became clear that Ginsberg had no intention of fading away quietly. He had written a fiery opinion piece for the *Washington Post* condemning the entire Republican apparatus, which Ginsberg said was complicit with the president's ongoing assault on democracy. The piece ran on September 8, two months before Election Day. "The president's actions—urging his followers to commit an illegal act [by voting twice] and seeking to undermine confidence in the credibility of election results—are doubly wrong," Ginsberg wrote. He blasted Trump and the Republican Party for fearmongering about voter fraud to help the GOP win more votes: "transactional hypocrisy designed to provide an electoral advantage," as Ginsberg put it. "The president's rhetoric has put my party in the position of a firefighter who deliberately sets fires to look like a hero putting them out. Republicans need to take a hard look before advocating laws that actually do limit the franchise of otherwise qualified voters. Calling elections 'fraudulent' and results 'rigged' with almost nonexistent evidence is antithetical to being the 'rule of law' party."

These were strong words, and they were made stronger because Ginsberg was a prominent Republican lawyer who, until very recently, had been representing the Trump campaign. Inside that campaign, Michael Glassner was already irate that Ginsberg was bailing so soon before the election. The *Post* piece felt like a betrayal. Glassner called Jones Day and lodged a complaint that Ginsberg, by attacking his recent client, was violating professional ethics.

To Ginsberg, this was exactly backward. Sticking to his core principles was the *embodiment* of ethics—even if it meant turning his back on a client. He couldn't afford to be complicit any longer.

Marc Elias read Ginsberg's piece in the *Post*. Now it made sense why he'd asked Elias, before *Meet the Press,* to avoid tarring him as part of the problem. Elias called Ginsberg. "Thank you," he said, "for standing up for democracy."

IN 2016, PENNSYLVANIA HAD been one of the formerly blue states that sent Trump to the White House; he nosed out Hillary Clinton by 44,000 votes out of nearly six million cast. Four years later, the Keystone State was again shaping up as a battleground. Trump, Biden, and their running mates had been crisscrossing the commonwealth, from rusty steel towns in the west to posh Philadelphia suburbs in the east. In the days before the election, most polls had Biden up by a few percentage points, but at least one gave Trump a slender lead, and in any case, polls were sometimes wrong. This thing was going to be close.

The previous year, the Pennsylvania legislature had dramatically expanded the use of mail-in voting. Now just about anyone could do it. This turned out to be a fortuitous change, since an airborne pandemic would soon transform in-person voting (and so many other once-routine activities) into risky endeavors. The only catch was that ballots had to be received by Election Day.

Normally this would not have posed a problem. But in the fall of 2020, the mail service had slowed to approximately the pace of chilled molasses. What's more, it had grown unpredictable. Sometimes letters zipped through the system; on other occasions they vanished for weeks. Maybe it was because so many stuck-at-home Americans were relying on Amazon and other delivery services. Maybe it was because the U.S. Postal Service was dysfunctional. Maybe it was both and more. Whatever the cause, there was no escaping the effect: People who sent their absentee ballots days before the election now risked having their votes lost to the sluggish and unreliable mail service.

At the urging of Pennsylvania's Democratic secretary of state, the commonwealth's Supreme Court in September 2020 concluded that—due to the combination of the importance of mail-in voting during a pandemic and the chaos engulfing the postal service—the requirement that ballots be received by Election Day risked disenfranchising voters and violating the state constitution's guarantee of "free and equal elections." The Pennsylvania court ordered that the deadline be extended by three days.

On its face, this shouldn't have been controversial. Nobody disputed that the pandemic had slowed the mail service—a circumstance that the legislature could not have anticipated when it crafted the law. Nor could anyone dispute (at least in good faith) that as a result of these unforeseeable events, maintaining the prior deadlines was likely to result in otherwise legitimate votes going uncounted.

But Trump had spent months railing against mail-in voting, and Republicans suspected that these ballots would skew heavily Democratic. And so the Pennsylvania Republican Party set out to enforce the Election Day deadline—and, in effect, to make it harder for those mail-in votes to count. To do that, the party turned to Jones Day.

The lead lawyer on the case was John Gore. He unfurled a series of arguments that appeared tailor-made to harm Democrats. His goal was to get the U.S. Supreme Court to strike down Pennsylvania's three-day extension. The foundation of his claim was that the extension violated the legislature's intent and that by granting those extra days, the state was essentially allowing "voters to cast or mail ballots after Election Day. . . . That outcome cannot be reconciled with federal statutes establishing a uniform nationwide Election Day." This was not true—the Pennsylvania court had specifically said that ballots needed to be postmarked by Election Day. But Gore was seizing on—in fact, his entire argument seemed to hinge on—a thin slice of the Pennsylvania ruling: If late-arriving ballots had illegible or missing postmarks, they would be presumed valid absent evidence to the contrary.

Gore claimed that this was an invitation to abuse. But how? And why? What incentive would people have to vote a day late? It conferred no advantage. It is "common sense" that "voters will know and seek to comply with the widely-publicized November 3 deadline for mailing ballots," a group of twelve prominent Republican officials from the Reagan and two Bush administrations wrote in a court filing that rebutted Gore's arguments. They added that rejecting Gore's claims "by the broadest majority possible will benefit this court, our country, and its precious tradition of the peaceful retention or transfer of power."

At the same time, Gore and Jones Day were representing Trump and the Republican Party on another matter involving Pennsylvania's absentee and mail-in ballots. In this case, they were trying to force county election boards to toss out ballots with signatures that they didn't think matched the voter registration records already on file. Otherwise, Gore said in a court filing, the door would be opened to "the counting of fraudulent mail-in and absentee ballots." He was giving voice—and legal backing—to the president's unsubstantiated fearmongering about the possibility of an election tainted by fraud. About two weeks before the election, the state supreme court rejected his claim as not being grounded in the law.

Gore and his colleagues framed these as principled arguments about weighty legal matters. But nobody disputed the bottom line, which was that he and Jones Day were advocating courses of action that would almost certainly disenfranchise voters.

AS THE RESULTS TRICKLED in on Election Night, Pennsylvania was tilting in Trump's favor. At one point the president led by nearly 700,000 votes. Trump declared victory.

But there were a lot of mail-in ballots—well over 2.6 million in the end—and those would take time to tally. The day after the election, with Trump's lead dwindling, his lawyers filed a motion to join the litigation over Pennsylvania's three-day extension, which Jones Day was trying to get the U.S. Supreme Court to intervene on. Trump made clear that he was pinning his hopes in large part on this action. The outcome, his team wrote in a motion, "may well dictate who will become the next president."

Two days later, the Friday after the election, Gore filed a Supreme Court petition directly to Justice Samuel Alito. It asked the court to order Pennsylvania to segregate any mail-in ballots that arrived after Election Day—and to stop counting them. Gore raised questions about whether the state's county election boards were properly handling the late-arriving ballots and warned that the state was at risk of mixing "invalid" votes with legitimate ones—without presenting any evidence that this was actually happening. Within hours, Alito ordered that the election boards keep late-arriving ballots separate.

As it turned out, this wouldn't matter. Barely 10,000 mail-in ballots arrived during the three-day extension period, and by the weekend after the election Biden was up by more than 30,000 votes in Pennsylvania. (His margin ultimately would be more than 80,000.) At 11:25 a.m. on Saturday, November 7, the Associated Press called Pennsylvania—and with it, the whole election—for Biden. In the end, more than three out of every four mail-in ballots went for Biden. It was easy to see why Republicans had been so eager to curtail the counting of those votes.

Jones Day would later insist that the firm was simply raising legitimate, hard-to-settle constitutional questions that only the Supreme Court could adjudicate. As Mike Carvin put it in an email to me, "there is an obvious, dispositive, universally recognized distinction between a (pre-election defensive) challenge to *voting rules as unconstitutional* . . . and a post-election challenge alleging that the election was stolen because voting rules were broken when the ballots were cast and counted. The former is universally accepted as being in the best traditions of the bar because it is, among other things, the only way to determine whether a voting rule is constitutional or not." (The firm didn't participate in the outlandish vote-rigging lawsuits that Trump and his allies would file in the weeks ahead.)

This blurred a basic fact: Jones Day and its lawyers were trying to stop votes from being counted—not because they thought there was something improper underway (there was zero evidence of that), but because they detected an opportunity to use the law to give their side a political edge. In the firm's calculus, the consequences—fanning fears of fraud that would, two months later, erupt into a violent assault on democracy—were immaterial.

In short, these lawyers were operating just as they had been programmed to do. The same go-all-the-way instincts that led down this road in Pennsylvania had also spurred Jones Day to coach witnesses in the Abbott Laboratories depositions, to make a $10,000 campaign contribution on Charles Keating's behalf, to hurl ethical allegations to help Walmart, to threaten a small Massachusetts town that dared challenge Big Tobacco. The law had long ago ceased to serve as a vehicle for achieving justice, for assuring fairness. It had become something to exploit. And Jones Day—and, for that matter, the entire modern legal industry—had become really good at doing exactly that.

29

WE DISSENT

A week and a half after the election, Kevyn Orr convened back-to-back videoconference calls for Jones Day's lawyers in Washington. The son of a teacher-turned-school-superintendent (mom) and a teacher-turned-minister (dad), Orr had joined Jones Day in 2001 after years of serving as a lawyer for various arms of the federal government. He was impressed by the firm's "stellar reputation for integrity and superior legal work." Orr was friendly and charismatic and "very conscientious about being an attorney of color in a big law firm," one of his former colleagues, Ritu Cooper, told me. He went out of his way to mentor young lawyers and "has a way of making everyone feel special and important."

For years, Orr had been privately grumbling to colleagues about his distaste for the work that the D.C. office—of which he was ostensibly in charge—was performing for Trump. It was more than disliking Trump's politics. Orr told other lawyers that he feared that Jones Day was debasing itself through its close ties to an administration that had little interest in the rule of law. Orr loved Jones Day, and he admired Brogan, and he worried that the stain on the firm's reputation could be dark and indelible.

Now his fears were being realized. In the days after the election, as Trump made clear that he would not be going quietly, that he would resort to dangerous tactics to cling to power, the outside world began waking up to the role that Jones Day had played for the past five years in getting Trump into office and keeping him there. And with the action in Pennsylvania, Jones Day was arming Trump with ammunition to stop the vote-counting and preserve his fast-shrinking lead.

In San Francisco, activists on November 6 created a 240-foot mural on the street outside Jones Day's offices. On a rust-colored backdrop, the words "Jones Day: Hands Off Our Ballots" were painted in white. The silhouette of a hand reached across the letter "H," as if to steal a ballot.

A networking organization for young lawyers called on law students not to take jobs at Jones Day. A group called Rise and Resist held a protest outside the firm's New York office. At the University of Michigan School of Law (Orr's alma mater), a group of students pledged not to interview at Jones Day. A Stanford Law professor and leading legal ethicist said she would warn students about working for the firm.

In Texas, Lizanne Thomas, the partner in charge of the southeastern region for Jones Day and the head of its corporate governance practice, received emails from partners complaining that their firm was demeaning itself. (Thomas told me that she had "always been comfortable with our firm's principled stand in representing unpopular or controversial clients.") The general counsel of a company in Texas wrote to his point of contact at Jones Day that he was deeply disappointed in the firm. Another partner got a slightly apologetic note from a longtime client, who said he was urging people he knew at other Jones Day clients to protest to the firm about its work for Trump. The partner forwarded the email to Orr.

Even with everyone working from home, Orr could feel the temperature rising. It was getting to the point where a trusted leader could no longer pretend that he didn't know how his troops were feeling. Orr's instinct was to address this head-on. As it turned out, he'd already scheduled a partners' meeting for Thursday, November 12. Before Covid, Orr would invite the Washington partners for lunch at least once a month. He'd kept it up, virtually, during the pandemic. The ostensible purpose of this particular meeting, held over the digital-conferencing platform Webex, was for Orr to nudge partners to nudge their clients to pay their bills. The year was ending, and it was important that all accounts get settled so that the office would hit its budget target.

After Orr reminded his colleagues about money, and after he gave an update on recruitment and business development, Orr said he'd like to address the Trump controversy. He got as far as asserting that Jones Day was not trying to overturn the election, that it was litigating a legitimate constitutional issue. Then the normally staid meeting disintegrated. *That's a semantic distinction!* one partner angrily interjected. *You're drawing way too fine a line.* The call intensified, lawyers drawing emotional energy from each previous speaker. A number of partners declared that they were so upset that they were considering quitting. Julie McEvoy—who'd held a senior role in the Obama Justice Department—said she'd joined Jones Day a quarter century earlier in part because it wasn't affiliated with a particular political party. Those days were gone, she noted; this no longer felt like the place she'd picked to spend the bulk of her career. She told her colleagues that she "wanted to speak up because the firm's identity seemed to be at a crossroads, and it was not clear which way we were headed," as she put it to me a year later.

At one point, Orr tried to turn the tables by accusing Jones Day's rivals of whipping up the controversy around its work on the Pennsylvania lawsuit. Partners could see each other rolling their eyes. When Orr insisted that the firm couldn't abruptly ditch a client, partners protested that neither could the firm wantonly threaten the rule of law.

It was an extraordinary uprising—especially at a place like Jones Day, whose culture under Steve Brogan rewarded deference. There was "more blowback than I've ever heard" at a Jones Day meeting, one participant told me. Whining was supposed to be off-limits; flagrantly challenging authority like this would normally be a recipe for getting fired. Now, though, a bunch of partners seemed willing to take that risk.

Among those who spoke up was Sparkle Sooknanan, one of the firm's young stars. Born in Trinidad and Tobago, she had set out to New York at age sixteen to attend college and then law school, working full-time at night to pay her way. After graduating she landed jobs at the Justice Department and then as a clerk for a series of federal judges, including Justice Sonia Sotomayor, who became her most cherished mentor. Sooknanan joined Jones Day in 2014 and became a partner at the beginning of 2020 at age thirty-six. She was winning cases and earning professional plaudits, but her heart lay in using the law to pursue justice.

Now, on the video call, Sooknanan's voice trembled as she decried Jones Day's work in Pennsylvania. "This lawsuit was brought for no other reason than to deprive poor people of the right to vote," she said. Most of the partners' lines were muted, and Sooknanan's remarks were greeted with silence.

FOR ALL THE ANGER on the partners' call, the associates in Jones Day's D.C. office were even more restive. The day after the Webex meeting, they were invited to participate in their own video meeting with Orr.

When the gathering got underway, it looked like most of the office was online, participants' faces compressed into tiny squares to squeeze into the on-screen grid. Orr spent about fifteen minutes reciting corporate boilerplate: *It's our job to take hard clients—remember Art Modell!—and we don't abandon them midstream.* (As Orr put it to me, "Our strongest cultural norm perhaps is the resolute belief that we will not yield in our commitment to our clients even though some on the outside may find those representations objectionable or even offensive.") As Orr finished, a lawyer named Robin Overby spoke up. "Kevyn, are you taking questions?" she asked.

"No," Orr replied. "I'll take them seriatim." It was a bit of Latin legalese: People could ask him questions privately, one by one. The call ended.

This was not what Overby had expected. Given Orr's reputation as a listener, she and others had figured there would be an opportunity to ask questions or maybe even vent a little. After consulting with colleagues, she and another associate, Parker Rider-Longmaid, had drafted a statement that they'd hoped to read aloud on the call. But they didn't get the chance.

Slim and sandy-haired, Rider-Longmaid had an idealistic streak. He'd spent nearly two years in Teach for America as an eighth-grade math and science teacher in Philadelphia. Now, as a lawyer, he had a promising career in front of him. He'd clerked on the Supreme Court for Ruth Bader Ginsburg. Then he was lured to Jones Day and its six-figure signing bonuses. He had a reputation as a reserved, careful lawyer, a bit of a nerd, the last guy to rock the boat. But shortly after Orr ended the meeting, Rider-Longmaid did something unexpected. He sent an email to everyone in Jones Day's Washington office. It was the statement that he and Overby had hoped to read aloud.

"We dissent," it began.

The question, Rider-Longmaid wrote, was not whether the Pennsylvania case did or did not have technical legal merit. That was beside the point.

> I believe the question is whether this firm should lend its prestige and credibility to the project of an administration bent on undermining our democracy and our rule of law.
>
> Make no mistake. From the outset, this petition [the Pennsylvania litigation] was designed to suppress the vote, to ensure that fewer of our fellow Americans' voices would be heard, in the midst of a global pandemic like we have never seen in our lifetimes.
>
> And now, it is being weaponized to threaten our generations-long tradition in this country of peaceful and democratic transition of power.

I believe that our society should strive to become a more just and inclusive representative democracy. And this petition, and the project to which it lends our collective prestige, stands firmly in the way of that ideal.

We as lawyers choose our clients and our causes. We choose what we stand for. And this project, I submit, should not be one of those things.

As an American, I am today deeply disappointed in this firm. I do not accept as simply unpopular what is profoundly undemocratic. We are better than this. And yesterday should be no excuse for tomorrow.

We dissent.

A COUPLE OF MONTHS later, shortly after Joe Biden was sworn in as the forty-sixth president, a memo went out to Jones Day's lawyers. It announced the firm's latest comings and goings. "The following lawyers are leaving the Firm," the memo said. There were six lawyers on the list—including Sparkle Sooknanan and Parker Rider-Longmaid. "We wish you all the best!"

EPILOGUE

THE BLACK BOOK

As the Trump administration came to an ignominious end—democracy in doubt, cherished institutions trampled, violence in the streets—its alumni scurried toward the friendly confines of Jones Day's landmark building. A quarter of a mile away, a statue of "Freedom" was perched atop the Capitol dome, and the bronze female figure was visible from the steps leading up to the law firm's heavy front doors. On January 6, months of fearmongering and lies about voter fraud and a stolen election exploded into a deadly insurrection. Jones Day wasn't to blame, but it wasn't *not* to blame either. The firm had contributed to misapprehensions about the vulnerability of the electoral system. More important, it had nurtured, protected, and enabled Donald Trump since long before anyone took his candidacy seriously and for long after his demagogy was impossible to miss. Now the costs were clear.

The day after the riot, Eric Dreiband announced his resignation from the Justice Department; he would rejoin Jones Day the next month.* It was an interesting juxtaposition: As a lawyer in public service, Dreiband was perfectly willing to call it quits as his "client" (the president) pushed the bounds of propriety, even as his once-and-future employer in the private sector insisted on maintaining loyalty, no matter what.

---

* Dreiband told me he'd decided to quit in late December 2020.

In March, David Morrell returned to Jones Day, which promoted him to partner; in the Justice Department, in addition to his work on the Walmart case, he'd defended federal agents' detention of rioters in Portland. That month, Scott Brady—whose efforts as U.S. attorney in Pittsburgh to investigate Hunter Biden had raised concerns inside the Justice Department that he was trying to hurt Joe Biden's candidacy*—also came back to Jones Day, where he'd worked a few jobs earlier. In his new job, he'd focus in part on defending companies that were targets of federal investigations.

In April, Brinton Lucas, who also worked in the Justice Department, returned to the firm. ("Brinton will add great value to the representation of our clients in the highest courts," Noel Francisco predicted.) In May, Kate O'Scannlain, the top lawyer in Trump's Labor Department, signed on. And in June, Hashim Mooppan returned after four years at the Justice Department. (He had defended Trump's ban on travelers from Muslim countries.)

Finally, in September 2021, James Burnham came full circle. He had been an associate when he left with what amounted to an extra year's salary in his pocket. Now, following stints in the White House and Justice Department (where he'd sat in on the Walmart meetings) and a Supreme Court clerkship for Neil Gorsuch, he was hired back by Francisco—as a partner.

A couple of week later, Francisco told me that he thought Jones Day's exertions for Trump were going to pay dividends. "I believe the firm's work in this area has afforded incredible professional opportunities for many of our lawyers, and that those opportunities will redound to the firm's long-term benefit as many of those lawyers return to the firm."

---

* Brady denied trying to influence the 2020 election. He said that "any fair review of the facts would conclude that I handled [the situation] with the professionalism and discretion expected of all senior DOJ officials."

• • •

In the spring of 2021, Johnson & Johnson turned to Jones Day for help. Thousands of people were claiming to have contracted cancer via regular use of J&J's talcum baby powder, which for years had been marketed as a feminine hygiene product. While J&J denied that the powder contained carcinogens or caused cancer, this was threatening to become a very costly problem for America's largest health care company. Jones Day, of course, had a well-thumbed playbook for such situations: Blur the science, blame the victims, question the consequences. But there was another reason J&J had turned to its longtime law firm: Jones Day had pioneered the use of a brutally effective legal maneuver to help companies shed their liabilities as easily as a dirty pair of pants.

The tactic was known as the Texas two-step. It worked like this: A company facing a ruinous wave of lawsuits registers as a Texas corporation and then splits itself into two separate entities. One contains the ongoing operating business. The other houses the original company's legal liabilities—the costs arising from litigation, government investigations, and the like. Then that second entity files for bankruptcy, leaving plaintiffs, the government, and anyone else with a legal claim to fight for financial scraps.

By the time Jones Day pitched this strategy to J&J, the firm had already executed it with great results on behalf of other companies, including one owned by Koch Industries. It couldn't have been a hard sell for J&J, eager to insulate itself from a flood of lawsuits. Under tight secrecy, work began on what the lawyers codenamed Project Plato.

In October 2021, J&J spun off a newly created subsidiary called LTL Management, which immediately filed for bankruptcy. J&J infused LTL with more than $2 billion to handle payouts to thousands of cancer victims, which the company described as a magnanimous effort to "equitably resolve" current and future lawsuits.

But the money seemed grossly inadequate considering that a court had recently ordered J&J to pay more than $2 billion to a group of only twenty-two women with ovarian cancer. (Five days after the LTL spinoff and bankruptcy filing, J&J announced that it had earned about $4 billion in profits in the prior three months.)

This was bad news for cancer patients but a proud moment for Jones Day, which was pulling in millions for its work on the spinoff and bankruptcy. (Partners were billing as much as $1,450 an hour.) The *Financial Times* noted that Jones Day was reaping a "fee bonanza" by helping J&J and other companies dance the Texas two-step.

Jones Day's role attracted criticism—not just from plaintiffs' lawyers and activists, who argued that the two-step was a flagrant abuse of the bankruptcy system, but also from the Biden administration. The U.S. Trustee, an arm of the Justice Department, objected to Jones Day representing LTL, on the grounds that the law firm was a years-long adviser to J&J, an apparent conflict of interest. Legal scholars also cried foul. "For Jones Day," one professor asked, "the question is: What is the boundary of zealous representation?"

In fact, it was hard to detect any boundary whatsoever. In early 2022, reporters at Reuters were preparing an article critical of J&J's efforts to limit payments to cancer patients. Jones Day asked a federal judge to issue an injunction blocking the news agency from publishing its article. Reuters rushed out its exposé the next day, rendering moot the requested injunction. Even so, Jones Day's attempt to take a hammer to the First Amendment—which courts have long interpreted as prohibiting such prior restraint of published speech—seemed to reflect the law firm's increasing radicalization.

There were plenty of other signs as well. In 2021, Jones Day filed a lawsuit arguing that the setup of the Consumer Product Safety Commission, where Dana Baiocco remained a commissioner, was unconstitutional—and that the agency's actions were therefore legally void. The firm successfully sued on behalf of two Realtors' associations to block the Biden administration's moratorium on evictions during the pandemic.

Not long after, McGahn and Francisco submitted a Supreme Court brief on behalf of Mitch McConnell. The "friend of the court" filing was related to a lawsuit by Ted Cruz, who was seeking to invalidate an obscure provision of the landmark McCain-Feingold campaign-finance law. What made the Jones Day brief notable was its ambitious embrace of judicial activism. McGahn and Francisco argued that the Supreme Court should strike down the entirety of the 2003 law, not just the one provision at issue in Cruz's lawsuit. Their claim was that because other parts of the statute had already been invalidated, the remainder was "a patchwork of provisions that Congress never would have approved." This was a weak argument—the original law stipulated that even if certain elements were deemed unconstitutional, the rest should remain intact—but here was Jones Day, again, trying to advance a tenuous position that happened to align with its leaders' ideology. As the *Washington Post*'s Ruth Marcus put it, "There is, it seems, no argument too extreme for this crowd in their effort to reshape the law to their liking."

Jones Day, in short, was not chastened and was not backing down. This was a pattern, and it should not have surprised anyone. Jones Day was a corporate law firm, and a little public outrage wasn't going to fundamentally alter its character. It was going to remain devoted to its causes and clients, the same way that Paul Weiss and Skadden Arps and Gibson Dunn and Baker McKenzie and all the other megafirms would remain devoted to theirs, regardless of how far they had strayed from their original missions or their profession's sacred creeds. These firms were rich, their top partners pocketing many millions a year. They were strong, teeming with thousands of lawyers in dozens of offices. And nobody had the power to stop them—least of all anyone with a compelling interest to do so.

And yet some of Jones Day's left-leaning lawyers had drawn

solace from the firm's occasional liberal overtures. In Minneapolis, for example, where the partner in charge of the office was a former Obama administration official, Jones Day had launched a pro bono project to help the city government deal with the problems of police violence against Black residents. While the firm largely kept quiet about its work on the conservative front, it was quick to crow about this one. In the fall of 2021, Jones Day created a colorful eight-page brochure titled "Do You Know Us? Jones Day and Our Pro Bono Culture." It highlighted work like the Laredo Project (since renamed The Border Project) and the policing initiative in Minneapolis. "The Firm's Managing Partner initiated the effort to demonstrate Jones Day's commitment 'to advancing the rule of law governing policing in the minority communities,'" the brochure stated.

In September 2021, the Jones Day partner in charge of pro bono work sent me the brochure. That same week, another partner told me a story that highlighted the conflict that was continuing to simmer inside the firm. Two decades earlier, Jones Day had stopped working for the Center to Prevent Handgun Violence after the firm took on the firearms manufacturer Colt. In the ensuing years, Jones Day's liberal lawyers had managed to resume doing some pro bono work for gun control groups like Everytown for Gun Safety. This was feasible only because Jones Day, for whatever reason, had stopped working for gun companies. The liberals convinced themselves that this was a sign that their firm, despite its conservative reputation, was really willing to take on both sides, left and right. Some even believed that Jones Day's leadership had taken a principled stand against representing gun companies (following the lead of other major law firms).

Then, in August 2021, the Mexican government filed a lawsuit in federal court against the world's leading gun companies: Colt, Smith & Wesson, Glock, Sturm Ruger. The suit accused the companies of illegally trafficking "a torrent of guns" to Mexican drug cartels. A month later, a handful of law firms announced they were lining up to defend the gun companies. Most of the firms were small or midsized, with one exception: Jones Day was defending Smith & Wesson. And it wasn't just anyone at Jones Day. It was Noel Francisco, whom Brogan, the day after Biden's inauguration, had promoted to run the firm's Washington office. (He replaced Kevyn Orr, who was given the new job of partner in charge of U.S. offices.) In defending Smith & Wesson, Francisco was teaming up with a former federal prosecutor, Andrew Lelling, whom the firm had hired in early 2021 from the Trump administration.

The partner who brought this to my attention guessed that Jones Day would, once again, have to halt its gun-control work. "It's so disappointing," he told me.

AFTER TRUMP LOST THE election, his campaign was converted into political action committees. It was the outcome that Ginsberg and McGahn had expected back in 2015 when they began representing the Trump campaign and figured it would quickly fizzle out. Their hope at the time was that once Trump realized he had no shot of winning a Republican primary, much less capturing the nomination, much less prevailing in a national election, and settled instead on creating an influence-buying PAC, Jones Day would get the job of setting up the entity and making sure it complied with the relevant regulations. More than five years later, the PACs were all that was left, and Jones Day was their law firm.

In the 2012 election cycle, before Jones Day hired the Patton Boggs crew, the firm had pocketed a grand total of $169,541 working on federal campaigns. Eight years later, the windfall was well over $19 million. Some of that (about $6 million) came from the Trump campaign, but the remainder was spread across a wide variety of Republican candidates and committees, ranging from the RNC (almost $5 million) to a Republican congressman's Warrior Diplomat PAC ($450).

In the 2022 election cycle, with democracy on the ballot as much as any candidate, the gusher continued. Trump's shadow loomed large, and his PACs and affiliated groups were still creating lots of work for Jones Day (and were still spewing lots of lies about the election). And so were other Republicans, including the RNC and the Republican Senate fundraising committee and Senator Ron Johnson, a prolific peddler of misinformation about the 2020 election, and Trump wannabes in Pennsylvania and Alabama. Jones Day was in their corner, and it was good at its job, and it wasn't going to stop.

Steve Brogan and his colleagues had wagered that representing Trump—and staffing his administration—would help transform Jones Day into a go-to firm for Republicans, mainstream and fringe alike. Their bet was paying off.

THE BLACK LEATHER COVER was cracked and discolored with age. Lissy Gulick sat at a table in her home, a converted gray farmhouse built in the mid-1800s, several miles outside Cleveland. She inspected the seventy-two-year-old volume, oversized and heavy like a photo album. Gulick hadn't looked at it—hell, she hadn't even *thought* about it—in what felt like decades. But she had spare time these days, thanks to the pandemic and her recent retirement as an actress. (She'd had small roles in a bunch of films, including as a social worker in Denzel Washington's *Antwone Fisher.*) There were only two and a half words on the book's dimpled cover, and they were etched in tiny golden calligraphy: *Thomas H. Jones.*

Gulick knew her grandfather as Tom Tom. Though he had died when Gulick was only four, she felt close to the great man, her memories kept alight by family lore and evocative photos.

Here he was sailing, the strong Lake Erie wind tilting his boat far to the port side. Once, Gulick had dropped a favorite toy overboard, and Tom Tom had calculated wind and drift and navigated the craft to fetch the special piece of rubber bobbing in the choppy lake.

Here he was on a sunny day, outside their home, wearing a brown flannel suit, deep creases lining his face, beaming at his granddaughter in his arms. More than seven decades later, Gulick could still feel the warmth kindled by Tom Tom's "wonderful smile-wrinkles."

She opened the book. Inside was a collection of letters, proclamations, and newspaper clippings commemorating the role her grandfather had played at the small law firm that he had joined straight out of Ohio State in 1911—and that, more than a century later, still bore his surname. Tom Jones had been in the prime of his career when a heart attack killed him at age sixty. The resolutions adopted by the boards of directors of the numerous companies he advised—reproduced in the book with their ornate lettering and the curling signatures of the companies' board members—were testament to that. "He was naturally modest and unassuming and so won and held the affection and friendship of his acquaintances and associates," read one proclamation, issued by the board of the Warner & Swasey Company, a local machine-making concern. "We shall sadly miss his wise counsel, but even more we shall miss him as a friend."

The book brimmed with similar testimonials, and Gulick skimmed them and smiled as she leafed through the still-glossy pages. It was a cold day in November 2020. Two weeks earlier, Trump had lost the election—and that was why Gulick had rummaged around in her house to retrieve the nearly forgotten memorial book.

For Gulick, Jones Day had long been a family affair. In addition to Tom Tom, Gulick's father had been a partner. So had her other grandfather and his son, Gulick's uncle. In the 1940s and '50s, she had tagged along with her father to the office on Saturday mornings and sat at the phone operator's desk, playing with the manual switchboard. When she was an adult, the firm had been the place that she could count on to perform mundane tasks like tidying up this relative's will or that one's mortgage. "We just thought that Jones Day was the last word," she reminisced.

Gulick wasn't naive. She had known for some time that this was no longer Tom Tom's firm, that the world had changed irrevocably since the days when her grandfather's colleagues counseled the East Ohio Gas Company to promptly make whole those harmed by its deadly explosions. By the late 1970s—around the time that the firm's leaders had set their sights on conquering first the country, then the world—Gulick's phone calls had stopped getting returned. "It had gone from the place where my granddad could suggest a nice young lawyer to a place that seemed unapproachable," she said.

And then, as the 2020 election came and went, Gulick learned that this once-familiar law firm was working for the president and his allies, who seemed to be playing Russian roulette with American democracy. "I am just so outraged that a company with my grandfather's name on the door would act in this way," she told me. She flipped through the memorial book, and she considered what his law firm had become, and she fumed.

"Tom Tom would have probably said they got too big for their britches. It's one thing representing a client. But it's another . . ." She trailed off, too angry to complete her sentence.

ACKNOWLEDGMENTS

Like any other work of journalism, this book would not exist were it not for the sources who spent hours patiently recounting to me the events I've described (as well as many others that didn't make the final cut). More than a few people—in particular some who currently work at Jones Day—risked their jobs by speaking to me, and I am especially grateful for their trust.

This book is a project of the pandemic, a period in which many of us have endured prolonged periods of painful isolation. I feel blessed to have largely avoided this fate. The help and camaraderie of a wonderful group of family, friends, and colleagues kept me sane and made this book possible.

As Trump and his allies lied about the results of the 2020 election, my *New York Times* colleagues Rachel Abrams and Jessica Silver-Greenberg and I wrote an article about Jones Day's work for the Trump campaign. Rachel and Jessica are masters at identifying sources and persuading them to talk, and when I began researching this book, they handed off some of these people to me—an act of generosity that gave me a running start. Other *Times* colleagues—including Mike Schmidt, Emily Steel, Matt Goldstein, Jesse Drucker, Sue Dominus, Jim Stewart, Kashmir Hill, and Katie Rosman—provided reporting assistance, advice, and/or encouragement. Jessica Silver-Greenberg and Emily Flitter read the manuscript. Their edits were golden and saved me from embarrassing mistakes.

I'm grateful to Ellen Pollock for permitting me to work on this project (and for regaling me with tales about the *American Lawyer*). I'm indebted to the many colleagues—including Rich Barbieri (another *American Lawyer* alum), Mohammed Hadi, Virginia Hughes, Dagny Salas, Sharon O'Neal, Dave Schmidt, Justin Swanson, Ashwin Seshagiri, and Greg Schmidt—who picked up my slack at points along the way. Thank you as well to A. G. Sulzberger, Dean Baquet, Joe Kahn, Matt Purdy, Carolyn Ryan, and Rebecca Blumenstein for their leadership of the *Times*.

A handful of good friends deserve special acknowledgment. Mark and Lisa have been regular sounding boards and sources of stability (and of a car, which they lent me so I could collect documents from a source). Carolina and Tom were enthusiastic backers of this project. Jason, Brad, Matt, and Ed were sparring partners as I tested the book's themes. And Dominic, Kevin, Pete, and Ray felt like a second family. I am grateful for all of you.

My agent Dan Mandel has been a loyal and savvy advocate for seven years, and he was a consistent source of encouragement about this project.

At Mariner Books and HarperCollins, thank you to Peter Hubbard, who immediately embraced this book and deftly edited and championed it. Molly Gendell kept everything running smoothly and dealt with my annoyingly regular requests for other HarperCollins titles. Karen Richardson expertly copyedited. Maureen Cole helped drum up publicity, and Tavia Kowalchuk handled marketing. Kyran Cassidy and Rachel McGhee provided a vigorous legal scrubbing and handled incoming flak. Thank you as well to Liate Stehlik and Ben Steinberg.

This brings me to my family.

Carole Paul and Albert Leutwyler lent me their Manhattan apartment to use as a refuge for writing. Lisa Benhammou has been an unflappable source of support.

My father, Peter Enrich, a recently retired Northeastern University law professor, helped me appreciate the power of the law and the legal profession at a young age. He read an early draft of this book and offered superb advice. My mother, Dr. Peggy Enrich, a psychologist, helped me understand the mindsets of the book's characters (and chauffeured me on a Jones Day recon mission). This book is dedicated to both of you.

Liza and Jay and Nick and Jords are always there for me. A special shout-out to Zander and Hazel for being my biggest boosters.

Henry and Jasper: You have had to endure way too many mornings, evenings, and weekends with your dad working. I am eternally grateful for your patience, love, and curiosity, about the book-writing process and everything else (Pokémon, baseball, cooking, *Sing 2*, technology, skiing). I adore you both and am so proud of who you are. And Milkshake, I love you, too.

Kirsten: When I first mentioned this project to you in late 2020, I could practically see the conflicting emotions colliding in your brain. You liked the idea but instantly recognized what this would mean for you: more work, more stress, less husband. Still, you got on board and did not waver, even as you lost your father. Throughout, you provided me with sage edits and, just as important, reassurance that the book did not suck.

For all that and so much more, thank you, Kirsten. I love you.

NOTES

Prologue: Power Play

2 they had never done so: Joe Sims email to author.

2 "That is one great building": Betsy Pisik, "Big law firm plans move near Capitol," *Washington Times,* 5/7/1996.

2 This was when the problems began: Jennifer Yachnin, "Senate Overrules Zoning Board," *Roll Call,* 6/30/2005.

3 essentially blocked the building's construction: Yachnin, 2005.

5 touched that Jones Day: Don McGahn email to author.

5 a handful of prominent Democrats: Kevyn Orr email to author.

8 Supreme Court orator Daniel Webster: Adam Winkler, *We the Corporations: How American Businesses Won Their Civil Rights,* 2018, 71–72.

Chapter 1: A Hustling Business

13 Four hulking steel tanks: John Stark Bellamy II, *They Died Crawling: True Stories of the Foulest Crimes and Worst Disasters in Cleveland History,* 1995, 63.

13 50 million cubic feet: Alvin Silverman, "34 Dead, Scores Missing, 10,000 Driven Out in Blast," *Plain Dealer,* 10/21/1944.

13 twice the volume: Grant Segall, "'I knew everything was gone'—the East Ohio Gas explosion," *Plain Dealer,* 10/16/1994.

13 "one of the scientific wonders": Silverman, 1944.

14 Neighbors noticed white mist: Bellamy, 66.

14 "a big balloon of fire": Fred McGunagle, "Gas Explosion Rocks East Side," *Plain Dealer,* 12/6/1998.

14 sky turned orange: Silverman, 1944.

14 flames leaping a half mile up: Bellamy, 62.

14 enough to melt coins: Bellamy, 62.

14 "It was as if a flame-thrower": Eric Sandy, "The Day Cleveland Exploded," *Cleveland Scene,* 10/15/2014.

14 Charred sparrows fell: Silverman, 1944.

14 car tires blew out: Bellamy, 68–69.

14 manhole covers shooting: Silverman, 1944.

14 The fire smoldered: Segall, 1994.

14 The occasional lonely tree: Segall, 1994.

14 they couldn't be identified: Michael Sangiacomo and James Ewinger, "East Ohio Gas Explosions—60 Years Later," *Plain Dealer,* 10/18/2004.

14 Some were found kneeling: Segall, 1994.

15 one of the three largest: Jim Dubelko, "The Union Trust Building," Cleveland Historical Society.

15 East Ohio's best bet: Albert Borowitz, *Jones, Day, Reavis & Pogue: The First Century,* 1993, 94–95.

16 The next day: Borowitz, 94–95.

16 "It is not necessary": Segall, 1994.

16 Only twenty-four lawsuits: Borowitz, 94–95.

16 remained in the neighborhood: Sangiacomo and Ewinger, 2004.

16 fast and fair: Segall, 1994.

16 was not libelous: Borowitz, 13–14.

17 he was found lying: Borowitz, 15–16.

17 the case was never cracked: Borowitz, 16–17.

17 building a mythology: Jones Day presentation to new hires, October 2017.

17 Jack Reavis, chuckled: Reavis speech to Jones Day associates, 1983.

17 Lawyers who assembled: Mitt Regan and Lisa H. Rohrer, *BigLaw: Money and Meaning in the Modern Law Firm,* 2021, 17–18.

17 "a hustling business": Regan and Rohrer, 19.

17 The profession's response: Regan and Rohrer, 19.

18 "This young man": Jones Day presentation to new hires, October 2017.

18 "just as local": Reavis speech to associates, 1983.

18 in a cape and top hat: Borowitz, 47–48.

18 "A young lawyer": Janet H. Cho, "A global venue," *Plain Dealer,* 6/19/2006.

18 "He completely dominated": Borowitz, 47.

18 "If you are not willing": Jones Day website, "Firm History."

18 Jones represented: Borowitz, 24–25.

19 alongside his brother Tat: Borowitz, 35.

19 "this god-awful alcohol": Reavis speech to associates, 1983.

19 it was a prank: Borowitz, 35.

19 Ginn selected Jones: Borowitz, 64.

19 four weeks of vacation time: Borowitz, 75–77.

19 "possibly the greatest trial lawyer": Borowitz, 66.

19 He focused on keeping: Borowitz, 68–73.

20 the last clerk to serve: Nick Ravo, "Chapman Rose, 83, Lawyer Who Served In 2 Administrations," *New York Times,* 2/20/1990.

20 "Dullness is not diminished": Author interview of a Rose family member.

20 "Sonny, go home": Borowitz, 95.

20 his starting salary: Reavis speech to associates, 1983.

20 the rank of colonel: Ravo, 1990.

20 Washington was poised: Borowitz, 95–97.

20 representing storied companies: Borowitz, 116.

20 a client of Luther Day's: Borowitz, 99–100.

21 "What in the world": Brooks Jones notebook, provided to author by Lissy Gulick.

21 "Your father is dead": Jones notebook.

Chapter 2: The Independence Principle

22 prowling the offices: Stephen Adler, "Antonin Scalia: The affable arch-conservative," *American Lawyer,* March 1985.

23 that year's going rate: Marc Galanter and Thomas Palay, *Tournament of Lawyers: The Transformation of the Big Law Firm,* 1991, 24.

23 about $4,000: Erwin O. Smigel, "The Impact of Recruitment on the Organization of the Large Law Firm," *American Sociological Review,* February 1960.

23 Firms also sent notices: Smigel, 1960.

23 "summer boarders": Smigel, 1960.

23 "irritates many lawyers": Smigel, 1960.

23 "not going to talk to you": Dick Pogue interview with author.

24 he planned to accept: E. R. Shipp, "Scalia's Midwest Colleagues Cite His Love of Debate, Poker and Piano," *New York Times,* 7/26/1986.

24 Lynn had persuaded: Adler, 1985.

24 thought to himself: Bloomberg Law, "Scalia's Six-Year Stint as a Big Law Associate," 2/17/2016.

24 The debate wore on: Adler, 1985.

24 Scalia summered: Antonin Scalia interview by Judith R. Hope, Oral History Project of the Historical Society of the District of Columbia Circuit, 12/5/1992.

25 played the piano: Jane Morice, "Former Jones Day colleague remembers Scalia as conscientious lawyer with 'twinkle in his eye,'" Cleveland.com, 2/14/2016.

25 "likes to hammer": Shipp, 1986.

25 wearing a fishing hat: James B. Staab, *The Political Thought of Justice Antonin Scalia: A Hamiltonian on the Supreme Court,* 2006, 6.

25 At lunch, he'd debate: Shipp, 1986.

25 "I got a really good look": Scalia interview, 1992.

25 "longer than I should have": Scalia interview, 1992.

25 Scalia grew bored: Bloomberg Law, 2016.

25 "such a liberal place": Adler, 1985.

25 "a sharp tongue": Borowitz, 129.

26 the names of partners' wives: Borowitz, 130.

26 "Sierra Club 'Soot Award'": Roldo Bartimole, "Scrooge Awards," *Point of View,* 12/20/1971.

26 "another fat cat": Roldo Bartimole, "Many Roads Lead to Jack Reavis," *Point of View,* 4/21/1968.

26 He used his clout: Borowitz, 136–37.

27 sixteen-year-old farm boy: Adam Bernstein, "L. Welch Pogue Dies," *Washington Post,* 5/14/2003.

27 Among his clients were Bell: Borowitz, 152–53.

27 he helped negotiate: Bernstein, 2003.

27 fourteen lawyers: Pogue interview.

27 its first winner: Bernstein, 2003.

27 was completely reliant: Nicholas Lemann, "The Split," *Washington Post Magazine,* 3/23/1980.

27 He immediately hit it off: Mark Stevens, *Power of Attorney: The Rise of the Giant Law Firms,* 1987, 132.

27 Pogue could tell: Stevens, 130–31.

27 more than doubled: Borowitz, 154.

27 Pan Am, its biggest customer: Lemann, 1980.

28 landed him: Erwin N. Griswold, *Ould Fields, New Corne: The Personal Memoirs of a Twentieth Century Lawyer,* 1992, 353–54.

28 first met Nixon: Ravo, 1990.

28 became friends: *New York Times,* "Lawyer Affirms Nixon Consulted Him," 7/15/1973.

28 a big donor: Ravo, 1990.

28 regularly called Rose: John W. Dean, *The Nixon Defense: What He Knew and When He Knew It,* 2014, 422.

28 "glad to offer it": *New York Times,* 1973.

29 Jonathan Rose would say: Borowitz, 242.

29 "a supreme demonstration": Borowitz, 242.

29 "The Independence Principle": Jones Day website, "Firm History."

Chapter 3: A Truly National Firm

30 "much like Silicon Valley": Naomi R. Lamoreaux, Margaret Levenstein, and Kenneth L. Sokoloff, "Mobilizing Venture Capital During the Second Industrial Revolution: Cleveland, Ohio, 1870–1920," *Capitalism and Society,* 2006.

30 brilliant but mercurial: Borowitz, 188.

31 "got tired of bed": Borowitz, 191–92.

31 Holmes didn't care: Pogue interview.

31 *Let's follow it west*: Pogue interview.

31 serve as a model: Borowitz, 158–59.

31 "a dramatic symbol": Dick Pogue, "Inside Jones Day: Cleveland, 1893 to Donald Trump," *Big Law Business Podcast,* 3/17/2017.

32 the bar association caved: Borowitz, 160–61.

32 The California experiment proved humbling: Pogue podcast, 2017.

32 it became a joke: Borowitz, 165–66.

32 a self-sufficient fiefdom: Griswold, 366.

32 expelled the leaders: Lemann, 1980.

32 Pogue was impressed: Pogue email to author.

32 left the firm: Griswold, 418.

33 Lynn endorsed Scalia: Adler, 1985.

33 following a recommendation from Jonathan Rose: Adler, 1985.

33 where he helped establish: Michael Kruse, "The Weekend at Yale That Changed American Politics," *Politico Magazine,* September/October 2018.

33 Rose recommended him: Adler, 1985.

Chapter 4: Advertisers-at-Law

34 He started looking: John Bates interview with author.

35 sounded pretty good: Bates interview.

35 They became friends: Author interviews with Bates and Van O'Steen.

35 "this gigantic gap": Bates interview.

36 "a neighborhood drunk": John Tierney, "Van O'Steen Brings the Law to the People," *Esquire,* December 1985.

36 could spend their time: David L. Hudson Jr., "Bates Participants Reflect on Landmark Case," Freedom Forum Institute, 11/18/2004.

36 "defy the traditions": Galanter and Palay, 69–70.

36 "shall not publicize himself": Wade H. Logan III, "Lawyer Advertising and Solicitation: The Birth of the Marlboro Man," *South Carolina Law Review,* Summer 1991, 860.

36 had been disciplined: Galanter and Palay, 70.

38 agreed to run the ad: O'Steen interview.

38 That week was a blur: Bates interview.

39 Lewis and Ruth Goldfarb: Louis M. Kohlmeier, "Price-Fixing in the Professions," *New York Times,* 4/18/1976.

39 "committing economic suicide": Alan B. Morrison, oral arguments in *Goldfarb v. State Bar of Virginia,* 3/25/1975.

40 "one of the most farsighted": Winkler, 299.

41 fast-track the case: O'Steen interview.

41 rejected their arguments: Hudson, 2004.

41 like their faces were burning: O'Steen interview.

42 "Did you hear that?": Bates and O'Steen interviews.

43 "You won": O'Steen interview.

44 a decent-sized firm: O'Steen interview.

44 The two old friends: Bates interview.

45 the number would soar: Galanter and Palay, 53.

45 National Association of Law Firm Marketing Administrators: David Margolick, "They're Selling Lawyers on Selling Their Services," *New York Times,* 3/26/1993.

45 "came down the wrong way": Pogue interview.

45 "It worked!": Pogue interview.

46 brought in folks: Cora Daniels, "The Man in the Tan Khaki Pants," *Fortune,* May 2000.

46 The venue: Terry Pristin, "The Suits Loosen Up, in an Uneasy Way," *New York Times,* 4/6/2000.

46 strutted their khakis: Daniels, 2000.

Chapter 5: Creating a Monster

47 "Try to put yourself": Steve Brill, "Dark World of the Wino," *New York Times,* 12/31/1970.

48 had gone viral: Steven Brill interview with author.

49 "The law is moving rapidly": Brill memo, reviewed by author.

49 fifteen minutes left: Brill interview.

49 "stories that should be written": Jim Stewart interview with author.

50 attendees were besieged: Arthur John Keeffe, "Everyone Wants to Get into the Act," *American Bar Association Journal,* November 1978.

51 "a scurrilous publication": Patricia Bellew Gray, "Steven Brill, the Terror of Legal Journalism, Is Building an Empire," *Wall Street Journal,* 3/26/1986.

51 "run you out of town": Laura Mansnerus, "As Brash Publisher's Empire Ends, Quest Begins for Another," *New York Times,* 3/3/1997.

51 The greatest indignity: Brill interview.

51 a group of reporters would smoke pot: Jill Abramson interview with author.

52 Stewart was embarrassed: Stewart interview.

52 he'd scrawl insults: Mansnerus, 1997.

52 "Is English your second language?": Gray, 1986.

52 "You should be fired": James J. Cramer, *Confessions of a Street Addict,* 2003, 11.

52 "a real S.O.B.": Gray, 1986.

52 threatened to stab: Abramson interview.

53 sank his teeth: Gray, 1986.

53 trail of blood: Cramer, 12.

53 bloody scratches: Stewart interview.

53 "all with one bite": Cramer, 12.

54 Most Friday evenings: Brill interview.

54 His idea was this: Brill interview.

55 Reporters could use the clue: Bob Windrem interview with author.

57 "one of the most antisocial acts": Brill, 30–31.

57 That was what it took: Andrew Bruck and Andrew Canter, "Supply, Demand, and the Changing Economics of Large Law Firms," *Stanford Law Review,* April 2008.

57 doubled between 1985 and 1998: Galanter and Palay, 46, and David Segal, "In the Business of Billing?," *Washington Post,* 3/22/1998.

57 seventeen did: Bernard Ascher, "The Threat to U.S. Lawyers from Competition by Multidisciplinary Practices," American Antitrust Institute Working Paper, November 2006, 16.

57 at least a billion dollars: Regan and Rohrer, 3.

57 rivaled the auto sector: Brill, 30.

57 did so with gusto: James F. Fitzpatrick, "Legal Future Shock: The Role of Larger Law Firms by the End of the Century," *Indiana Law Journal,* Summer 1989.

57 The number of recruiting firms: Galanter and Palay, 54.

57 "can create immense risks": Fitzpatrick, 1989.

57 "Growth changes the character": Galanter and Palay, 3.

58 more than 1,300 billable hours: Bruck and Canter, 2008.

58 at least 2,000 hours: Segal, 1998.

58 2,500 billable hours: Bruck and Canter, 2008.

58 52 consecutive all-nighters: Segal, 1998.

58 a national survey of lawyers: Segal, 1998.

58 "ethical gray zones": Marc Galanter and William Henderson, "The Elastic Tournament: A Second Transformation of the Big Law Firm," *Stanford Law Review,* April 2008.

58 "The leaders of the law": Sol M. Linowitz and Martin Mayer, *The Betrayed Profession: Lawyering at the End of the Twentieth Century,* 1994, 227.

59 "The only question": Segal, 1998.

59 "It's all my fault": Linowitz and Mayer, 32.

Chapter 6: Keeping Up with the Jones Days

60 Dick Pogue was in his office: Pogue email.

60 even as a baby: Borowitz, 350.

60 poker and the saxophone: Borowitz, 352.

60 "more hours than I do": Borowitz, 351.

60 two main priorities: Pogue email.

60 "Everyone else was going": Pogue interview.

61 The firm had a jump: Borowitz, 174–75.

61 seized on the deal: Stuart Taylor, "Law Firms Becoming National in Scope," *New York Times,* 1/11/1981.

61 in five offices: Larkin, 2018.

61 an office in Austin: Borowitz, 177.

61 Kneipper and a small team: Rick Kneipper interview with author.

61 "we needed to be international": Pogue podcast, 2017.

62 their frugality appealed: Pogue email.

62 a total of 572: Borowitz, 178–79.

62 "the primary attraction": *New York Times,* "2 Law Firms In a Merger," 1/7/1986.

62 "the unique distinction": Borowitz, 238–41.

63 South African Sugar Association: Jones Day FARA disclosure, 6/26/1988.

63 the Chinese government: Jones Day FARA disclosures, 1/31/1986 and 7/22/1987.

63 ended up serving the weapons factory: Robert J. McCartney, "4 Firms Linked to Libyan Plant," *Washington Post,* 1/10/1989.

63 officials denied wrongdoing: Stephen Engelberg, "U.S. Says an Iraqi Had Role in Libyan Plant," *New York Times,* 1/10/1989.

63 already in hot water: McCartney, 1989.

63 "guilty until proven innocent": John McCain, *Congressional Record—Senate,* 1/25/1989, 500.

64 "Proposal for Representation": Jones Day FARA disclosure, 2/17/1989.

65 signed on as a client: Jones Day FARA disclosure, 2/17/1989.

65 Senate aides said: Mark Hosenball, "Law Firm's German Client Alleged to Have Ties with Libya," *Washington Post,* 6/13/1989.

65 went on a spree: Borowitz, 179–83.

65 more than one thousand lawyers: Gayle Young, "Jones Day to merge, creating second largest law firm," United Press International, 5/11/1989.

65 "awesome to behold": Stevens, 146

65 "keeping up with the Jones Days": Steven Greenhouse, "U.S. Lawyers Flock to Brussels," *New York Times,* 5/13/1991.

65 Under Pogue's watch: Larkin, 2018.

66 Pogue would insist: John R. Brandt, "The light at the end of the tunnel," *Corporate Cleveland,* January 1993.

66 "a sparkling personality": Stevens, 136.

66 prone to repeating: Stevens, 149–50.

66 ill-fitting suits: Stevens, 136.

Chapter 7: The Greatest Client

67 McCartan's defense was that: Michael L. King, "Top Trial Lawyer Gets Firms Out of Trouble With Quiet Efficiency," *Wall Street Journal,* 11/2/1982.

67 never been forced to pay: Philip Hager, "Cigarette Makers Sued," *Los Angeles Times,* 8/5/1985.

68 courts increasingly held: Frank V. Tursi, Susan E. White, and Steve McQuilkin, *Lost Empire: The Fall of R.J. Reynolds Tobacco Company,* 2000, 242–43.

68 got permission to appoint: Pogue email.

68 Pogue promised Henderson: Borowitz, 234–35.

69 a large team set up shop: Tursi, White, and McQuilkin, 246.

69 Small squads of attorneys: "RJR Response to Attorney General Humphrey Comments," 4/22/1998. This document and others cited below—including internal RJR records and correspondence between company executives and Jones Day lawyers—are available in the vast "Truth Tobacco Industry Documents" archive maintained by the University of California, San Francisco.

69 a long report: "Jones, Day, Reavis & Pogue Draft: Corporate Activity Project," 11/17/1986.

70 "The key defense strategy": "Corporate Activity Project," 1986.

70 "waging a definitional battle": Tursi, White, and McQuilkin, 342.

70 directed to find experts: Peter Biersteker letter to RJR and Womble Carlyle, 8/12/1992.

70 Camel Lights smoker: John Strauch email to author.

70 high school football star: Bill Lubinger, "Latest Win for the Defense," *Plain Dealer,* 8/27/2000.

71 During jury selection: Lubinger, 2000.

71 Folks like that: Tom Jackson, "Jones Day partner wins big for Big Blue," *Crain's Cleveland Business,* 4/5/2004.

72 "He was raised": Lubinger, 2000.

72 "we're in control": Lubinger, 2000.

72 Weber composed a handbook: Bob Weber, *Some Few Thoughts on Trial Law and Trial Lawyers,* 2005.

72 Belli thought he'd found: Tursi, White, and McQuilkin, 244.
73 he generally appeared: Oliver, 1996.
73 "live like the king of torts": Tursi, White, and McQuilkin, 245.
73 Galbraith would sneak smokes: Marcia Chambers, "Suit to Link Smoking and Death Opens This Week," *New York Times,* 11/12/1985.
73 more addictive than alcohol: Hager, 1985.
73 similar lawsuits: Chambers, 1985.
74 Jones Day demanded: Sara D. Guardino and Richard A. Daynard, "Punishing Tobacco Industry Misconduct," *University of Pittsburgh Law Review,* 2005.
74 The RJR contingent subpoenaed: *Dallas Times Herald,* "Giant Tobacco Firm Deploys Small Army to Fight Lawsuit," 12/8/1985.
74 hobbies and eating habits: Tursi, White, and McQuilkin, 249–50.
74 "The aggressive posture": Laurie P. Cohen and Alix M. Freedman, "Smoke and Mirrors: The Tobacco Industry's Response to Health Fears," *Wall Street Journal,* 2/11/1993.
75 surveyed the crowded courtroom: Gene Marlowe, "Legal Forces Are Gathering in Reynolds Cigarette Case," *Richmond Times-Dispatch,* 11/9/1985.
75 it convinced the judge: *Dallas Times Herald,* 1985.
75 a regular audience of analysts: Marlowe, 1985.
75 a surprisingly long life: Morton Mintz, "R.J. Reynolds Upbeat as Court Date Looms," *Washington Post,* 11/10/1985.
75 "who helped him obtain cigarettes": Marlowe, 1985.
76 Strauch crowed to reporters: Linda Deutsch, "Tobacco Company Wins Suit Over Death of Man Who Smoked for 50 Years," Associated Press, 12/23/1985.
76 had approached Huber: Deposition of Gary Huber, 9/20/1997, 11.
76 "the P.R. value": Final opinion in *US v. Philip Morris USA et al.,* 8/17/2006, 148.
76 inhaling the smoke deeper: Final opinion in *US v. Philip Morris,* 284.
77 "people who worship": Huber deposition, 53–54.
77 the visit from Jones Day: Huber deposition, 85.
77 "shoddy and poorly conceived": Lee Hancock and Mark Curriden, "Ex-tobacco insider says lawyers were in control," *Dallas Morning News,* 12/21/1997.
77 "so highly diluted": Dick Stanley, "Texas professor questions secondhand smoke claims," *Austin American-Statesman,* 7/18/1994.
77 "Is smoking beneficial": Shane, 1997.
77 pointed reporters toward Huber's research: Hancock and Curriden, 1997.
77 "one of the most cited researchers": Stanley, 1994.
77 "Modern Puritans want to control": William Murchison, "Modern Puritans want to control us through government," *Dallas Morning News,* 10/19/1994.

77 Congressional Research Service report: Hancock and Curriden, 1997.

77 cited Huber's research in ads: Hancock and Curriden, 1997.

77 a lawsuit against the U.S.: Stanley, 1994.

77 into the millions of dollars: Hancock and Curriden, 1997.

78 Jones Day helped craft: "Statement of R.J. Reynolds Tobacco Company," submitted to House Energy and Commerce Committee, 4/14/1994.

78 "I was shocked and appalled": Letter to RJR's James Johnston from Jones Day's Jean Firestone, 4/21/1994.

78 "Jones Day's representation of RJR": Letter from Chuck Brixt to Pat McCartan, 4/24/1995.

78 a weekend of golf: Blixt letter to Bob Weber, 6/3/1997.

78 a $2 billion racketeering case: Emily Heller, "Playing defense on a high wire," *National Law Journal,* 6/21/2004.

78 At RJR's instruction: Letter from Jones Day's Barbara Kacir to RJR's Daniel Donahue, 4/17/1992.

78 RJR cited those papers: RJR, "Issues Related to Allegations Made by 27 State Attorneys General," September 1993.

78 a total of about $1 million: Tursi, White, and McQuilkin, 247.

78 $7.8 million in a typical month: R.J. Reynolds Tobacco Company, "Estimated RJRT liabilities as of 9/15/98," 9/21/1998, 8.

78 the firm's total revenue: "Jones Day," *ALM Intelligence* website.

79 "extremely angry": Hancock and Curriden, 1997.

79 "My prayers are with you": Hancock and Curriden, 1997.

79 "worried about a lot of things": Huber deposition, 108.

79 offered him the protection: Hancock and Curriden, 1997.

80 a crucial piece of his argument: Don Homa, "Where There's Smoke, There's Distortion," *Arizona Republic,* 6/8/2002.

Chapter 8: Aiding and Abetting

82 the firm could pitch itself: Kneipper interview.

82 about two hundred thrifts: Wade Lambert, "Jones Day Will Pay $51 Million to Settle Lincoln Savings Case," *Wall Street Journal,* 4/20/1993.

82 Immediately before arriving: Office of Thrift Supervision, "Jones Day Settles OTS Case Involving Lincoln Savings," PR Newswire, 4/19/1993.

82 "the same type of violations": Susan Schmidt, "Law Firm Sued Over Keating Aid," *Washington Post,* 4/4/1991.

82 His hope was that Schilling: Rita Jensen, "In Whose Best Interests?," Fellowship paper, Alicia Patterson Foundation, 1994.

82 eager to show his new colleagues: Kneipper interview.

83 Word had reached Jones Day: Kneipper interview.

83 an eleven-page letter: Jensen, 1994.
83 Their pitch was that: Jensen, 1994.
83 "is made for us": James S. Granelli, "Keating's Advisers Under Fire," *Los Angeles Times,* 3/14/1992.
83 showed off the $250,000 check: Jensen, 1994.
83 about thirty colleagues: Diane Solov, "Jones Day Still Dealing With Fallout of Failed S&L," *Plain Dealer,* 3/21/1993.
83 round-the-clock operation: Jensen, 1994.
83 Jones Day had somehow learned: Solov, 3/21/1993.
83 "the client": Jensen, 1994.
83 Within three weeks: Jensen, 1994.
84 the lawyers told their client: Tim Smart, "Jones Day: Did It Do Its Duty in the Keating Affair?," Bloomberg News, 5/4/1992.
84 an entity controlled by Keating: Smart, 1992.
84 "They reported the crimes": Solov, 3/21/1993.
84 a bank employee told the lawyers: Jensen, 1994.
84 The retroactive cleanup: Jensen, 1994.
84 another two years: Solov, 3/21/1993.
85 the largest PAC: Saundra Torry, "Presents From Deep Pockets for Election Season," *Washington Post,* 11/4/1996.
85 "we could bill liberally": Granelli, 1992.
85 "Shame on them": Granelli, 1992.
86 $1,000 denominations: Keith R. Fisher, "The Higher Calling: Regulation of Lawyers Post-Enron," *University of Michigan Journal of Law Reform,* Volume 37, 2004.
86 a secretary at Jones Day noticed: Jensen, 1994.
86 More than twenty thousand: Jensen, 1994.
87 Pogue flew down to Texas: Stuart Taylor Jr., "Did Jones, Day's Slick Deals Cross the Line?," *American Lawyer,* March 1991.
87 a former bank employee told: Taylor, 1991.
87 "aided and abetted": Stephen Labaton, "Regulators Suing Law Firm They Use," *New York Times,* 11/4/1990.
88 might have been averted: Schmidt, 1991.
88 Pogue was furious: Taylor, 1991.
88 regulators and lawmakers criticized: Ricardo Sandoval, "Top S&L regulator to join law firm that represented American Continental," *Orange County Register,* 8/21/1990.
88 the two Texas thrifts: Taylor, 1991.
88 "This type of thing": Sandoval, 1990.
88 Pogue had entrusted this plotting: Brandt, 1993.

89 Pogue decided that the right thing: Pogue email.

89 barely made a dent: Kirk Ladendorf, "$16.5 Million Fine Settles S&L Suit," *Austin American-Statesman,* 10/10/1992.

89 "There was an increasing risk": Alison Leigh Cowan, "Big Law and Auditing Firms to Pay Millions in S.&L. Suit," *New York Times,* 3/31/1992.

89 The partners themselves: Wade Lambert and Amy Stevens, "Jones Day Girds for Unusual Fight With RTC Over Lincoln Savings," *Wall Street Journal,* 4/13/1993.

90 delayed a week: Diane Solov, "'Call Me Every 10 Minutes': How Jones Day Made the RTC Deal," *Plain Dealer,* 4/25/1993.

90 the largest penalty levied: Cushman, 1993.

90 "This is really an instance": Granelli, 1993.

90 one Jones Day lawyer smirked: Diane Solov, "Jones Day Agrees to Pay $51 Million in S&L Case," *Plain Dealer,* 4/20/1993.

90 $395 million: "Jones Day," *ALM Intelligence.*

91 "If it was me alone": Solov, 4/25/1993.

91 "The oft-heard justification": Fisher, 2004.

Chapter 9: Judas Day

92 "His playground was a field": Brandt, 1993.

92 until he discovered the magic: Stephen J. Brogan, "Jones Day recalls with gratitude Pat McCartan's leadership," Jones Day website, 12/1/2020.

92 As an undergrad: King, 1982.

92 A few years later: Brandt, 1993.

92 Eating lunch with other clerks: King, 1982.

92 became lifelong friends: Brogan, 2020.

92 Jack Reavis saw something: Brogan, 2020.

93 trotting out a chalkboard: King, 1982.

93 "as primped and pressed": King, 1982.

93 "I was dealing with an individual": King, 1982.

93 "He taught them to be lawyers": Brandt, 1993.

94 "I would like to think": Griswold, 389.

94 "I think it's now apparent": Brandt, 1993.

94 roster of lawyers declined: *New York Times,* "Survey Finds Retrenching in Law Firms," 9/20/1993.

94 shut down the firm's Austin office: Bruce Hight, "Jones Day attorneys finding new jobs after surprise announcement that Austin office will soon be closed," *Austin American-Statesman,* 8/21/1994.

95 One fabled episode: Steven L. Kent, *The Ultimate History of Video Games: From Pong to Pokémon and Beyond,* 2010, 394–95.

96 The jurors loved it: Kent, 394–95.

96 one of the largest awards ever: Teresa Riordan, "Nintendo Is Ordered to Pay $208 Million in Patent Case," *New York Times,* 8/2/1994.

96 If they're hiding this: Jackson, 2004.

97 Weber grilled a professor: Lubinger, 2000.

97 The president then watched the game: Fran Henry, "The Beginning of a Whole New Ballgame," *Plain Dealer,* 4/7/1994.

98 The decision ticked off partners: Pogue email.

98 "Another tough day": Jack Torry, *Endless Summers: The Fall and Rise of the Cleveland Indians,* 1996, 235–36.

98 Modell was in the box: Henry, 1994.

98 "A crummy old silo": Dick Feagler, "For Mum Modell, It's a Case of Hurt Feelings," *Plain Dealer,* 9/1/1995.

99 Reporters tracked down Modell: Timothy Heider and Steven Koff, "Modell Declares That Browns Not for Sale to Quelch Rumor," *Plain Dealer,* 11/3/1995.

99 wearing a bulletproof vest: Bart Hubbuch, "Shaken Modell lets lawyers plead his case," *York Daily Record,* 1/18/1996.

99 season ticket holders accused: Christopher Evans, "Every Fan Meet Howard Beder," *Plain Dealer Sunday Magazine,* 3/21/1999.

100 "Cleveland will long remember": Joe Dirck, "Callers Scorn Idea of Team Poaching," *Plain Dealer,* 11/14/1995.

100 called for Weber to resign: Daniel W. Hammer and David J. Hooker, "The Right to Legal Counsel," *Plain Dealer,* 2/9/1996.

100 "serious personal threats": Diane Solov, "Taking the Heat," *Plain Dealer,* 2/13/1996.

100 Clients pulled their business: Solov, 1996.

100 fax lines were sabotaged: Lubinger, 2000.

100 "have a chilling effect": Evans, 1999.

100 "It was kind of comical": John C. Kuehner, "Little Guys Take on Big Boys From Browns," *Plain Dealer,* 12/7/1995.

100 "Gazing upon wave after wave": Dirck, 1995.

101 in orange face paint: Dirck, 1995.

101 "The life of a lawyer": Robert J. Vickers, "Lawyer Is on His Own Turf for Browns," *Plain Dealer,* 11/25/1995.

101 The headline on the front page: Brogan, 2020.

101 "Professionals do not walk away": Solov, 1996.

Chapter 10: The Full Fredo

105 "That tells you the incredible": Melissa Isaacson, "Power Behind Irish," *Chicago Tribune,* 12/12/2004.

105 opened offices: Jones Day website, "Firm History."

105 "It's been in there": Peter Krouse, "Choosing Jones Day's next leader," *Plain Dealer,* 1/12/2002.

106 Brogan was only thirty-seven: Jones Day, "Jones Day Introduces Seventh Managing Partner," 11/18/2002.

106 the office was booming: Sims email.

106 one of his associates told me: Mike Gurdak email to author.

107 his mother suffered from health problems: Elizabeth Auster, "Jones Day's Brogan: A man who doesn't budge," *Plain Dealer,* 12/21/2002.

107 his father, a lieutenant: Jones Day, 2002.

108 "Your dad just reeks": Auster, 2002.

108 the Crusaders' starting catcher: Bergen Catholic yearbook via Classmates .com.

108 "He didn't back down": Auster, 2002.

108 a degree in English: Boston College yearbook, 1974, 221

108 fantasized about being a cop: Auster, 2002.

108 "was an accomplished guy": Auster, 2002.

108 As an up-and-coming lawyer, he represented: Jones Day, 2002.

108 the bin Laden family: Brogan letter to 9/11 Commission, 4/30/2004.

109 his favorite authors: Auster, 2002.

111 Pogue similarly cautioned: Pogue email.

111 To celebrate his mentor: Sims email.

112 Some four hundred: *Inside Business,* "Reception for new managing partner of Jones Day," 1/1/2003.

112 pay their respects: Brian Tucker, "McCartan to leave wide-reaching legacy," *Crain's Cleveland Business,* 11/25/2002.

112 McCartan told attendees: Auster, 2002.

112 "Cop shoes": Michael K. McIntyre and Jennifer Scott Cimperman, "Swearing commitment to Cleveland," *Plain Dealer,* 11/20/2002.

112 "He's an Irish Catholic": McIntyre and Cimperman, 2002.

Chapter 11: Try to Save the Culture

113 its seventh iteration: Borowitz, 384.

113 "The move to 'Jones Day'": *Jones Day Quarterly,* "Jones, Day, Reavis & Pogue Becomes Jones Day," Spring 2003.

114 "We're the investment banking people": Alison Frankel, "And The Winner Is . . ." *Corporate Counsel,* 3/30/2002.

114 unveiled the day before: Jennifer Scott Cimperman, "Jones Day acquires London law firm," *Plain Dealer,* 2/7/2003.

115 posed for photos: Photo from *Jones Day Quarterly,* Spring 2003.

115 Jones Day agreed to buy: Jonathan D. Glater, "Pennie & Edmonds Says It Is Being Acquired by Jones Day," *New York Times,* 12/12/2003.

115 doubled in size: Adelle Waldman, "Jones Day now nation's 2nd largest," *Plain Dealer,* 1/25/2004.

115 "an important market for our clients": Jones Day, "Jones Day Opens Moscow Office, Further Expanding Its International Presence," *Business Wire,* 9/28/2004.

115 adviser to oligarch-owned conglomerates: Vladimir Lechtman profile on Jones Day website.

115 One of the firm's senior associates: LinkedIn profile for Alexei Kostin.

115 Putin's inner circle: Joanna Partridge, "Alisher Usmanov: Ex-fencer who 'solves Putin's business problems,'" *Guardian,* 3/3/2022.

115 "A firm spokesman declined comment": Roy Strom, "Jones Day's Brogan Stays in Top Role, Francisco, Orr Promoted," Bloomberg Law, 1/26/2021.

116 Most major law firms: Regan and Rohrer, 132.

118 successfully defended IBM: Heller, 2004.

119 a pack-a-day smoker: Rick Merritt and Mike Santarini, "IBM begins building defense in chemical lawsuit," *EE Times,* 11/9/2003.

119 Palmisano told him: Sam Palmisano interview with author.

121 Jones Day sent word: Paul Hodkinson, "Jones Day hits Gouldens staff with US-style billing," *Legal Week,* 4/17/2003.

123 showed up in Colt's corner: *City of Cincinnati v. Beretta Corporation,* Supreme Court of Ohio, 6/12/2002.

123 "From handguns to tobacco": Matt Fleischer-Black, "Hard Cases," *American Lawyer,* January 2004.

Chapter 12: Rogue Lawyers

125 Christian Meister was one of the first: Meister interview with author.

125 one of its four inaugural partners: *Legal Week,* "Four-partner raid secures Jones Day Munich launch," 10/11/2002.

125 Before Brogan came to christen: Meister interview.

126 "You cannot do this": Meister interview.

127 "That's what friends are good for": Meister interview.

127 Ricker left voluntarily: John Normile email to author.

127 The firm concluded: Normile email.

127 "Over the course of the last several years": Jones Day letter to Falcon Waterfree Technologies, 12/21/2006, reviewed by author.

127 small amounts: Normile email.

127 a sentiment shared: Normile email.

128 hadn't billed enough hours: Normile email.

128 noted in a report: Munich public prosecutor's report, 6/21/2010, reviewed by author.

129 paint Meister as unhinged: Sebastian Orton interview with author.

130 barred foreign law firms: Nathan Koppel, "Shadow Practices," *American Lawyer*, 11/1/2004.

130 Jones Day covered the costs: *Jones Day v. Anand Pathak*, Cuyahoga County Court of Common Pleas, 4/17/2014.

130 "establishing a practice in India": Jones Day, "Jones Day establishes practice in India," *Business Wire*, 11/1/1995.

131 later left Jones Day: *National Law Journal*, "Gibson poaches Jones Day for Singapore post," 5/26/2008.

132 Brogan suggested that he oversee: Geoff Stewart email to author.

132 P&A was legally required: Koppel, 2004.

132 told his American colleagues: Anand Pathak interview with author.

132 To emphasize the separation: Pathak interview

133 "our heart belongs to Jones Day": Koppel, 2004.

133 "to apply the funds": *Jones Day v. Pathak*, 2014.

133 $250,000 to the American Indian Foundation: *Jones Day v. Pathak*, 2014.

133 and $500,000: Stewart email.

134 Brogan himself got on the phone: Pathak interview.

134 He wrote a letter: Stewart email.

134 Jones Day's foundation contributed: Jones Day Foundation, 2012 Form 990.

134 Brogan and Stewart traveled: Stewart email.

135 highlighted the Holy Cross gift: Jones Day, "Materials Prepared for City of Detroit," 3/5/2013.

136 dismissing the complaint: Pathak interview.

Chapter 13: Burning the Envelope

137 Megan had struggled: Megan Surber interview with author.

137 spruced up with carpet: Troy Kunkel interview with author.

137 Megan sanitized a bottle: *Security National Bank of Sioux City, Iowa, vs. Abbott Laboratories*, trial transcript, 2/15/2011.

138 The most common way: *Security National Bank of Sioux City, Iowa, vs. Abbott Laboratories*, complaint and jury demand.

138 didn't get sick: Trial transcript, 2/15/2011.

140 Megan and Troy felt hope: Kunkel interview.

140 become an issue: Tim Bottaro interview with author.

141 Since 1987: Dan Reidy email to author.

141 pitch documents seeking new customers: Jones Day, "Materials Prepared for City of Detroit," 3/5/2013.

141 the law firm had sued: Jones Day, "Abbott launches patent litigation against Sandoz," January 2007.

141 It had defended Abbott: Jones Day, "Abbott prevails on appeal of first products liability trial involving Lupron," May 2013.

141 one case in rural North Carolina: *Sisk v. Abbott Laboratories,* plaintiff's memorandum in opposition of Abbott's motion to dismiss, 7/13/2011.

141 In another case: *Burks et al. v. Abbott et al.,* second amended complaint, 10/17/2008.

142 Reidy was the partner responsible: Reidy email.

142 Ghezzi had a specialty: Frankel, 2002.

142 He liked Ghezzi: Reidy email.

142 As he entered his chambers: Mark Bennett interview with author.

143 "incredible obstructionist conduct": U.S. Court of Appeals, Eighth Circuit, ruling 8/27/2015.

143 an Eighth Amendment violation: Bennett interview.

143 "a lot of associates to keep busy": Stephen Rathke interview with author.

144 federal rules of civil procedure: Eighth Circuit ruling, 2015.

144 interrupted 115 times: Eighth Circuit ruling, 2015.

144 Over and over and over: Judge Mark W. Bennett, "Memorandum Opinion and Order Regarding Sanctions," 7/28/2014.

145 Abbott unsuccessfully sought a summary judgment: Eighth Circuit ruling, 2015.

145 There was no telling: Bennett interview.

146 Jones Day lawyers shut him down: Rathke interview.

148 "We're not trying to blame": Nick Hytrek, "Lawyers debate source of bacteria that caused Sioux City girl's brain damage," *Sioux City Journal,* 1/6/2014.

148 for seven hours: Nick Hytrek, "Jury finds baby formula maker not liable for Sioux City girl's brain damage," *Sioux City Journal,* 1/17/2014.

148 "I hate to tell you": Kunkel interview.

149 "Well, I'm sorry": Bennett memo on sanctions.

150 he got creative: Bennett memo on sanctions.

150 Bennett soon was fielding: Bennett interview.

Chapter 14: Make It Go Away

153 on display in his office: Sims email.

154 once gave a presentation: Exhibit in *Tolton et al. v. Jones Day,* Document 145.24.

154 Lovitt later described it: Traci Lovitt email to author.

157 The lawsuit ticked off: *Tolton et al. v. Jones Day,* 6/24/2019.

157 a partner warned her: *Tolton et al. v. Jones Day,* plaintiffs' supplemental memorandum, 10/24/2019.

157 "You usually have to knock": Vivia Chen, "Jones Day Partner Tells All (About Getting an Offer)," *The Careerist,* 5/21/2010.

158 played the game Fuck, Marry, Kill: Plaintiffs' supplemental memorandum.

159 Jones Day informed her: Tolton deposition, 9/17/2019.

160 Tolton was struggling: Tolton deposition.

160 Jones Day, up until that point: Plaintiffs' supplemental memorandum.

160 Their vitriol was so intense: Tolton deposition.

161 "What a royal tease": Vivia Chen, "A Waste of Time? The War Against Jones Day Over Sex Bias Claims," Bloomberg Law, 3/26/2021.

161 a confidential memo: Brogan memo, 3/11/2021, reviewed by author.

Chapter 15: Psychological Combat

162 inhabited the area: Sippican Historical Society website, "History of Marion, Massachusetts."

163 decided to move there: Jason Reynolds interview with author.

163 more than murders: Campaign for Tobacco-Free Kids, "The Toll of Tobacco in the United States," 11/3/2021.

164 From a legal standpoint: Cheryl Sbarra interview with author.

164 more dangerous than normal tobacco: Centers for Disease Control and Prevention, "Menthol and Cigarettes," 7/16/2021.

164 mentioned the proposals: Jean Perry, "Marion to Ban Synthetic Drugs, Menthol Cigarettes," *The Wanderer,* 8/12/2016.

164 the tobacco industry might sue: Jean Perry, "BOH Risks Lawsuit With Menthol Cig Ban," *The Wanderer,* 8/25/2016.

165 It was steady, profitable: George Manning interview with author.

165 "We have a relationship": Waldman, 2004.

166 "You can't just pick": Manning interview.

167 The trial was split: Tobacco Control Legal Consortium, "What Is the '*Engle* Progeny' Litigation?," September 2015.

167 Judges in Florida would instruct: Tobacco Control Legal Consortium, 2015.

167 Jones Day was averaging: Law.com, "No Egos Allowed: Jones Day, Winner of the Litigation Department of the Year," 12/19/2017.

168 contesting its authority: Katie Buehler, "Tobacco Cos. Seek Extra Delay Of Graphic Cigarette Warnings," *Law360,* 11/23/2020.

168 created a year earlier: Coalition for Responsible Retailing website, archived at Archive.org.

169 He was a spokesman: Robert Preer, "Heart of the matter," *Boston Globe,* 7/3/2010.

169 since the mid-1990s: John H. Kennedy, "The cost of cutting back," *Boston Globe,* 4/12/1994.

169 "Don't discriminate": Jean Perry, "BOH Hears From Retailers on Menthol Ban," *The Wanderer,* 9/28/2017.

170 empowered states and localities: Tobacco Control Legal Consortium, "Fact Sheet 4: Unchanged State and Local Authority," July 2009.

171 the only body in town: Reynolds interview.

171 a one-day alcohol license: Marion Board of Selectmen, Meeting Minutes, 10/4/2016.

171 Lane had already lobbied: Perry, 9/28/2017.

171 "put on the back burner": Jean Perry, "Menthol Cigs on Back Burner," *The Wanderer,* 4/27/2017.

171 would soon send flyers: Jean Perry, "Board Won't Quit Nicotine Flavor Ban Pursuit," *The Wanderer,* 11/21/2017.

172 "You're essentially shutting us down": Jean Perry, "More Opposition to Menthol Cig Ban," *The Wanderer,* 10/27/2017.

172 "The town has limited resources": Michael J. DeCicco, "Town prepares for possible tobacco industry lawsuit," *South Coast Today,* 10/5/2016.

172 The guy shrugged: Reynolds interview.

Chapter 16: Dirty, Dirty, Dirty

174 industry mints money: *American Lawyer* rankings in 1985, 2020.

175 "We don't do business": Baker McKenzie website, "Code of Business Conduct."

175 Baker McKenzie stands out: Sydney P. Freedberg, Agustin Armendariz, and Jesús Escudero, "How America's biggest law firm drives global wealth into tax havens," International Consortium of Investigative Journalists, 10/4/2021.

176 "an architect and pillar": Freedberg, Armendariz, and Escudero, 2021.

176 "I was comforted that": Freedberg, Armendariz, and Escudero, 2021.

177 That is what happened: David Enrich, *The Spider Network: The Wild Story of a Math Genius, a Gang of Backstabbing Bankers, and One of the Greatest Scams in Financial History,* 2017, 316–19.

179 hired private investigators: Ronan Farrow, "Harvey Weinstein's Army of Spies," *New Yorker,* 11/6/2017.

179 surveilled the company's critics: John Carreyrou, *Bad Blood: Secrets and Lies in a Silicon Valley Startup,* 2018, 135.

179 kept tabs on Carreyrou's reporting: Barry Meier, *Spooked: The Trump Dossier, Black Cube, and the Rise of Private Spies,* 2021, 92–93.

180 more than $100 million a year: Casey Sullivan, "Inside Paul Weiss' Relationship With Apollo Global Management," *Insider,* 6/30/2021.

180 turned out to be true: Matthew Goldstein and Katherine Rosman, "Apollo C.E.O. to Step Down After Firm Finds More Payments to Jeffrey Epstein," *New York Times,* 1/25/2021.

181 He warned that Paul Weiss: William D. Cohan, "'The Truth Turns Out to Be Ugly,'" *Vanity Fair,* 4/27/2021.

182 eight cease-and-desist letters: Liz Day, Emily Steel, Rachel Abrams, and Samantha Stark, "Britney Spears Felt Trapped. Her Business Manager Benefited," *New York Times,* 12/19/2021.

182 unwilling to risk litigation: Jim Waterson, "Bookshops threatened with legal action over book about Malaysian 'playboy banker,'" *Guardian,* 9/14/2018.

182 agreed to hand over: Bruce Birenboim email to author.

183 Birenboim wasn't done: Birenboim letter to Waxman, 2/24/2020, reviewed by author.

184 $1 trillion in mergers: *American Lawyer,* "With DuPont Deal, Skadden Breaks $1 Trillion M&A Barrier for 2015," 12/11/2015.

185 died of heart failure: Jonathan D. Glater, "Joseph H. Flom, Pioneering Lawyer in Mergers and Acquisitions, Dies at 87," *New York Times,* 2/23/2011.

185 He enlisted Skadden: Kenneth P. Vogel, "Skadden Said to Have Paid $11 Million to Settle Ukraine Dispute," *New York Times,* 5/10/2020.

185 went to bat for Manafort: Sharon LaFraniere, "Trial of High-Powered Lawyer Gregory Craig Exposes Seamy Side of Washington Elite," *New York Times,* 8/26/2019.

185 found no evidence: David M. Herszenhorn and David E. Sanger, "Failings Found in Trial of Ukrainian Ex-Premier," *New York Times,* 12/12/2012.

185 more than $5 million: Vogel, 2020.

185 other Western governments: Kenneth P. Vogel and Andrew E. Kramer, "Skadden, Big New York Law Firm, Faces Questions on Work With Manafort," *New York Times,* 9/21/2017.

186 at least $11 million: Vogel, 2020.

186 frail, wheelchair-bound, and very angry: David M. Herszenhorn, "Fresh From Prison, a Former Prime Minister Returns to the Political Stage," *New York Times,* 2/23/14.

186 "dirty, dirty, dirty contract": Vogel, 2020.

Chapter 17: Lurching to the Right

187 contacted dozens of Catholic organizations: Marcia Coyle, "Jones Day Is on a Mission," *National Law Journal,* 2/17/2014.

187 "You have walked": Dennis Brown, "In memoriam: Board chair emeritus Patrick F. McCartan," *Notre Dame News,* 12/2/2020.

188 the plaintiffs ultimately collected: Ed Housewright and Brooks Egerton, "Diocese blames insurers in lack of Kos settlement," *Dallas Morning News,* 10/30/1997; Rachel Zoll, "Dioceses sell land, borrow to pay for abuse," *Morning Journal,* 3/4/2002.

188 was close with McCartan: Catholic Diocese of Cleveland, "Patrick F. McCartan left his mark as a man of faith, philanthropy and professionalism," 12/10/2020.

188 seven-month grand jury inquiry: Regina Brett, "Diocese's secrecy speaks volumes," *Plain Dealer,* 3/5/2003.

188 exceeding the statute of limitations: Cory Shaffer, "Will Cleveland-area residents ever get to know the names of priests accused in the past?," Cleveland.com, 10/2/2018.

188 open his office's files: James F. McCarty, "Church, county at odds in priest scandal," *Plain Dealer,* 2/9/2003.

188 a letter to Mason: McCarty, 2003.

188 The files would never: Shaffer, 2018.

189 a regular venue: Event invitations via politicalpartytime.org.

189 an academic paper: Adam Bonica, Adam S. Chilton, and Maya Sen, "The Political Ideologies of American Lawyers," *Harvard Kennedy School Faculty Research Working Paper Series,* August 2015.

189 represent them pro bono: Rachel Zoll, "Catholic dioceses, colleges sue over Obama birth control mandate," Associated Press, 5/21/2012.

190 "It's a firmwide commitment": Coyle, 2014.

191 a textile salesman: Sheryl Gay Stolberg, "A Lawyer Taking Aim at the Health Care Act Gets a Supreme Court Rematch," *New York Times,* 3/4/2015.

191 viewed liberal politics as irrational: Mike Carvin email to author.

191 "I had no marketable skills": Carvin email.

191 Matalin gushed: Mary Matalin interview with author.

192 left him for James Carville: Lois Romano, "The Reliable Source," *Washington Post,* 11/17/1993.

192 *Vincere aut Mori*: Otis Bilodeau, "How Cooper Carvin Came Apart," *National Law Journal,* May 2001.

192 son of a Filipino immigrant: Mark Weiner, "Oswego's Noel Francisco, likely solicitor general," Syracuse.com, 3/10/2017.

192 shaping his conservative philosophy: Noel Francisco email to author.

193 With Steve Brogan's backing: Carvin email to author.

193 "I've done a lot": Vivia Chen, "Rise of the Right," *American Lawyer,* July 2007.

194 one of the country's sharpest: Francisco email.

194 promoted a lawyer: Chad Readler, Senate Judiciary Committee, Questionnaire for Judicial Nominees, 2018.

194 argued against a ban: Chad A. Readler, "Make Death Penalty for Youth Widely Available," *Los Angeles Daily Journal*, 2/24/2004.

194 an elementary school teacher: "Senate Judiciary Committee Hearing on Pending Nominations," *CQ Transcriptions*, 10/10/2018.

194 called for eliminating: Carol Biliczky, "Constitution Phrase Troubles State Leader," *Akron Beacon Journal*, 4/15/2014.

195 firms bragged: John Shiffman, "Former clerks: Today's prospects, tomorrow's elite," Reuters, 12/8/2014.

195 about $100,000: Tony Mauro, "Competition for Supreme Court Clerks Intensifies," *Legal Intelligencer*, 6/21/2004.

195 a total of about thirty: Tony Mauro, "Jones Day Continues Its Run on Former Supreme Court Clerks," *National Law Journal*, 11/2/2015.

195 "When the numbers get so high": Mauro, 2015.

196 "It's really not that much": Mauro, 2004.

196 sent to trade publications: Shiffman, 2014.

196 "There's going to be a number": Shiffman, 2014.

197 at one point fantasized: Greg Veis, "Megyn Kelly on Working for Fox News and Leaving Her Law Career," *GQ*, 11/21/2010.

197 successfully defended the network: Jones Day, "Fox defeats first amendment lawsuit relating to COVID-19 news coverage," May 2020.

197 the firm shielded Fox: Jones Day, "Fox's dismissal of defamation and intentional infliction of emotional distress claims brought by former employee affirmed by D.C. Circuit," March 2021.

197 an unsuccessful attempt to neuter: Ashby Jones, "The Jones Day Lawyers Looking to Take Down SOX," *Wall Street Journal*, 11/20/2019.

197 briefs on Buckeye's behalf: Buckeye Institute, "The Buckeye Institute Files Legal Briefs Supporting Ohio Election Laws," 7/12/2016.

197 helped advance Buckeye's argument: Jones Day, "Buckeye Institute submits brief in support of certiorari in challenge of CFPB structure," October 2018.

197 "for the public good": American Bar Association, "A Guide and Explanation to Pro Bono Services," 5/13/2021.

198 about one speech a month: Noel Francisco, Senate Judiciary Committee questionnaire, 2017.

198 "I always say yes": Federalist Society video, *The Second Amendment: Enforcing the Heller Decision*, 11/19/2016.

198 "The government's tentacles invade": Jones Day promotional video, *Government Regulation and Overreach Challenges*, 8/10/2015.

201 "Jones Day's Moby Dick": James Schroeder, "Fight Club: Jones Day is ready, willing and able to go toe-to-toe with the feds," *American Lawyer,* January 2016.

201 In another, Carvin represented: Coyle, 2014.

201 his first defeat: Stolberg, 2015.

201 "Take a breath": Stolberg, 2015.

201 he would later explain: Marcia Coyle and Mike Scarcella, "What to Know About Noel Francisco as the New SCOTUS Term Nears," *New York Law Journal,* 9/22/2017.

202 went to check on him: Alan Blinder and Manny Fernandez, "Ranch Owner Recalls Finding Justice Antonin Scalia's Body," *New York Times,* 2/14/2016.

202 "Justice Scalia did not just defend": "The Legacy of Justice Scalia," Heritage Foundation event, 5/19/2016.

203 "assaults on freedom of religion": Ann Rodgers, "Diocese says government slow to resolve contraception impasse," *Catholic News Service,* 8/25/2016.

Chapter 18: The Bloody Eighth

207 in four straight elections: Dirk Johnson, "The 2000 Campaign: An Indiana Race," *New York Times,* 10/10/2000.

207 a three-member committee: Julian E. Zelizer, "A 1985 Recount Is Suddenly Relevant Again," *Atlantic,* 11/12/2018.

208 failed the bar exam: Jan Baran interview with author.

208 assigned Ginsberg the task: Baran interview.

209 radicalized Ginsberg: Jake Tapper, *Down and Dirty: The Plot to Steal the Presidency,* 2001, 47.

210 known as Project Ratfuck: David Daley, *Ratf**ked: Why Your Vote Doesn't Count,* 2016, 34–36.

210 elevated him to national prominence: Tapper, 39.

210 helped the Swift Boat Veterans: Patrick Healy, "Bush lawyer quits over tie to anti-Kerry veterans," *Boston Globe,* 8/26/2004.

210 McGahn thought to himself: Don McGahn speech at Widener University, 2/25/2020.

211 partly a byproduct: Jeffrey Toobin, "The Great Election Grab," *New Yorker,* 12/8/2003.

211 McGahn's phone rang: McGahn speech at Widener.

211 didn't hang with the jocks: *New York Times' The Weekly*, "Mr. McGahn," 10/25/2019.

211 "to work harder than those": McGahn email to author.

211 Republicans were galvanized: McGahn speech at Widener.

211 "I ended up latching onto Ben": McGahn speech at Stockton University, 1/30/2020.

211 the more McGahn learned: McGahn speech at Widener.

212 rock group that billed itself: Andy Kroll, "Better call Don," *Mother Jones,* May 2017.

212 more than thirty guitars: Clifford Hall, "Former White House official Don McGahn: 'I know how tough the life of a musician is,'" *Guitar World,* 8/10/2020.

212 "It was extra-Constitutional": "Discussion and Q&A with Don McGahn," Federalist Society's Florida chapter, 2/1/2020.

213 caused such an uproar: Ben Terris, "Trump's own Beltway establishment guy: The curious journey of Don McGahn," *Washington Post,* 4/11/2016.

213 blocking the investigation: Matt Zapotosky and Sari Horwitz, "Who is Donald McGahn, the fiery lawyer at the center of virtually every Trump controversy?," *Washington Post,* 2/15/2017.

213 "in a death spiral": McGahn speech at Widener.

214 Francisco cheered: Wilson and Ho, 2014.

Chapter 19: Trump's Stallion

215 pledging $1.5 million: *American Lawyer,* "How Don McGahn Introduced Jones Day to Politics," March 2017.

215 defending the National Rifle Association: McGahn letter to Federal Election Commission, 8/5/2015.

215 a group affiliated with the Koch brothers: *American Lawyer,* 2017.

215 one other key client: C. Ryan Barber and Katelyn Polantz, "Trump Lawyers' Financial Disclosures Reveal Big Law Salaries, Client Lists," *National Law Journal,* April 2017.

216 become his first client: *American Lawyer,* 2017.

216 "Everyone in Washington knows": Eric Lichtblau, "A Combative Counsel for Trump White House," *New York Times,* 12/13/2016.

216 at his Fifth Avenue skyscraper: One America News, "OAN Exclusive: Don McGahn," 7/20/2016.

216 Trump signed a book: McGahn speech at Widener.

216 a power broker: Iver Peterson, "Patrick T. McGahn Jr., 72, Lawyer for Casinos," *New York Times,* 8/3/2000.

216 sued his former lawyer: Schmidt, 132.

216 heaped praise on the man: McGahn at Stockton University.

217 resonated with McGahn: McGahn at Stockton University.

217 "Good for you": *New York Times' The Weekly*, 2019.

217 To underscore his seriousness: Robert Costa, "Trump says he is serious about 2016 bid, is hiring staff and delaying TV gig," *Washington Post,* 2/25/2015.

218 On April 23, 2015: Federal Election Commission records.

219 more than $29,000: FEC records.

220 He stood on the mezzanine: Adam Wren, Tom LoBianco, Warren Rojas, Nicole Gaudiano, and Darren Samuelsohn, "The definitive oral history of how Trump took over the GOP," *Insider,* 7/18/2021.

221 McGahn beat back: Heather Haddon, "Effort to Knock Donald Trump Off N.H. Ballot Fails," *Wall Street Journal,* 11/24/2015.

221 handling the selection and wrangling: McGahn at Stockton University.

221 nearly $600,000: FEC records.

Chapter 20: You Can Count Me In

222 It was Trump's idea: McGahn at Federalist Society's Florida chapter.

224 McGahn's judicial philosophy: Jason Zengerle, "How the Trump Administration Is Remaking the Courts," *New York Times Magazine,* 8/22/2018.

225 quite the conversation starter: McGahn Lunch Address to Federalist Society Western Chapters Conference, 2/19/2019.

225 McGahn called Bunch: McGahn speech to Federalist Society, "17th Annual Barbara K. Olson Memorial Lecture," 11/18/2017.

226 showed up at Jones Day's Capitol Hill office: Paul Kane, "Trump courts lawmakers at Capitol Hill law firm, wins lobbyist backing," *Washington Post,* 3/21/2016.

226 instructed everyone to enter: *New York Times' The Weekly,* 2019.

226 "to assure he would be seen": Kane, 2016.

226 "Why don't I put out a list": Don McGahn and Mitch McConnell, "Judicial Nominations in the Trump Administration," Federalist Society Kentucky Chapters Conference, 10/7/2019.

227 a bit more than an hour: Kane, 2016.

227 "making America great again": Kane, 2016.

227 "It was a beginning meeting": Kristina Peterson, "Newt Gingrich, GOP Lawmakers Huddle With Donald Trump," *Dow Jones Newswires,* 3/21/2016.

227 a team led by McGahn and Leo: McGahn at Federalist Society's Florida chapter.

227 "The list reassured": McGahn and McConnell, 2019.

Chapter 21: A Lawless Hobbesian Nightmare

228 one lawyer vented: David Lat, "Jones Day: Helping Donald Trump to Make America Great Again," *Above the Law,* 3/21/2016.

229 Jones Day notified its staff: Susan Beck, "Trump's Lawyers to Close Office During Convention," *New York Law Journal,* 5/13/2016.

229 splashed behind each of them: Jones Day, "Jones Day Presidential Forum: 2016 Policy Insights," 8/2/2016.

230 the idea was vetoed: Jones Day list of approved/unapproved items bearing firm name/logo, reviewed by author.

230 the lawyers made no effort: Susan Beck, "During RNC, Jones Day Hosts Panel," *National Law Journal,* 7/25/2016.

230 "It's a great day": One America News, 2016.

232 infuriated the business lobby: Michael Isikoff, "No. 2 Aide at Justice Quits Post," *Washington Post,* 5/12/1990.

232 after six months: Ronald J. Ostrow, "Aide Says Thornburgh Meddled in Leak Probe," *Los Angeles Times,* 5/20/1990.

232 a top Thornburgh aide sniffed: Isikoff, 1990.

232 "Donald Trump's impulsive temperament": "Statement by Former U.S. Department of Justice Officials," 10/10/2016, reviewed by author.

233 filed a complaint: Campaign Legal Center, "Donald Trump Is Illegally Soliciting Money from Foreign Nationals to Fund His Presidential Campaign," 6/29/2016.

Chapter 22: A Nice Little Cushion

235 "You've got to get everybody": Eric Heisig, "Judge's order aims to head off voter intimidation," *Plain Dealer,* 11/5/2016.

235 "racially charged calls": Mark Gillispie, "Judge issues order to stop voter harassment by Trump backers," Associated Press, 11/4/2016.

236 "are perfectly within their rights": Eric Heisig, "Trump campaign lawyer defends 'poll watching' targeted in lawsuit," *Plain Dealer,* 11/3/2016.

236 Did Readler truly believe: Heisig, 11/5/2016.

237 preparing to fight recounts: McGahn at Stockton University.

239 a break from the tradition: Zengerle, 2018.

239 half as many unfilled judgeships: Zengerle, 2018.

239 "Just do this yourself": McGahn and McConnell, 2019.

239 Trump agreed: Schmidt, 7.

240 The firm's lawyers were responsible: Zoe Tillman, "Trump Taps Kirkland, Jones Day Lawyers to Lead DOJ Transition," *New York Law Journal,* 11/22/2016.

240 definition of pro bono work: ABA, 2021.

241 Reporters at the event noticed: Mike Moffitt, "Were folders stuffed with Trump's 'business plan' papers blank props?," *SFGate,* 1/12/2017.

241 surrounded with his colleagues: "President Donald J. Trump Announces Key Additions to the Office of the White House Counsel," WhiteHouse.gov, 3/7/2017.

241 Brinton Lucas: Jones Day, "Brinton Lucas rejoins Jones Day's Issues & Appeals Practice in Washington," April 2021.

241 recently had helped defend: Astead W. Herndon, "Trump civil rights nominee went from government advocate to corporate hired gun," *Boston Globe*, 7/10/2017.

241 company was a Jones Day client: Search for "WL Ross" on Jones Day website.

242 "I don't know of a precedent": Paul Barrett, "Donald Trump's Favorite Law Firm," Bloomberg News, 3/16/2017.

242 a grand total of three partners: *Jones Day Quarterly*, "Justice Is Served," Fall 2001.

242 permitted Brogan to make these payments: Sims email.

242 "I don't think that's true": Recorded conversation disclosed in *Tolton, et al. v. Jones Day*, Document 115–11.

243 Every four years: Carvin email.

243 "Light meals and refreshments": Ellevate, "Inauguration Day Open House with Ellevate and Jones Day."

243 including Mike Carvin and Noel Francisco: Carvin and Francisco emails.

Chapter 23: Rich, Pissed Off, and Wrong

244 One was Mike Carvin: David Lat, "Jones Day in the (White) House," *Above The Law*, 1/19/2017.

245 McGahn had recommended him: McGahn email.

246 "Noel and I have been": Ted Cruz, "Sen. Cruz Praises Nomination of Noel Francisco as U.S. Solicitor General," Ted Cruz's Senate website, 3/10/2017.

246 "Frankly the most interesting law practice": Francisco interview at Catholic University, 1/24/2018.

247 considered it his dream job: Jasmin Melvin, Maya Weber, and Christopher Newkumet, "In wake of McIntyre death, attention turns to replacement," *Platts Inside FERC*, 1/7/2019.

247 diagnosed with a brain tumor: Kevin McIntyre, "Letter From FERC Chairman Kevin McIntyre," FERC, 10/22/2018.

247 shot down a push: Steven Mufson, "Kevin McIntyre, Federal Energy Regulatory Commission chairman, dies at 58," *Washington Post*, 1/3/2019.

247 "his high civic calling": Mufson, 2019.

248 developed a specialty in: Sheila Kaplan, "Trump Pick to Head Con-

sumer Safety Board Is Seen as Too Close to Industries," *New York Times*, 12/6/2017.

248 She represented Honeywell: C. Ryan Barber, "Jones Day Partner Picked to Flip Product Safety Agency," *National Law Journal*, 9/22/2017.

248 In a booklet for clients: Jones Day, "The Era of the Global Product Recall: Overview of Issues," May 2008.

249 were on the rise: Barber, 2017.

249 didn't penalize a single company: Todd C. Frankel, "Product recalls under Trump fall to lowest level in 16 years," *Washington Post*, 1/13/2020.

250 the CPSC had previously signed off: Paul Nathanson, Britax spokesman, email to author.

250 "I think it was good": Todd C. Frankel, "After hundreds of crashes, this Britax jogging stroller faced recall. Then Trump appointees stepped in," *Washington Post*, 4/2/2019.

250 replacement bolts proved defective: Todd C. Frankel, "Britax avoided one recall for its BOB stroller. But its crash fix leads to a recall now," *Washington Post*, 7/25/2019.

251 similar events in the past: Sims email.

252 "tacky, tasteless, bush league": Joe Patrice, "Jones Day Advertising Its Trump Admin Ties Because They Have No Shame," *Above the Law*, 4/25/2017.

Chapter 24: Subsidizing Trump

253 filed the paperwork: Trump letter to Federal Election Commission, 1/20/2017.

254 fell to Jones Day: Kenneth P. Vogel and Rachel Shorey, "Trump Campaign Spending on Legal Fees Surges as Russia Inquiries Widen," *New York Times*, 10/15/2017.

254 Jones Day also would handle: Kenneth P. Vogel and Rachel Shorey, "About 25% of Trump's Re-election Spending Continues to Go to Lawyers," *New York Times*, 2/1/2018.

254 relationship with Cambridge Analytica: Stewart Crosland letter to FEC, 5/25/2018.

254 Brogan, too, took part: McGahn email.

255 White House lawyers waived: White House memo from Stefan C. Passantino and James D. Schultz, 4/26/2017.

256 "I rated the ability": McGahn speech at Oxford Union, 4/22/2019.

256 noticing strangers in airports: McGahn at Federalist Society Western Conference.

256 "Their clashes were primal": Schmidt, 5.

257 "We're proud to have represented": Roy Strom, "A Quiet Firm With a Famous Client," *American Lawyer*, March 2017.

258 Jones Day broadened this effort: Jones Day website, "Pro Bono: Immigration—The Border Project."

258 representing hundreds of women and children: Jones Day website, "Pro Bono: Immigration—The Border Project."

258 nearly $200 million: Laura Tuell email to author.

258 clients sent their in-house lawyers: Tuell email.

259 In a 2018 interview: Larkin, 2018.

260 Jones Day helped file the paperwork: Tom LoBianco and Dave Levinthal, "Jared Kushner helped create a Trump campaign shell company that secretly paid the president's family members and spent $617 million in reelection cash, a source tells Insider," *Insider,* 12/18/2020.

260 Nearly $800 million: Center for Responsive Politics, "Vendor/Recipient Profile: American Made Media Consultants," 2/1/2021.

260 at Jones Day's D.C. offices: Sarah N. Lynch, "U.S. Justice Dept targets discrimination against houses of worship," Reuters, 6/13/2018.

260 a total of $7.5 million: Author's analysis of Trump federal election filings.

260 hadn't pocketed more than $1 million: Center for Responsive Politics, "Vendor/Recipient Profile: Jones Day."

Chapter 25: Bizarre Coincidences

262 a well-known phenomenon: Jesse Drucker and Danny Hakim, "How Accounting Giants Craft Favorable Tax Rules From Inside Government," *New York Times,* 9/19/2021.

263 signed their names: Justice Department settlement agreement with Catholic organizations, 10/13/2017.

263 "For too long": Administration of Donald J. Trump, "Remarks on Signing a Proclamation on the National Day of Prayer," 5/4/2017.

263 issued a rule: Michelle Hackman, "Trump Administration Rolls Back Obama Rule on Birth-Control Coverage," Dow Jones Newswires, 10/6/2017.

264 handled the talks: Carol Zimmerman, "Groups settle in lawsuit against HHS contraceptive mandate," *Catholic Telegraph,* 10/17/2017.

264 pay Jones Day $3 million: Zoe Tillman, "The Trump Administration Agreed to Pay More Than $3 Million in Legal Fees to Settle Contraception Mandate Lawsuits," *BuzzFeed News,* 1/9/2018.

264 hired as a partner: Jones Day, "Jones Day adds Brett Shumate, Margaret 'Peggy' Blake in Washington," August 2019.

265 "Shamoil was an energetic leader": Mark Curriden, "Shipchandler resigns as SEC regional director," *Texas Lawbook,* 1/25/2019.

265 trying to derail those state inquiries: Associated Press, "SEC drops investigation into Exxon climate change response," 8/3/2018.

265 "We have concluded the investigation": Shipchandler letter to Woodcock, 8/2/2018, reviewed by author.

265 trumpeted the letter to the media: Associated Press, 2018.

Chapter 26: Redefining Shamefulness

267 would adjudicate sibling spats: Natalie Posgate, "Joshua Russ: The Whistleblower," *Texas Lawbook*, 8/10/2021.

267 "I like to be able to sleep": Posgate, 2021.

268 "I liked that Josh": Posgate, 2021.

268 The prosecutors soon discovered: *USA v. Walmart*, Complaint, 12/22/2020.

270 they were preparing to indict: Jesse Eisinger and James Bandler, "Walmart Was Almost Charged Criminally Over Opioids. Trump Appointees Killed the Indictment," *ProPublica*, 3/25/2020.

271 to resolve the two cases: Eisinger and Bandler, 2020.

271 taken a job at Jones Day: Jason Varnado email to author.

272 "We are not about self-protection": Schroeder, 2016.

272 a letter to the deputy U.S. attorney general: Eisinger and Bandler, 2020.

272 a subsequent letter to DOJ: Eisinger and Bandler, 2020.

273 instructed him to halt: Eisinger and Bandler, 2020.

274 on the department's org chart: Justice Department, "DOJ GEN Chart on DOJ Leadership," 10/22/2018.

274 helped the firm line up: Emails between Readler and Curt Kirschner, 12/2017, obtained by author via FOIA.

274 also working with Mike Carvin: Email between Readler and Alex Haas, 5/11/17, obtained by author via FOIA.

274 more than a dozen Jones Day: Search for "Purdue" on Jones Day website.

274 "Not that there isn't room": Patrick Radden Keefe, *Empire of Pain: The Secret History of the Sackler Dynasty*, 2021, 381.

275 boasted about: Jones Day, "Materials Prepared for City of Detroit," 3/5/2013.

275 *increased* overdose rates: Keefe, 346, 408.

275 now turned instead: Keefe, 312.

276 decided to stop complying: Hewitt letter to Eyler, 9/27/2019.

277 told to stand down: Posgate, 2021.

277 Trump visited a Walmart: Matthew Adams, "Ivanka Trump to visit Mesquite on Friday to see how Walmart trains workers for today's economy," *Dallas Morning News*, 9/19/2018.

279 a farewell letter: Russ letter, 10/25/2019.

279 FedExed a complaint: Posgate, 2021.

279 cowrote an article: Eisinger and Bandler, 2020.

279 issued a public statement: Justice Department, "U.S. Attorney Brown Announces Departure from Office," 5/26/2020.

280 "The President has clearly conveyed": Tom Hamburger and Devlin Barrett, "Former U.S. attorneys—all Republicans—back Biden, saying Trump threatens 'the rule of law,'" *Washington Post*, 10/27/2020.

281 Walmart sued: *Walmart v. Justice Department*, Drug Enforcement Administration, et al., 10/22/2020.

281 Justice Department filed: *USA v. Walmart*, Complaint, 12/22/2020.

Chapter 27: No Vacancy Left Behind

282 had to leave in a hurry: Charlie Savage, "Counsel Quietly Trying to Corral Trump While Pushing G.O.P.'s Agenda," *New York Times*, 1/26/2018.

282 "I can't believe you didn't": Schmidt, 344.

282 had drawn Trump's ire: Michael S. Schmidt and Maggie Haberman, "McGahn, Soldier for Trump and Witness Against Him, Leaves White House," *New York Times*, 10/17/2018.

282 more than 150 judges: McGahn speech at Widener.

283 "I am you": McGahn at Federalist Society Western Conference.

283 "Why the Left is triggered": *New York Times' The Weekly*, 2019.

283 write him a letter of recommendation: Schmidt, 346.

283 Monday in March 2019: Jones Day, "Former White House Counsel Donald F. McGahn II returns to Jones Day as Practice Leader of Government Regulation," 3/4/2019.

284 a few days after: Schmidt, 350.

284 passing on their résumés: Rob Luther email to Stephen Vaden, 4/2/2017, obtained by author via FOIA.

285 "The insights and understanding": Jones Day, "Jones Day adds Brett Shumate, Margaret 'Peggy' Blake in Washington," August 2019.

285 Gore was accused in court: Caroline Spiezio, "Former senior DOJ attorney rejoins Jones Day," Reuters Legal, 11/11/2019.

285 which a federal judge emphasized: Brian Flood, "Trump Administration Sanctioned in 2020 Citizenship Case," Bloomberg Law, 5/21/2020.

285 argued seventeen cases: Justice Department, "Solicitor General Noel Francisco Announces Departure from Department of Justice," 6/17/2020.

287 Katsas swore Readler in: Readler email to Civil Division staff, 3/12/2019.

287 "We're very proud": Jones Day, "Former Jones Day lawyers Chad Readler, Eric E. Murphy confirmed to U.S. Sixth Circuit seats," March 2019.

287 "I am honored to serve": Emails between Vaden, Luther, and Tim Murtaugh, obtained by author via FOIA.

287 Vaden was unpopular: Catherine Boudreau, "Low morale plagues USDA legal team under Trump's general counsel nominee," *Politico Pro Agriculture,* 12/4/2017.

287 "I selected Jones Day": Jones Day promotional video, *Former U.S. Supreme Court Clerks Join Jones Day's Issues & Appeals Practice,* 3/11/2020.

288 deemed her "not qualified": Letter from ABA to Lindsey Graham and Dianne Feinstein, 9/8/2020.

288 Jones Day hired Chad: Jones Day, "Jones Day welcomes Chad Mizelle to Government Regulation Practice in Miami and Washington," January 2021.

Chapter 28: Fearmongering

291 a fiery opinion piece: Benjamin L. Ginsberg, "Republicans have insufficient evidence to call elections 'rigged' and 'fraudulent,'" *Washington Post,* 9/8/2020.

294 a group of twelve prominent Republican officials: Amicus curiae brief filed by Tom Ridge et al. in *Republican Party of Pennsylvania v. Boockvar,* 10/2/2020.

295 Barely 10,000 mail-in ballots arrived: Pennsylvania Department of State, "Department of State Provides Update on Election Results," 11/13/2020.

295 At 11:25 a.m. on Saturday: Brian Slodysko, "Explainer: Why AP called Pennsylvania for Biden," Associated Press, 11/7/2020.

295 more than three out of every four mail-in ballots: Pennsylvania election results at electionreturns.pa.gov.

Chapter 29: We Dissent

297 The son of a teacher-turned-school-superintendent: Tom Hals, "Newsmaker: Detroit financial manager steps up from second fiddle," Reuters, 3/14/2013.

297 "stellar reputation for integrity": Kevyn Orr email to author.

298 A group called Rise and Resist: Arriana McLymore, "Law student group aims one-two punch at Big Law over Trump ties," Reuters Legal, 11/14/2020.

298 warn students about working for the firm: Dan Packel, "Polarizing Election Work, Discrimination Suits May Dent Jones Day's Appeal to Young Lawyers," *American Lawyer,* 12/17/2020.

300 Sparkle Sooknanan: *American Lawyer,* "DC Rising Stars: Sparkle Sooknanan, 36," 8/3/2020.

301 he'd spent nearly two years: Parker Rider-Longmaid profile on LinkedIn.

302 "The following lawyers are leaving": Internal Jones Day memo, 1/29/2021, reviewed by author.

Epilogue: The Black Book

304 he'd defended federal agents' detention: Clare Roth and Malathi Nayak, "Oregon Battles With U.S. in Court on Federal Agents in Portland," Bloomberg Law, 7/22/2020.

304 raised concerns inside the Justice Department: Adam Goldman, Katie Benner, and Ben Protess, "Material From Giuliani Spurred a Separate Justice Dept. Pursuit of Hunter Biden," *New York Times*, 12/11/2020.

304 In his new job: Jones Day, "Scott Brady, former U.S. Attorney for Western District of Pennsylvania, joins Jones Day in Pittsburgh," March 2021.

304 "Brinton will add great value": Jones Day, "Brinton Lucas rejoins Jones Day's Issues & Appeals Practice in Washington," April 2021.

304 He had defended Trump's ban: Yeganeh Torbati and Mica Rosenberg, "U.S. lawyer defending travel ban grilled in court over Trump's tweets," Reuters, 12/8/2017.

304 hired back by Francisco: Jones Day, "James Burnham returns to Jones Day as partner in Firm's Issues & Appeals Practice in Washington," September 2021.

305 In the spring of 2021: Mike Spector and Dan Levine, "Inside J&J's secret plan to cap litigation payouts to cancer victims," Reuters, 2/4/2022.

305 already executed this strategy: Jamie Smyth, Kate Beioley, and Sujeet Indap, "'Texas two-step' outcry risks ending fee bonanza for law firm Jones Day," *Financial Times*, 2/6/2022.

305 codenamed Project Plato: Spector and Levine, 2022.

305 the company framed this: Johnson & Johnson news release, "Johnson & Johnson Takes Steps to Equitably Resolve All Current and Future Talc Claims," 10/14/2021.

306 "a fee bonanza": Smyth, Beioley, and Indap, 2022.

306 Legal scholars cried foul: Smyth, Beioley, and Indap, 2022.

306 claimed that this structure was unconstitutional: *Consumers' Research v. CPSC*, complaint, 7/2/2021.

307 "no argument too extreme": Ruth Marcus, "Opinion: Mitch McConnell's un-conservative plea to the Supreme Court," *Washington Post*, 12/30/2021.

309 well over $19 million: FEC records via Open Secrets.

310 spewing lies about the election: Josh Dawsey and Rosalind S. Helderman, "Trump's PAC collected $75 million this year," *Washington Post*, 7/22/2021.

310 a prolific peddler of misinformation: John Nichols, "Ron Johnson Gets Caught Debunking the Big Lie," *The Nation*, 9/2/2021.

310 Trump wannabes in Pennsylvania: Mike Scarcella, "Dr. Oz turns to law firm Jones Day for consulting in U.S. Senate bid," Reuters, 2/1/2022.

310 and Alabama: Federal Election Commission spending records for Durant for Senate.

310 Gulick sat at a table in her home: Lissy Gulick interview with author.

311 Inside was a collection of letters: Thomas H. Jones memorial book, reviewed by author.

INDEX

ABOUT

MARINER BOOKS

MARINER BOOKS TRACES ITS BEGINNINGS TO 1832 WHEN William Ticknor cofounded the Old Corner Bookstore in Boston, from which he would run the legendary firm Ticknor and Fields, publisher of Ralph Waldo Emerson, Harriet Beecher Stowe, Nathaniel Hawthorne, and Henry David Thoreau. Following Ticknor's death, Henry Oscar Houghton acquired Ticknor and Fields and, in 1880, formed Houghton Mifflin, which later merged with venerable Harcourt Publishing to form Houghton Mifflin Harcourt. HarperCollins purchased HMH's trade publishing business in 2021 and reestablished their storied lists and editorial team under the name Mariner Books.

Uniting the legacies of Houghton Mifflin, Harcourt Brace, and Ticknor and Fields, Mariner Books continues one of the great traditions in American bookselling. Our imprints have introduced an incomparable roster of enduring classics, including Hawthorne's *The Scarlet Letter,* Thoreau's *Walden,* Willa Cather's *O Pioneers!,* Virginia Woolf's *To the Lighthouse,* W.E.B. Du Bois's *Black Reconstruction,* J.R.R. Tolkien's *The Lord of the Rings,* Carson McCullers's *The Heart Is a Lonely Hunter,* Ann Petry's *The Narrows,* George Orwell's *Animal Farm* and *Nineteen Eighty-Four,* Rachel Carson's *Silent Spring,* Margaret Walker's *Jubilee,* Italo Calvino's *Invisible Cities,* Alice Walker's *The Color Purple,* Margaret Atwood's *The Handmaid's Tale,* Tim O'Brien's *The Things They Carried,* Philip Roth's *The Plot Against America,* Jhumpa Lahiri's *Interpreter of Maladies,* and many others. Today Mariner Books remains proudly committed to the craft of fine publishing established nearly two centuries ago at the Old Corner Bookstore.